horage—Hotel Captain Cook * Atlanta—Colony Square Hotel * Atlanta—The Ritz-Carlton Atlanta * Baden-Baden—
nner's Park-Hotel * Baltimore—Harbor Court Hotel * Bangkok—The Dusit Thani * Boston—The Colonnade * Cape Cod/
atham, MA—Wequassett Inn * Carmel—Quail Lodge * Charlotte—The Park Hotel * Chicago—The Barclay Chicago *
cago/Oak Brook—Oak Brook Hills Hotel * Cincinnati—The Cincinnatian Hotel * Cologne—Excelsior Hotel Ernst * Dallas—
el Crescent Court * Dallas—The Mansion on Turtle Creek * Denver—The Brown Palace Hotel * Düsseldorf—Hotel
idenbacher Hof * Fort Lauderdale—Pier 66 Hotel and Marina * Frankfurt/Wiesbaden—Hotel Nassauer Hof * Hong Kong—
Peninsula * Honolulu—Halekulani * Houston—The Warwick * Indianapolis—The Canterbury Hotel * Kansas City—
meda Plaza Hotel * Keystone, CO—Keystone Lodge * Las Vegas—Desert Inn Hotel & Casino * London—The Dorchester *
s Angeles—Westwood Marquis Hotel & Gardens * Lucerne—Grand Hotel National * Lucerne/Vitznau—Park Hotel Vitznau
Madrid—Palace Hotel * Malaga—Hotel Byblos Andaluz * Manila—The Manila Peninsula * Maui—Maui Prince Hotel *
mphis—The Peabody * Milwaukee—The Pfister Hotel * Minneapolis—The Whitney Hotel * Montreal—Le Grand Hotel
Munich—Hotel Bayerischer Hof * Napa Valley/St. Helena—Meadowood Resort Hotel * New York City—Grand Bay Hotel at
uitable Center * New York City—United Nations Plaza Hotel * New York City/Long Island—The Garden City Hotel *
lando—The Peabody * Osaka—Royal Hotel * Palm Beach—The Breakers * Paris—Hotel Le Bristol * Phoenix—The Pointe at
uth Mountain * Portland—The Heathman Hotel * Rome—Ambasciatori Palace Hotel * San Antonio—La Mansión del Rio *
n Diego—U.S. Grant Hotel * San Diego/La Jolla—La Valencia Hotel—San Francisco—The Stanford Court Hotel * San
ancisco/Oakland—The Claremont Resort Hotel & Tennis Club * San Juan—El San Juan Hotel & Casino * Seattle—The
rrento Hotel * Seoul—Hotel Lotte * Singapore—Goodwood Park Hotel * Sonoma—Sonoma Mission Inn & Spa * Tokyo—
perial Hotel * Toronto—Park Plaza Hotel * Toronto—The Prince Hotel * Vienna—Hotel Im Palais Schwarzenberg *
shington, D.C.—The Hay-Adams Hotel * Washington, D.C.—The Watergate Hotel * Washington, D.C./Alexandria—
rrison House * Wilmington—Hotel du Pont * Zurich—Hotel Baur Au Lac * Anchorage—Hotel Captain Cook * Atlanta—
ony Square Hotel * Atlanta—The Ritz-Carlton Atlanta * Baden-Baden—Brenner's Park-Hotel * Baltimore—Harbor Court
tel * Bangkok—The Dusit Thani * Boston—The Colonnade * Cape Cod/Chatham, MA—Wequassett Inn * Carmel—Quail
dge * Charlotte—The Park Hotel * Chicago—The Barclay Chicago * Chicago/Oak Brook—Oak Brook Hills Hotel *
cinnati—The Cincinnatian Hotel * Cologne—Excelsior Hotel Ernst * Dallas—Hotel Crescent Court * Dallas—The Mansion
Turtle Creek * Denver—The Brown Palace Hotel * Düsseldorf—Hotel Breidenbacher Hof * Fort Lauderdale—Pier 66 Hotel
Marina * Frankfurt/Wiesbaden—Hotel Nassauer Hof * Hong Kong—The Peninsula * Honolulu—Halekulani * Houston—
e Warwick * Indianapolis—The Canterbury Hotel * Kansas City—Alameda Plaza Hotel * Keystone, CO—Keystone Lodge
Vegas—Desert Inn Hotel & Casino * London—The Dorchester * Los Angeles—Westwood Marquis Hotel & Gardens
ucerne—Grand Hotel National * Lucerne/Vitznau—Park Hotel Vitznau * Madrid—Palace Hotel * Malaga—Hotel Byblos
daluz * Manila—The Manila Peninsula * Maui—Maui Prince Hotel * Memphis—The Peabody * Milwaukee—The Pfister
tel * Minneapolis—The Whitney Hotel * Montreal—Le Grand Hotel * Munich—Hotel Bayerischer Hof * Napa Valley/St.
lena—Meadowood Resort Hotel * New York City—Grand Bay Hotel at Equitable Center * New York City—United Nations
za Hotel * New York City/Long Island—The Garden City Hotel * Orlando—The Peabody * Osaka—Royal Hotel * Palm
ach—The Breakers * Paris—Hotel Le Bristol * Phoenix—The Pointe at South Mountain * Portland—The Heathman Hotel *
me—Ambasciatori Palace Hotel * San Antonio—La Mansión del Rio * San Diego—U.S. Grant Hotel * San Diego/La Jolla—La
encia Hotel—San Francisco—The Stanford Court Hotel * San Francisco/Oakland—The Claremont Resort Hotel & Tennis Club
San Juan—El San Juan Hotel & Casino * Seattle—The Sorrento Hotel * Seoul—Hotel Lotte * Singapore—Goodwood Park
tel * Sonoma—Sonoma Mission Inn & Spa * Tokyo—Imperial Hotel * Toronto—Park Plaza Hotel * Toronto—The Prince
tel * Vienna—Hotel Im Palais Schwarzenberg * Washington, D.C.—The Hay-Adams Hotel * Washington, D.C.—The
tergate Hotel * Washington, D.C./Alexandria—Morrison House * Wilmington—Hotel du Pont * Zurich—Hotel Baur Au Lac
nver—The Brown Palace Hotel * Düsseldorf—Hotel Breidenbacher Hof * Fort Lauderdale—Pier 66 Hotel and Marina
Frankfurt/Wiesbaden—Hotel Nassauer Hof * Hong Kong—The Peninsula * Honolulu—Halekulani * Houston—The Warwick
Indianapolis—The Canterbury Hotel * Kansas City—Alameda Plaza Hotel * Keystone, CO—Keystone Lodge
chorage—Hotel Captain Cook * Atlanta—Colony Square Hotel * Atlanta—The Ritz-Carlton Atlanta * Baden-Baden—
enner's Park-Hotel * Baltimore—Harbor Court Hotel * Bangkok—The Dusit Thani * Boston—The Colonnade * Cape Cod/
atham, MA—Wequassett Inn * Carmel—Quail Lodge * Charlotte—The Park Hotel * Chicago—The Barclay Chicago *
icago/Oak Brook—Oak Brook Hills Hotel * Cincinnati—The Cincinnatian Hotel * Cologne—Excelsior Hotel Ernst * Dallas—
tel Crescent Court * Dallas—The Mansion on Turtle Creek * Denver—The Brown Palace Hotel * Düsseldorf—Hotel
eidenbacher Hof * Fort Lauderdale—Pier 66 Hotel and Marina * Frankfurt/Wiesbaden—Hotel Nassauer Hof * Hong Kong—
e Peninsula * Honolulu—Halekulani * Houston—The Warwick * Indianapolis—The Canterbury Hotel * Kansas City—
ameda Plaza Hotel * Keystone, CO—Keystone Lodge * Las Vegas—Desert Inn Hotel & Casino * London—The Dorchester *
s Angeles—Westwood Marquis Hotel & Gardens * Lucerne—Grand Hotel National * Lucerne/Vitznau—Park Hotel Vitznau
Madrid—Palace Hotel * Malaga—Hotel Bvblos Andaluz * Manila—The Manila Peninsula * Maui—Maui Prince Hotel *
emphis—The Peabody * Milwaukee—The Pfister Hotel * Minneapolis—The Whitney Hotel * Montreal—Le Grand Hotel
Munich—Hotel Bayerischer Hof * Napa Valley/St. Helena—Meadowood Resort Hotel * New York City—Grand Bay Hotel at
uitable Center * New York City—United Nations Plaza Hotel * New York City/Long Island—The Garden City Hotel *
lando—The Peabody * Osaka—Royal Hotel * Palm Beach—The Breakers * Paris—Hotel Le Bristol * Phoenix—The Pointe at
uth Mountain * Portland—The Heathman Hotel * Rome—Ambasciatori Palace Hotel * San Antonio—La Mansión del Rio *
n Diego—U.S. Grant Hotel * San Diego/La Jolla—La Valencia Hotel—San Francisco—The Stanford Court Hotel * San
ancisco/Oakland—The Claremont Resort Hotel & Tennis Club * San Juan—El San Juan Hotel & Casino * Seattle—
rrento Hotel * Seoul—Hotel Lotte * Singapore—Goodwood Park Hotel * Sonoma—Sonoma Mission Inn & Spa * Tokyo—
perial Hotel * Toronto—Park Plaza Hotel * Toronto—The Prince Hotel * Vienna—Hotel Im Palais Schwarzenberg *
shington, D.C.—The Hay-Adams Hotel * Washington, D.C.—The Watergate Hotel * Washington, D.C./Alexandria—Mor-
on House * Wilmington—Hotel du Pont * Zurich—Hotel Baur Au Lac * Anchorage—Hotel Captain Cook * Atlanta—Colony

The Chef Prefers

Favorite Recipes by
the Chefs of

PREFERRED HOTELS®
WORLDWIDE

ALLAN PUBLISHERS, INC.

ISBN 0-8241-4010-9

Acknowledgement

Many thanks for the contents of this book go to the Chefs of Preferred Hotels; for sharing their creativity, their expertise, and for their invaluable contributions to these hotels.

Dedication

What is it that makes Preferred Hotels truly great? Our guests, of course. It is to these people that this book is dedicated. Thank you.

CONTENTS

Introduction

This is a cookbook for those who value the very best in fine food and wine...those who wish to duplicate the kind of dining experiences which can only be found in the best restaurants of the world. For it is from the Chefs of some of the world's best restaurants that this cookbook originates.

Restaurants renowned for their overall excellence...bastions of unique taste and style...reminding us of a time gone by. Places where courtesy and gracefulness, intimate luxuries and warm hospitality are the norm rather than the exception. Restaurants where dining is truly an experience to be relished...the restaurants of Preferred Hotels.

Of the thousands of luxury hotels throughout the world, only a handful in the United States, Canada, Europe, Asia and the Caribbean qualify as Preferred Hotels. What makes them so special? Quite simply, each must be established and recognized as the finest in its community.

Architectural appearance, staff, guest rooms and meeting facilities must be above reproach. Restaurants must offer superlative cuisine and ambiance proven by reviews, culinary awards, ratings, guests' comments and random inspections. And from the culinary awards and rave reviews these restaurants have received, the Chefs of these kitchens are the most talented in the world.

Each Chef was asked what he would personally recommend to a guest based on his years of training and experience. The menus in this book highlight the best from each restaurant, a unique compendium of tempting and exciting recipes which have never before been published.

The menus and recipes range from the traditional to the exotic. They reflect the interests and different ways of life of the national and international worlds they represent. Recipes range from tasty regional specialties and seasonal selections to elegant seafood dishes and unusual game entrees.

Recipes are included for appetizers such as Tenderloin of Baby Boston Turkey with Fresh Virginia Herbs from the award-winning Jean-Louis restaurant at The Watergate Hotel in Washington, D.C. Crabmeat Pancakes with White Butter Sauce is included from Gaddi's at The Peninsula in Hong Kong, one of the most fabled restaurants in the Orient.

The Mansion on Turtle Creek in Dallas, Texas, presents Tortilla Soup, a unique regional dish. Warm Squab Breast and Duck Foie Gras Salad, represents true continental cuisine, from the United Nations Plaza Hotel in New York City. And entrees such as Saddle of Lamb with a Garlic Cream Sauce from Hotel Le Bristol, situated in the heart of Paris, reflect the diverse backgrounds of the Chefs from these fine hotels.

What menu would be complete without mouth-watering desserts? Key Lime Pie from The Breakers in Palm Beach, or Bread and Butter Pudding from the Dorchester in London, both local specialties, are a few of the delicious desserts presented.

An accomplished cook or a frequent entertainer looking for menu ideas can find a wealth of suggestions to delight the eye and please the palate. Ideas abound that are right for every occasion...ideas which can make every dining experience delightfully easy and eminently successful.

Originality and versatility...these are the qualities that make a dining experience truly memorable. These same qualities make the restaurants of Preferred Hotels internationally renowned. This cookbook is a resource to be treasured, as there is no better endorsement than *"The Chef Prefers."*

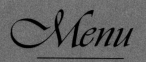

Menu

Deep-Fried "Clam Gulch" Clam Strips

Beer Batter Alaskan Halibut Cheeks

Dandelion and Fiddlehead Fern Salad
Hot Bacon Dressing

Wild Redcurrant Sherbet

Cook Inlet King Salmon
Quarter Deck Style

Rhubarb Blueberry Crisp

The Hotel Captain Cook, in downtown Anchorage, offers a variety of dining experiences unmatched elsewhere in town. "The Crow's Nest" offers simply the best French cuisine. Pizzas and sandwiches are served at "Fletcher's," a spirited English pub. New American cuisine is the specialty in the private club, "The Quarter Deck."

Deep-Fried "Clam Gulch" Clam Strips

Servings—12
Portion—1 clam

12 Alaska razor clams (or 24 Cherrystone clams)
2 cups (500 g) cornmeal
2 cups (115 g) breadcrumbs
2 cups (450 g) flour
6–8 eggs, beaten
1 tablespoon (15 g) paprika
Seasoned salt to taste

Soak clams overnight in milk to cover. Open clams and cut muscles connecting meat to shell; remove and discard bellies. Cut meat into ½-inch (1 cm) strips. Mix seasoned salt with flour. Combine cornmeal, breadcrumbs, and paprika, mixing thoroughly. Dip clam strips in seasoned flour, then in the beaten eggs. Cover in cornmeal/breadcrumb mixture. Deep fry in 400°F (200°C) oil for 1 minute. Serve with either tartar sauce or cranberry sauce.

Beer Batter Alaskan Halibut Cheeks

Servings—12
Portion—3 ounces (85 g)

2 pounds (900 g) Alaskan halibut cheeks
5 cups (1 k) flour
½ cup (125 g) cornstarch
1 egg
1 teaspoon (5 g) paprika
1 teaspoon (5 g) baking soda
1 teaspoon (5 g) baking powder
2 teaspoons (10 g) granulated garlic
4¾ cups (1¼ L) of beer (not dark)
Seasoned salt to taste
Parsley for garnish

Seasoned Flour—

Mix 1 cup (225 g) flour, cornstarch, 1 teaspoon (5 g) granulated garlic and seasoned salt.

Beer Batter—

Mix 4 cups (900 g) flour, paprika, baking soda, baking powder, remaining granulated garlic, and seasoned salt. Add egg and beer. Mix well to form a smooth batter.

Cut halibut cheeks into approximately 1-ounce (30 g) pieces. Dip in seasoned flour and then beer batter to coat. Deep fry in 375°F (190°C) for 1–2 minutes. Garnish with sprigs of parsley.

Cook Inlet King Salmon Quarter Deck Style

Servings—1
Portion—8 ounces (225 g)

½ pound (225 g) Alaska king salmon fillet
¼ cup (60 g) finely chopped onion
2 hard-cooked egg yolks, sieved
2 hard-cooked egg whites, sieved
Salt and white pepper to taste
Chive butter
Fresh chives for garnish

Chive Butter—

- **½ cup (115 g) unsalted butter, melted**
- **3 tablespoons (30 ml) white wine**
- **¼ cup (60 g) chopped fresh chives**
- **1 teaspoon (5 ml) lemon juice**
- **Dash of cayenne**
- **Dash of white wine Worcestershire sauce**

Combine all of the Chive Butter ingredients thoroughly.

Cut parchment paper into 7 inch (18 cm) hearts. Brush paper with clarified butter and place salmon in center. Spread chive butter evenly over fish. Starting on the diagonal, arrange alternate lines of the chopped onion, the sieved egg yolk, and the sieved egg white until fish is covered. Fold long sides of parchment paper together, and crimp edges to seal. Bake at 400°F (200°C) for 5 minutes. Garnish with fresh chives.

Rhubarb Blueberry Crisp

Servings—12
Portion—1 square

- **2 cups (500 g) rhubarb, cut into ½-inch (1.3 cm) pieces**
- **3 cups (700 g) blueberries**
- **2 cups (500 g) flour**
- **2¾ cups (410 g) sugar**
- **1½ teaspoons (7.5 g) salt**
- **2 teaspoons (10 g) baking powder**
- **2 eggs, slightly beaten**
- **1¾ cups (420 g) unsalted butter, melted**
- **3 cups (¾ L) crème chantilly**

Preheat oven to 350°F (180°C). Grease a 9 × 13 inch (23 × 38 cm) baking dish.

Wash blueberries and mix with rhubarb. Put fruit into prepared baking dish and sprinkle with ¾ cup (185 g) of sugar.

Topping—

Mix flour, remaining sugar, salt, and baking powder together. Add eggs and stir with fork until mixture resembles coarse meal. Sprinkle mixture on top of fruit. Pour melted butter over top. Bake at 350°F (180°C) for approximately 1 hour, or until the top is golden brown.

Serve portion with ¼ cup (60 ml) crème chantilly.

COLONY SQUARE HOTEL

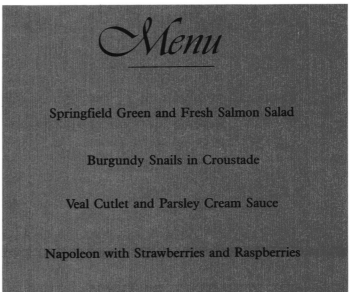

Menu

Springfield Green and Fresh Salmon Salad

Burgundy Snails in Croustade

Veal Cutlet and Parsley Cream Sauce

Napoleon with Strawberries and Raspberries

While you're staying at Colony Square Hotel, you needn't go far for a great place to dine. "Trellises of Midtown" is well known for its superlative menus, along with impeccable service and cheerful environment. "The Crown Room", atop the Hotel, offers a buffet of exceptional variety and taste.

Springfield Green and Fresh Salmon Salad

Servings—4
Portion—4 slices

   1 pound (450 g) fresh salmon fillets cut into 16 small slices

   16 fresh asparagus tips

   1 head red oak leaf lettuce

   ½ head chicore frise lettuce

   1 head Bibb lettuce

   ½ red bell pepper, finely diced

   2 tablespoons (30 g) chopped Italian parsley

   4 leaves cilantro

Vinaigrette—

   2 tablespoons (30 ml) finely chopped shallots

   3 teaspoons (15 ml) virgin olive oil

   3 teaspoons (15 ml) salad oil

   2 teaspoons (10 ml) lemon juice

   Salt and pepper to taste

Cook the salmon pieces in butter for 1 minute on each side. Set aside. Cook the asparagus for 4 minutes only. Clean and wash assorted greens and place alternately on dinner plates. Place pieces of salmon on top of the salad with asparagus tips crossing the plate. Sprinkle red bell pepper over the dish with finely chopped cilantro and Italian parsley. Heat the vinaigrette, lightly pour over the dish and serve.

Burgundy Snails in Croustade

Servings—4
Portion—1 pastry

   26 medium snails

   ¾ cup (180 ml) wine

   ¼ cup (60 g) shallots

   ⅓ cup (75 g) parsley

   2 tablespoons (30 g) garlic

   ½ cup (125 g) white mushrooms

   4 artichoke hearts

   ½ cup (120 ml) heavy cream

   ¼ cup (60 g) butter

   ½ cup (50 g) gruyère or Swiss cheese

   4 rounds frozen prepared puff pastry

   Salt and pepper to taste

Prepare 4 5-inch (13 cm) rounds of frozen puff pastry sheet dough. Cook snails in butter and shallots. Deglaze with white wine and reduce to half. Add fresh cream, finely chopped white mushrooms, and sliced artichoke hearts. Cook for 5 minutes. Add fresh chopped parsley and garlic. Place in croustades. Split in two lengthwise. Cover with cheese and place in broiler until tops are golden. Place on salad plate and cover with the second part of the prepared puff pastry.

Veal Cutlet and Parsley Cream Sauce

Servings—4
Portion—1 cutlet

- 24 ounces (675 g) boneless loin of veal cut into 4 6-ounce (180 g) portions
- ½ cup (120 g) oil
- ¼ cup (60 g) sweet butter
- 4 tablespoons (60 g) Italian parsley
- ¼ cup (60 g) carrots cut into very fine julienne strips
- 2 tablespoons (30 g) finely chopped shallots
- ¾ cup (180 ml) half-and-half
- ⅓ cup (75 ml) white wine
- 1 tablespoon (15 g) pink pepper

Sauté veal cutlets and shallots in oil and butter. When veal cutlets are cooked, set aside. Deglaze pan of cooked veal with white wine, add carrots. Reduce to half. Add fresh cream. Reduce to ⅓.

Add fresh sweet butter, Italian parsley, and pink pepper. Pour sauce over veal cutlets and garnish with green tips of baby carrots.

Napoleon with Strawberries and Raspberries

Servings—4
Portion—1 pastry

- 1 puff pastry sheet
- 1 cup (250 ml) pastry cream
- ½ cup (125 g) fresh raspberries
- ½ cup (125 g) fresh strawberries
- Raspberry and Strawberry coulis
- Cherry liqueur
- Angel hair sugar
- Confectioner's sugar

Pastry Cream

- 2 cups (½ L) milk
- ½ fresh vanilla stick
- 1¼ cups (280 g) sugar
- 8 egg yolks
- ⅓ cup (75 g) flan powder

Bring milk and vanilla to a boil. After milk mixture has boiled, add other ingredients, mix, and cook until mixture comes to a boil again, stirring constantly.

Raspberry and Strawberry Coulis—

- 1 pound (45 g) fresh strawberries
- 1 pound (450 g) fresh raspberries
- 2¼ cup (505 g) granulated sugar
- Dash lemon juice
- 1 ounce (30 ml) cherry liqueur

Cook slowly together strawberries, raspberries, sugar, and lemon juice until reduced in half. Add cherry liqueur and keep in a cold place.

Angel Hair Sugar—

- 2¼ cups (505 g) granulated sugar
- Lemon juice
- ¼ cup (60 g) corn syrup

Cook granulated sugar with lemon juice and corn syrup to a light caramel color. Pour slowly over pre-oiled pastry grill, using a fork in an up and down motion until sugar hairs are separated. Take off the grill and set aside.

Prepare puff pastry and cut in 4-inch (10 cm) round portions. Split in two lengthwise. Use two rounds for one Napoleon. Cover first round with pastry cream sweetened with liqueur. Leave hole in the center and garnish with strawberry and raspberry coulis. Place fresh strawberry in round design. Cover second round as above, but garnish with raspberries. Cover third round with strawberries. Cover top with raspberries, sprinkle with confectioner's sugar, and finish with angel hair sugar over the top.

THE RITZ-CARLTON

Menu

Chilled Asparagus with Port Wine Vinaigrette

Blue Ridge Mountain Trout with
Braised Spinach and Red Wine Butter Sauce

Sautéed Soft Shell Crab
with Lime Butter and Chives

Roasted Semolina Soup
with Basil and Sundried Tomatoes

Baked Fresh Figs in Phyllo Pastry

In the heart of Atlanta's business and financial district, The Ritz-Carlton is the home of one of the finest collections of art and antiques in the Southeast. A traditional Continental cuisine is served in the restaurant. This club-like dining room features 18th and 19th century paintings of English hunting scenes.

Chilled Asparagus with Port Wine Vinaigrette

Servings—6
Portion—8 asparagus

48 medium-sized asparagus
½ cup (125 g) shallots
1 tablespoon (15 g) butter
2 cups (½ L) port wine
2 egg yolks
3 tablespoons (45 ml) raspberry vinegar
1 tablespoon (15 ml) white wine vinegar
Juice of 2 limes
1 tablespoon (15 ml) sesame oil
1 cup (250 ml) walnut oil
1 cup (250 ml) safflower oil
Salt and pepper to taste

In large saucepot, bring salt water to a boil. Add the asparagus and cook for about 2 minutes. Drain asparagus and rinse with cold water. Set aside.

Sauté shallots and butter in a small saucepan for about 2 minutes. Add port wine and reduce to one third. Let cool slightly and put in blender. Add egg yolks, raspberry vinegar, white wine vinegar, and lime juice. Blend on low speed for about 1 minute. Blend in sesame oil, walnut oil, and safflower oil, a little at a time. Season with salt and pepper.

Garnish plate with tomato rose in center, surrounded by asparagus. Serve with port wine vinaigrette.

Blue Ridge Mountain Trout with Braised Spinach and Red Wine Butter Sauce

Servings—6
Portion—1 trout

6 trout, head and tail removed
2 tablespoons (30 ml) lemon juice
¼ cup (60 g) sweet butter
½ cup (120 ml) white wine
¼ cup (60 g) chopped shallots
3 cups (650 g) spinach (dip in boiling water for 1 minute to wilt)
Salt and pepper to taste

Season trout with salt, pepper, lemon juice, and white wine. Sauté over medium heat about 6–8 minutes on each side. Remove from sauté pan and add chopped shallots. Cook for 2 minutes and add wilted spinach. Sauté for 2 minutes.

Red Wine Butter Sauce—

1 cup (225 g) butter
6 tablespoons (90 g) shallots
¾ cup (200 ml) heavy cream
¾ cup (200 ml) red wine
White vinegar to taste
Lemon juice to taste
Salt, pepper, cayenne to taste

Butter should be room temperature. Sauté the shallots until lightly colored. Add red wine. Reduce until almost dry. Add cream and reduce until thickened. Slowly add butter, making sure each spoonful is well mixed before continuing. Do not allow to boil. Season with vinegar, lemon, salt, and pepper. Strain before serving.

Spoon the sauce onto each plate. Center the braised spinach in the middle of the plate and top with a sautéed trout. Garnish with lemon segments and diced tomatoes.

Sautéed Soft Shell Crab with Lime Butter and Chives

Servings—6
Portion—1 crab

> **6 medium-sized soft shell crabs**
> **1 cup (225 g) flour**
> **½ cup (112 g) sweet butter**
> **½ cup (120 ml) white wine**
> **2 limes**
> **½ cup (120 g) chopped chives**
> **½ cup (120 g) chopped shallots**
> **2 cups (½ L) heavy cream**
> **Salt and pepper to taste**

Season crabs with salt, pepper, and juice of one half lime. Coat crabs with flour on all sides. Heat 1 tablespoon (15 g) butter in large sauté pan and sauté crabs for about 4 minutes. Set crabs aside on warm serving plates.

Add 1 tablespoon (15 g) of butter in the same sauté pan, add shallots and sauté for 3 minutes. Add white wine and reduce by half. Add heavy cream and reduce by half. Whip in the rest of the butter a little at a time. Do not boil. Season with lime, salt and pepper and strain through a fine strainer. Finish with the chopped chives. Pour sauce on center of each serving plate. Set one soft shell crab on top of each plate. Garnish with lime slice.

Roasted Semolina Soup with Basil and Sundried Tomatoes

Servings—6
Portion—¾ cup (200 ml)

> **1½ cups (375 g) semolina**
> **½ cup (125 g) chopped shallots or onions**
> **¼ cup (60 g) prosciutto ham, finely sliced**
> **½ cup (125 g) tomatoes, sliced and sundried**
> **1 tablespoon (15 g) basil, chopped**
> **½ cup (115 g) Parmesan cheese, freshly grated**
> **½ teaspoon (2.5 g) garlic purée**
> **5 cups (1¼ L) chicken broth**
> **1 tablespoon (15ml) olive oil**

Sauté shallots, prosciutto ham, and garlic in olive oil for about 3 minutes on medium heat in a large soup pot. Add semolina and roast over high heat for 3 more minutes. Add chicken stock and simmer for about 20 minutes. Remove from heat, stir in sundried tomatoes, chopped basil, and parmesan cheese. If soup is too thick, thin with some more chicken stock.

Garnish with parmesan cheese and basil leaf.

Baked Fresh Figs in Phyllo Pastry

Servings—6
Portion—1 pastry

> **6 large figs**
> **6 sheets phyllo pastry**
> **2 tablespoons (30 g) melted butter**
> **2 tablespoons (30 ml) marzipan (optional)**

Cut about a 1-inch (3 cm) hole from bottom of fig up into the middle. Stuff with marzipan. Brush first layer of phyllo pastry with melted butter. Layer a second sheet of pastry on top, brush with butter and repeat twice. Cut into 6 sections. Set one fig in the center of each pastry section and wrap the dough around the fig. Bake the wrapped figs in a 425°F (220°C) oven for about 10 minutes. Serve hot.

Garnish with cocoa powder and wild berries.

Brenner's Park-Hotel

Menu

Herb Soup Baden-Style

Lobster with Avocado Mousse
with Mixed Green Salad

Turbot with Salmon Filling

Neuweier Riesling Sauce

Medallion of Veal with Fresh Morels,
Carrots and Snow Peas and Schupfnudeln

Strawberries with White Cheese Gratinee

Centrally situated in a private park overlooking the Lichtentaler Allee, Brenner's Park-Hotel is ten minutes walking distance to downtown shopping. The elegant Restaurant with gourmet dining faces the park, and the rustically decorated "Schwarzwald-Stube" serves the same exquisite cuisine, yet requires less formal dressing.

Herb Soup Baden-Style

Servings—16
Portion—½ cup (120 ml)

Veal stock—
- **12 cups (3 L) water**
- **4½ pounds (2 kg) veal bones**
- **¼ cup (60 g) leek**
- **¼ cup (60 g) carrots**
- **¼ cup (60 g) celery**
- **1 twig thyme**
- **1 clove garlic**
- **½ onion with laurel and clove to taste**

Simmer for about 4 hours.

Veloute of Veal—
- **Strained veal stock (from above)**
- **3 cups (¾ L) cream**
- **2 tablespoons (30 g) shallots**
- **¼ cup (60 g) butter**
- **¼ cup (60 g) flour**
- **Baden Riesling wine to taste**
- **Salt and white pepper to taste**
- **Whipped cream**

Reduce cream to 2 cups (½ L) and add strained veal stock.

Sauté shallots in butter, add flour and veal stock with cream.

Add some Baden Riesling wine and simmer mixture for about 1 hour.

Season with salt and freshly ground white pepper. Add fresh butter and some whipped cream.

Herbs to Season—
- **1 tablespoon (15 g) parsley**
- **1 tablespoon (15 g) chives**
- **1 teaspoon (5 g) chervil**
- **Mint**
- **Balm mint**
- **Thyme**
- **Rosemary**
- **½ teaspoon (2.5 g) tarragon**
- **½ teaspoon (2.5 g) basil**
- **½ teaspoon (2.5 ml) Liebstöckel**

Chop herbs and add to veloute of veal.

Lobster with Avocado Mousse with Mixed Green Salad

Servings—4
Portion—½ lobster medallions

Avocado Mousse—
- **¾ cup (180 g) avocado**
- **2½ tablespoons (40 g) grated apple**
- **1 tablespoon (15 ml) broth**
- **2 leaves gelatin**
- **⅔ cup (150 ml) whipped cream**
- **Salt and white pepper to taste**
- **Dash lemon juice**
- **Finely mashed spinach (for color)**
- **2 lobsters, boiled and cut into medallions**

Press the avocados through a fine sieve, add the grated apple, salt, and freshly ground white pepper, stir well.

Soak the gelatin leaves in cold water for 10 minutes. Bring the broth to a boil, drain gelatin and add to broth, stirring until gelatin melts. Carefully fold this into the avocado mixture. Refrigerate for 1 hour.

Toss the mixed greens with salad dressing and arrange on plate. Place some medallions of lobster and a portion of the avocado mousse next to the salad.

Medallion of Veal with Fresh Morels, Carrots, Snow Peas, and Schupfnudeln

Servings—4
Portion—4 ounces veal (115 g)

1 pound (450 g) veal medallions
Salt and pepper to taste
Butter
1 cup (225 g) fresh morels
½ cup (115 g) shallots
½ cup (120 ml) cream

Season the veal with salt and pepper, sauté in butter, and set aside in a warm place.

Wash the fresh morels in plenty of cold water until free of sand. Dry and sauté with finely chopped shallots in butter. Thicken with cream. Cook until tender. Pour over the veal medallions.

Serve with glazed carrots, snow peas and schupfnudeln.

Schupfnudeln—

2¼ pounds (1 kg) raw potatoes
2 whole eggs
2 yolks
⅔ cup (150 g) flour
6 tablespoons (80 g) butter
Salt and nutmeg to taste

Boil and mash the potatoes. Add salt and nutmeg and cool. Beat eggs and yolks together, add flour and potatoes. Mix together into a dough and shape into "cigars" about 3 inches (8 cm) long. Boil in salted water for about 3 minutes, then sauté with butter.

Strawberries with White Cheese Gratinee

Servings—8
Portion—⅓–½ cup (80–100 g) per person

1¾ pounds (800 g) fresh strawberries
1⅛ cups (250 g) white cheese, 40% fat
1½ tablespoons (25 g) confectioner's sugar
2 eggs, separated
Grated lemon to taste

Arrange strawberries neatly in a pan. Mix all ingredients together in a bowl, except egg whites and sugar.

Beat egg whites and sugar together until soft peaks form. Fold this into the white cheese mixture. Pour the mixture over the strawberries and bake for 10 minutes in a (425°F) (220°C) oven. Serve with chocolate ice cream.

HARBOR COURT
HOTEL

Menu

Lobster Bisque

Sautéed Oysters with Fennel Butter

Rainbow Trout with Crabmeat

Pecan Rum Tart

"Hampton's," featuring New American cuisine, was recently voted Baltimore's "Best New Restaurant." The emphasis is on Chesapeake Bay regional and Southwestern offerings. "Hampton's" interior features traditional decor and enjoys a spectacular view of Baltimore's Inner Harbor.

Lobster Bisque

Servings—10
Portion—1 cup (250 ml)

3 lobsters, 1–1¼ pounds
    (450 g–565 g) each, broken

1 cup (225 g) butter

2 carrots, chopped

3 stalks celery, chopped

5 cloves garlic, chopped

¼ cup (60 g) tomato paste

1 cup (225 g) flour

2 cups (425 ml) white wine

¼ cup (60 ml) dry sherry

8 cups (2 L) fish stock

2 cups (425 ml) heavy cream

Cayenne pepper to taste

Place butter and vegetables in large stock pot and sauté. Add lobsters, tomato paste, then blend in flour and cook for 10 minutes or until lobsters are red. Pour in wine, sherry, and stock. Cook for about 1 hour. Remove lobsters and clean, saving meat. Add cream to soup and strain.

After straining, add meat and cayenne pepper to taste. Serve hot.

Sautéed Oysters with Fennel Butter

Servings—6
Portion—4 oysters

4 eggs

32 oysters

2 tablespoons (30 g) fennel seed

⅓ cup (75 ml) Pernod

¾ cup, (180 g) beurre blanc

2 bags spinach

½ cup (30 g) seasoned breadcrumbs

6 tablespoons (45 g) Parmesan
    cheese

Lemon

Parsley

½ cup (115 g) unsalted butter

¼ cup (60 ml) cream

Salt and pepper to taste

Drain oysters. Bread them by putting into flour, then into beaten eggs. Drain

and place into seasoned breadcrumbs with cheese. Blanch spinach in hot water with a little olive oil floating on top. Drain. Sauté oysters in oil until brown and crispy. Set aside.

Place Pernod in pan and reduce. Add fennel seeds and beurre blanc. Add cream to pan and reduce until thick, then whisk in butter, a small amount at a time. Add salt and pepper to taste.

To serve, place spinach in center of plate surrounded with fennel butter and place oysters on top of sauce.

Garnish with lemon and parsley.

Rainbow Trout with Crabmeat

Servings—1
Portion—1 trout

¾ pound (340 g) rainbow trout,
    boned

¼ cup (60 g) lump crabmeat

¼ bunch green onions, chopped

¼ cup (60 ml) cream sauce

½ tablespoon (7.5 g) Old Bay spice

6 leaves (20 g) fresh basil
8 large spinach leaves

Sauté green onions in butter, add crab-meat and cream and cook for 5 minutes. Season with Old Bay, then add the chopped basil.

Stuff the middle of the trout with crab-meat. Wrap trout in spinach and brush with butter. Bake in 400°F (200°C) oven for 15–20 minutes. Serve with Aioli Sauce.

Aioli Sauce—
  4 egg yolks
  2 cups (425 ml) oil
  ¼ cup (60 ml) lemon juice
  4 cloves garlic, chopped
  1 cup (240 g) fresh basil
  Salt and pepper to taste

In food processor, beat yolks, then add oil slowly in a light stream to emulsify. Thin with lemon juice, then add basil and garlic. Season with salt and pepper. Purée.

Pecan Rum Tart

Servings—8
Portion—⅛" (3 mm) slice

  Pastry dough for 1 pie crust
  Melted chocolate
  1½ cups (350 ml) light corn syrup
  ½ cup (115 g) butter
  2 tablespoons (30 g) flour
  1¼ cups (225 g) brown sugar
  4 eggs
  ½ cup (120 ml) dark rum
  ½ cup (115 g) solid pack pumpkin
  2 cups (200 g) chopped pecans

Prepare a pie tin or tart pan with your favorite pie dough or crust. Prebake blind for about 7 minutes. Line the lightly baked shell with a thin coating of melted chocolate. Leave at room temperature.

Heat corn syrup and butter until butter melts. Stir in flour, brown sugar and eggs until well blended. Add rum and pumpkin. Pour into prepared pie shell until half full. Sprinkle with nuts. Add more filling if necessary. Bake at 375°F (190°C) approximately 20 minutes. (Baking time will depend on depth of pan.)

Garnish with freshly whipped and spiced cream.

The Dusit Thani

Menu

Dragon Collation
(Cold Hors d'Oeuvres)

Braised Superior Shark's Fin

River Lobster Sautéed in Oyster Sauce

Mashed Shrimp with Crab Roe Sauce

Just as the attraction of Thailand lies in the variety it offers, The Dusit Thani Hotel offers a full variety of culinary styles, especially the delights of "Chinatown." Here is the perfect blend of East and West, of classical heritage lovingly preserved, combining Thai and Chinese decor with superb Chinese cuisine.

Dragon Collation

Servings—6
Portion—2 ounces (60 g)

¼ pound (100 g) pork sausage
¼ pound (100 g) cooked ham
¼ pound (100 g) stuffed pork leg
¼ pounds (100 g) shrimp
½ roasted duck, boned
7 tablespoons (100 g) black mushrooms
2 pigeon eggs
1 tomato
¼ cucumber
1 carrot

Slice all ingredients and arrange in a pleasing manner on serving plate.

Braised Superior Shark's Fin

Servings—6
Portion—½ cup (125 g)

1¼ cups (280 g) prepared, dried shark's fins
4 slices fresh ginger root

5 spring onions
2 tablespoons (30 ml) rice wine or dry sherry
2 cloves garlic

Superior Stock—

½ pig knuckle
½ chicken
6 chicken feet
½ pound (200 g) lean pork
¼ cup (60 g) cooked ham
6 cups (1½ L) water

Soak the sharks' fins in cold water for 2 hours, boil, and simmer for 30 minutes. Drain and cover with more cold water for 2 hours. Bring to a boil, and simmer again for 30 minutes. Repeat this process twice. When complete, rinse the fins well in cold water and drain.

Bring stock ingredients to a boil in a separate saucepan, and skim. Simmer covered for 3 hours until the liquid is well reduced.

Place sharks' fins on a closely woven bamboo rack. Arrange the ginger and

spring onions on top, sprinkle with wine. Place the rack in a casserole and pour stock over. Place on a rack in a wok or in a steamer, cover and steam for approximately 1½ hours over simmering water. Remember to replenish the water occasionally. Remove the sharks' fins from the rack and place on a serving plate. Bring the stock to a boil and thicken with cornstarch dissolved in a little cold water. Simmer until the sauce becomes transparent. Season to taste and pour sauce over fins.

Mashed Shrimp with Crab Roe Sauce

Servings—6
Portion—3 ounces (85 g)

½ pound (200 g) fresh shrimp
¼ cup (60 g) pork fat
7 tablespoons (100 g) crabmeat, white
1 cup (225 g) crab roe
1 cup (225 g) Chinese green vegetables

Skin of ½ chicken
Vegetable oil for deep frying
½ cup (120 ml) chicken stock
½ teaspoon (2.5 g) salt
½ teaspoon (2.5 g) sugar
½ tablespoon (7.5 g) cornstarch
2 tablespoons (30 ml) vegetable oil

Combine the pork fat and shrimp, mashing until well mixed. Lay the chicken skin on a flat surface and spread the shrimp and fat mixture ½ inch (13 mm) thick to a surface area of approximately 6 inch × 6 inch (15 cm × 15 cm). Carefully lift the square and deep-fry. When golden brown, remove and drain on a wire rack. Slice the square into fingers 1 inch × 3 inch (2.5 cm × 8 cm). Cook vegetables with a little salt in boiling water for approximately 3 minutes.

Heat 2 tablespoons (30 ml) oil. Add soup stock, salt, and sugar. Stir gently for 1½ minutes. Add cornstarch to thicken. Add white crabmeat and roe and heat for 1 minute. Pour the mixture in the center of a serving dish and arrange the shrimp cakes on top. Garnish with the Chinese green vegetables.

River Lobster Sautéed in Oyster Sauce

Servings—6
Portion—½ lobster

3 10½ ounce (300 g) lobsters
⅔ cup (150 ml) oyster sauce
10 tablespoons (150 ml) chicken stock
1½ tablespoons (25 g) corn flour
1½ tablespoons (45 ml) vegetable oil
½ tablespoon (7.5 g) white pepper
1 tablespoon (15 ml) black soy sauce
2 tablespoons (30 ml) Chinese rice wine

Clean the lobsters. Drain and dry thoroughly. Cut the tail lengthwise. Sprinkle the meat with cornstarch. Heat frying oil in a wok and deep-fry for 4–6 minutes, turning during cooking until golden.

Heat oil, add the wine, soup stock, oyster sauce, pepper, and soy sauce. Stir-fry for 30 seconds, add cornstarch and stir for 30 seconds. Pour sauce over the lobster.

Garnish with fresh asparagus spears.

The Colonnade

Menu

Breast of Duck Salad

Mussel Soup with Saffron

Paillard of Salmon with Chanterelles
and Basil Sauce

Earl Grey Tea Sorbet

Loin of Veal on the Bone with Watercress Sauce

Fresh Figs with Raspberries

Mocca Friandises

The Colonnade is an independently owned luxury hotel located in the heart of Boston's finest shopping, cultural and business areas. Contemporary in feeling, the European style luxury hotel is dedicated to individualized service. "Zachary's," the hotel's fine dining room, is renowned for its classical European cuisine.

Breast of Duck Salad

Servings—4
Portion—½ breast

2 duck breasts

2 tablespoons (30 g) butter

**1 rounded teaspoon (5 g) Dijon
mustard**

Coarse salt to taste

Freshly ground pepper to taste

¼ cup (60 ml) champagne vinegar

½ cup (120 ml) walnut oil

**2 young heads of chicory (use only
the yellow hearts)**

2 tomatoes

32 walnut halves, freshly shelled

Melt butter and arrange the duck breast in a casserole with butter. Cook slowly over medium to low heat, until golden brown on all sides turning frequently.

While the breasts are cooking, prepare vinaigrette sauce. Mix mustard with salt, pepper, and vinegar. Whisk the walnut oil into mustard slowly. Drop

the tomatoes in boiling water, count to 10, remove, and plunge into cold water. Peel tomatoes, cut in half and remove seeds. Squeeze lightly to remove excess water. Cut into quarters, lightly season with 2 tablespoons (30 ml) of vinaigrette and set aside.

Cut the breast meat into thin slices about 2½ inches (6.5 cm) long. Arrange on a plate and brush with strained juices, slightly warmed.

Separate the leaves of chicory, washing well. Shake and dry with a towel. To serve, mix the chicory with the vinaigrette and divide among 4 large plates. Lay the slices of duck on top of the chicory, harmoniously with the tomatoes and walnuts. Before serving, brush the duck meat again with the slightly warmed juices and serve immediately.

Mussel Soup with Saffron

Servings—4
Portion—3 ounces (75 ml)

2½ pounds (1¼ kg) mussels

½ cup (120 ml) dry white wine

¼ cup (60 ml) olive oil

1 onion, finely chopped

**1 leek (white part only), finely
chopped**

1 carrot, minced

1 clove garlic, finely chopped

3 tomatoes, peeled and chopped

**Bouquet garni (sprigs of thyme and
parsley and a bay leaf, tied
together)**

Saffron flowers—

2 cups (425 ml) fish stock

1 teaspoon (5 g) saffron threads

Coarse salt to taste

½ cup (120 ml) créme fraîche

Freshly ground pepper to taste

In preparing the mussels, choose large heavy mussels, alive and full of seawater. Scrape off the beards, scrub the mussels well, and rinse them in several changes of cold water without letting them soak. Place mussels in a casserole large enough to hold twice their volume. Pour the white wine over them and cover tighly. Cook about 4 minutes, turning once or twice. When mussels open, let cool enough to be handled, then remove the shells, dropping the mussels into a small bowl. Strain cooking liquid through a fine sieve lined with cheesecloth. Cover the mussels completely to keep them warm and moist. Save the remaining strained broth.

Heat the olive oil in a large casserole, and add the onion, leek, and carrot. Cover and cook over low heat for 15 minutes without browning. Stir frequently. Add the garlic, tomatoes, and bouquet garni. Cook 1 minute, then pour in the remaining mussel broth and the fish stock. Bring the liquid to a boil and skim the surface. Remove ½ cup (120 ml) of hot broth, blend it with the saffron, and return it to the soup. Add salt to taste, then cover, and simmer 40 minutes. Uncover the casserole and add the fresh cream. Return the soup to a gentle boil. Add salt and pepper to taste.

To serve, drain the mussels and place in a warmed soup tureen. Pour the boiling soup over the mussels and serve.

Paillard of Salmon with Chanterelles and Basil Sauce

Servings—6
Portion—8 ounces (225 g)

- 1 3-pound (1⅓ kg) salmon
- 10 shallots, peeled and minced
- 2 cups (240 g) fresh basil, cleaned and chopped
- 6 medium white mushrooms, cleaned and sliced
- 1 pound (450 g) fresh chanterelles, cleaned, with stems trimmed
- 1 cup (250 ml) dry white wine
- 1 cup (250 ml) heavy cream
- 1 quart (1 L) fish stock
- 1 cup (225 g) sweet butter
- ⅓ cup (75 ml) vegetable oil
- 2 cups (500 g) all-purpose flour

Paillards of Salmon—

Fillet salmon and cut into 8 ounce (225 g) portions. Place the salmon portions between plastic wrap, and lightly pound the pieces until about ⅛ inch (.32 cm) thick. In a separate saucepan, sauté the chanterelles in 2 tablespoons (30 ml) of sweet butter until golden brown on all sides. Add salt and pepper to taste. Immediately before serving, heat a large saucepan coated with vegetable oil until it smokes. Quickly place a portion of salmon in the pan. Sauté 30 seconds on each side. Serve the salmon on top of the sauce. Place the chanterelles on top of the salmon, and garnish with fresh basil leaves around the mushrooms.

Beurre Manie—

Combine 1 cup (225 g) of butter and 1 cup (225 g) of flour in a mixing bowl. Knead the mixture by hand, until smooth. Refrigerate.

Basil Sauce—

Lightly sauté shallots, mushrooms, and 1 cup (12 oz) of basil, for 3 minutes. Deglaze with white wine and reduce to ¼ cup (60 ml). Add the fish stock (see instructions below), and reduce by half. Add beurre manie small pieces at a time, until consistency coats the back of a spoon. (Not all the beurre manie will be necessary, but can be saved for future use). Add heavy cream and simmer for 20 minutes. Strain through a fine sieve. Add remaining chopped basil. Add salt and pepper to taste.

Fish Stock—

- ⅛ pound (56 g) sweet butter
- 1 onion, peeled and diced (medium-sized)
- 1 celery stalk, diced (medium-sized)
- 1 leek, washed thoroughly, diced (medium-sized)
- Pinch thyme
- 1 bay leaf
- 2 tablespoons (30 g) crushed black pepper
- 3 pounds (1⅓ kg) red snapper, striped bass or flat fish bones
- 1 cup (¼ L) white wine

Heat butter until melted. Add all the vegetables and herbs. Cover and sauté for 5 minutes. Add fish bones and white wine. Cover and sauté for 5 more minutes. Cover with water and simmer slowly for 45 minutes. Strain stock and return to stove. Reduce until 1 quart (1 L) of stock remains.

WEQUASSETT INN

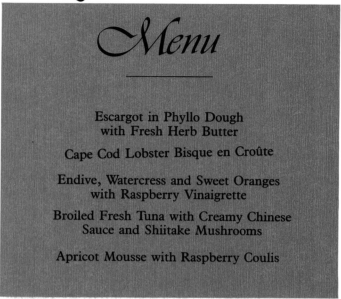

Menu

Escargot in Phyllo Dough
with Fresh Herb Butter

Cape Cod Lobster Bisque en Croûte

Endive, Watercress and Sweet Oranges
with Raspberry Vinaigrette

Broiled Fresh Tuna with Creamy Chinese
Sauce and Shiitake Mushrooms

Apricot Mousse with Raspberry Coulis

The Wequassett Inn is nestled amidst the pines overlooking Pleasant Bay. The guest rooms and elegant meeting facilities are all individually designed and decorated in the New England tradition. Dining is elegant in this lovely 18th century Sea Captain's home, offering continental cuisine and native seafood specialties.

Escargot in Phyllo Dough with Fresh Herb Butter

Servings—4
Portion—3 triangles

24 snails
2 tomatoes, peeled and diced
2 tablespoons (30 g) garlic, finely chopped
½ shallot, finely chopped
1 sprig of parsley, tarragon, thyme, and basil, finely chopped
6 ounce (185 g) box phyllo dough
¼ cup (60 g) pine nuts, toasted
¼ cup (60 ml) dry white wine
¼ cup (55 g) butter
¼ cup (60 ml) heavy cream
Egg wash

Sauté the snails in additional butter. Add ¼ of the chopped shallot, garlic, diced tomato, pine nuts, and half of the fresh herbs. Season with salt and pepper. Let snails cool. Wrap 2 snails with some of the sauté in a triangle of phyllo dough. Dip triangles in egg wash, then bake for 10 minutes at 375°F (190°C).

Fresh Herb Butter—

Reduce the white wine and remainder of the ¼ cup chopped shallot. Add heavy cream and reduce again by half. Add butter, little by little, and season to taste. Add the remaining fresh herbs and diced tomatoes.

Cover the bottom of a 9 inch (23 cm) plate with the herb butter and diced tomatoes. Place escargot triangles on top. Garnish with a sprig of basil.

Cape Cod Lobster Bisque en Croûte

Servings—4
Portion—8 ounces (250 ml)

2 1-pound (450 g) fresh lobsters
½ cup (125 ml) olive oil
1 bunch fresh tarragon
1 carrot, diced
1 onion, diced
¼ celery rib, diced
6 tablespoons (90 g) tomato paste
¼ cup (60 ml) dry white wine
¼ cup (60 ml) brandy
4 cups (1 L) fish stock
Thyme, bay leaf, salt, pepper, and cayenne to taste
¼ cup (60 ml) heavy cream
1½ cups (375 g) puff pastry dough

Cut the live lobsters in half and sauté in very hot olive oil. Add the carrots, onion, celery, thyme, bay leaf, tarragon, tomato paste, cayenne, salt, and pepper and flambé with brandy. Add the white wine and reduce, then add the fish stock and cook for 20 minutes. Remove meat from the lobster and dice for garnish. Strain the lobster bisque and reduce. Add heavy cream and diced lobsters to bisque and cool.

Place bisque in an 8 ounce (¼ L) cups containing some lobster meat. Cover the cups with pastry dough. Place in a water bath and bake at 425°F (220°C) for 25 minutes.

Endive, Watercress, and Sweet Oranges with Raspberry Vinaigrette

Servings—4
Portion—1 salad

2 endives
1 bunch of watercress
2 oranges
1 egg
¼ cup (60 ml) raspberry vinegar
1 teaspoon Dijon mustard
1 cup (250 ml) peanut oil
6 tablespoons (90 g) fresh raspberries, blended and seeded
Salt and pepper to taste

Wash and dry the endive and watercress. Peel and slice oranges. Break the egg into a bowl. Add mustard and raspberry vinegar, and blend very slowly. Add the fresh raspberries. Season to taste.

Arrange the endive and sliced oranges on the plate with the watercress in the middle. Top with raspberry vinaigrette just before serving.

Broiled Fresh Tuna with Creamy Chinese Sauce and Shiitake Mushrooms

Servings—4
Portion—8 ounces (250 g)

2 pounds (900 g) fresh yellowfin tuna, cut into 8 ounce (250 g) portions
6 tablespoons (90 g) fresh shiitake mushrooms, julienned
2 tablespoons (30 g) garlic, finely chopped
3 tablespoons (45 ml) soy sauce
3 tablespoons (45 ml) oyster sauce
2 tablespoons (30 ml) sesame oil
1 shallot, finely chopped
¼ cup (60 ml) dry white wine
1 cup (225 g) butter
½ cup (120 ml) heavy cream
Salt and pepper to taste
Pinch basil, tarragon, parsley, finely chopped

Marinate the tuna steaks in oil, soy sauce, and fresh herbs for 10 minutes. Broil until medium rare.

Reduce the white wine and shallots, then add heavy cream and reduce by half. Add the butter a little at a time with a whisk. Add garlic, oyster sauce, and sesame oil. Season to taste with salt and pepper. Sauté the mushrooms and add to the sauce.

Place sauce on the plate, and place the tuna steaks on the sauce. Serve with a vegetable and wild rice.

Apricot Mousse with Raspberry Coulis

Servings—4
Portion—4 ounces (125 g)

¾ cup (115 g) dried apricots
⅓ cup (75 g) apricot preserves
2 tablespoons (30 ml) apricot brandy
¾ cup (180 ml) heavy cream (whipped)
¾ cup (115 g) fresh raspberries

Purée the apricots, add the preserves, and apricot brandy. Add the whipped cream and serve in a lace tulip made of corn syrup and brown sugar.

Juice the raspberries and add sugar to taste for the coulis. Arrange a plate with the raspberry coulis, heavy cream, and the lace tulip on top for each serving.

QUAIL LODGE

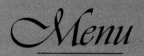

Menu

Mary Helen's Soup
Leek and Onion with Fresh Horseradish Cream

Roulade of Sole and Salmon
Paprika Sauce
Dilled Cucumbers

Breast of Range Hen
with Date and Walnut Stuffing
Cranberry Glaze

Green Salad with Nasturtium Leaves

Chocolate and Grand Marnier Mousse Torte

The casual elegance of Quail Lodge is conveyed through the natural wood interiors of "Covey Restaurant." Its large glass windows and sky-lights bring in the beauty of the outdoors. The menu combines quality and simplicity with a European touch, an International style that is perfectly suited to American tastes.

Mary Helen's Soup

Servings—16
Portion—6 ounces (200 ml)

   2 tablespoons (15 g) butter
   2 small leeks
   1 medium onion
   2 small boiling onions
   2 sprigs thyme (or ½ teaspoon (2.5 g) dried thyme)
   3 quarts (2¾ L) chicken broth
   ⅔ cup (155 g) scraped horseradish (or 2 tablespoons (30 g) prepared horseradish)
   1 cup (250 ml) whipping cream

Cut off the bottom third of the leeks and cut them across in regular slices, ³⁄₁₆ inch (48 cm). Wash well in cold water, separating the "rings" in the process. Split the remainder, wash well, and chop into large pieces. Dice the onion. Place the butter, chopped leek, diced onion, and thyme in a heavy saucepan and sauté over moderate heat 3–6 minutes. Add the chicken broth.

Bring to boil and simmer 15 minutes; strain.

Cut the boiling onions into rings and place them together with the leeks in the strained broth. Bring to a boil and simmer 5 minutes. Season to taste with salt and white pepper.

Whip the cream. Chop the scraped horseradish into large pieces and fold it into the cream, or fold prepared horseradish into the cream. Place in a serving bowl to accompany the soup.

Breast of Range Hen with Date and Walnut Stuffing

Servings—8
Portion—1 breast

   4 4-pound (1¾ kg) range hens or large frying chickens
   2 ribs celery
   1 leek
   1 medium onion
   2 bay leaves
   2 sprigs thyme (or ¼ teaspoon (1.2 ml) dried thyme)

   Small bunch of lovage (optional)
   1 inch (2.54 cm) piece ginger root
   8 cups (2 L) water
   3 tablespoons (45 g) clarified butter

Remove legs from hens and save for another use. Cut wings off just inside the second joint. Pull off skin, remove wishbone. Cut off breasts, leaving the wing bone attached to the breast. Refrigerate breasts while you prepare stock, sauce, and stuffing.

Stock—

Make a chicken stock with the carcasses, winglets, and trimmings by placing them in a stew pan with the vegetables, water, and herbs. Bring to a boil and simmer 2½–3 hours. Strain and skim. Reduce to approximately 1 cup (250 ml).

Sauce—

   4 cups (1¾ kg) cranberries
   2 tablespoons (9 g) sugar (or more to taste)
   2 cups (½ L) water
   3 tablespoons (25 g) butter, unsalted

1 tablespoon (15 g) arrowroot in 2 tablespoons (30 ml) water

Salt to taste

Cayenne pepper to taste

1 cup (250 ml) reduced chicken stock

Boil the cranberries, water, and sugar together until fruit is soft. Strain. Reduce to approximately 1 cup. Add the reduced chicken stock. Thicken with the arrowroot and then whisk in the unsalted butter. Season to taste with salt and cayenne.

Stuffing—

1 cup (150 g) pitted dates, coarsely chopped

⅔ cup (65 g) walnuts

1 tablespoon (15 g) chopped shallots

2 tablespoons (30 g) chopped parsley

½ cup (125 g) chopped ham

⅔ cup (50 g) white breadcrumbs

⅛ teaspoon (.6 ml) ground black pepper

Place all ingredients except breadcrumbs in food processor and blend together in short "pulses." Do not overprocess. Blend in breadcrumbs.

Place the chicken breasts skin-side down on a cutting board. Lift the tenderloin or fillets from each breast, and flatten the breasts and fillets with a meat mallet. Put some of the stuffing on each breast. Cover it with the fillets and fold over the breast meat to form a thick "package."

Season with salt and pepper, and dust with flour.

Heat 3 tablespoons (45 g) clarified butter in a heavy flat-bottom sauté pan. Place the breasts, folded side down, in the pan to seal the closure.

Bake the hen breasts 20 minutes at 350°F (177°C), basting frequently.

To serve, place wild rice in the center of each plate. Surround rice with cranberry sauce. Place a chicken breast on top of the rice and tuck broccoli florets around the chicken.

Chocolate and Grand Marnier Mousse Torte

Servings—12
Portion—1 slice

Base—

4 cups (240 g) soft cake crumbs

2 teaspoon (10 g) orange zest

4 tablespoons (60 g) clarified butter

2 tablespoons (30 ml) Grand Marnier

Mix the ingredients together and press evenly onto the bottom of a 12-inch (2.54 cm) springform pan.

Mousse—

12 ounces (375 g) Swiss chocolate

⅜ cup (90 ml) water

⅔ cup (175 g) sugar

5 egg yolks

3 egg whites

1½ cups (350 ml) whipping cream

⅓ cup (75 ml) strong coffee

3 tablespoons (45 ml) Grand Marnier

4½ tablespoons (100 g) soft butter (unsalted)

Slowly melt the chocolate over a double boiler, keeping chocolate mixture dry. Boil the water and sugar together for 3 minutes. Place the egg yolks in a bowl with the boiled syrup and coffee. Stand the bowl over boiling water, whisk over heat until it thickens to a creamy consistency. Remove from heat. Add the melted chocolate and whisk. Beat the egg whites and fold into chocolate mixture. Whip the cream and fold in mixture. Pour this mousse into the springform pan. Chill 1 hour.

Run a heated knife around the edge of the pan, then remove the rim. Smooth the edge of the mousse with a heated spatula. Chill while preparing the frosting.

Frosting—

12 ounces (340 g) Swiss chocolate

1½ cups (350 ml) cream

½ cup (120 ml) strong coffee

2 tablespoons (30 ml) Grand Marnier

½ cup (125 g) soft butter

Finely chop the chocolate. Bring the cream and coffee to a boil. Remove from heat and add chocolate. Mix with a wooden spoon until chocolate is fully blended. Add Grand Marnier. Reserve 1¼ cups (315 g) frosting.

Coat the mousse evenly with the warm remaining chocolate frosting. Chill. Remove mousse to serving platter. Warm reserved frosting over boiling water. Remove from heat and whisk in soft butter. Cool this mixture to a soft piping consistency, and with a pastry bag, decorate the torte.

Menu

She Crab Soup

Salad of Carolina Quail
Endive, Lemon Green Beans, and Foie Gras

Centercut Swordfish Steak Broiled
in White Butter Sauce
Roast Peppers and Crayfish, White Rice

Peanut Butter Tartlettes with
Carolina Peach Coulis

A rich and fiercely independent local heritage is echoed in the uncompromised tradition of unhurried attention and friendly service at Charlotte, North Carolina's Park Hotel. From a dinner menu that changes daily, "Morrocrofts" offers an eclectic blend of American and Continental cuisine, punctuated with a variety of regional favorites.

She Crab Soup

Servings—6
Portion—1 cup (¼ L)

   2 shallots, peeled and chopped
   2 tablespoons (30 ml) oil
   ½ cup (120 ml) sherry
   1 quart (1 L) clam juice
   2 cups (½ L) heavy cream
   ½ teaspoon (2.5 ml) pepper
   1 teaspoon (5 ml) salt
   ½ teaspoon (2.5 ml) thyme
   ¼ teaspoon (1.2 ml) basil
   Pinch red pepper
   ½ cup (125 g) cornstarch
   6 ounces (185 g) lump crabmeat

Sauté shallots in oil for 3 minutes. Add sherry and clam juice and bring to boil. Add cream and all spices. Simmer for 20 minutes.

Thicken with cornstarch that has been mixed with just enough water to make fluid paste. Simmer for another 5 minutes. Do not strain.

Add lump crabmeat and serve.

Centercut Swordfish Steak Broiled in White Butter Sauce

Servings—6
Portion—1 swordfish steak

   6–8 ounces (225 g) boneless
      swordfish steaks
   3 tablespoons (45 ml) olive oil
   1 tablespoon (15 g) salt
   1 tablespoon (15 g) pepper
   2 cups (500 g) red and green
      peppers, julienned
   3 tablespoons (45 g) butter
   ¾ cup ounces (180 g) crayfish
      tailmeat
   6 cups (2 kg) white rice, cooked

Sauce—

   2 chopped shallots
   ½ cup (120 ml) white wine
   ½ cup (120 ml) heavy cream
   3 tablespoons (45 g) butter, room
      temperature

Brush swordfish with olive oil. Salt and pepper both sides. Sauté on grill at high heat for 5–7 minutes, or to de-

sired doneness. Remove and keep warm.

Sauté peppers in butter. Season to taste. Add crayfish and sauté 2 minutes longer. Remove and keep warm.

For sauce, reduce white wine with shallots for 5 minutes. Add cream and simmer for 5 minutes. Mix room temperature butter into sauce slowly, stirring constantly after each addition with a wire whisk until combined. Do not boil.

Remove from heat and season to taste.

Arrange steak, sautéed peppers and crayfish, and rice on plate.

Salad of Carolina Quail

Servings—6
Portion—Pieces of ½ quail

   ½ box taboule
   1 tablespoon (15 ml) vinegar
   1 tablespoon (15 ml) oil
   1 tablespoon (15 ml) chopped
      parsley

Salt and pepper to taste

6 ounces (185 g) princess (young tender string) beans

3 quail, deboned and cut into pieces

4 tablespoons (60 ml) sherry vinegar

3 Belgian endive, cleaned

2 radicchio, cleaned

3 ounces foie gras, cut in sticks

Marinade—

1 shallot, chopped

3 tablespoons (45 ml) olive oil

1 tablespoon (5 ml) Dijon mustard

1 tablespoon (15 ml) lemon juice

Soak taboule as specified on label. Season with vinegar, oil, and salt and pepper to taste. Add fresh chopped parsley.

Blanch green beans in boiling water until just tender. Plunge into ice water to stop cooking and to retain green color. Drain. Put beans into marinade of shallots, lemon juice, mustard, and olive oil.

Sauté deboned pieces of quail with a little oil. Add salt and pepper to taste. Remove from pan when golden brown. Deglaze residue in pan with sherry vinegar and reduce to about 3 tablespoons (45 ml).

Arrange endive spears in fan shape. Place one soupspoon of taboule in center. Decorate with radicchio. Place quail between endive spears and add glaze. Arrange string beans and foie gras on the centered taboule.

Peanut Butter Tartlettes with Carolina Peach Coulis

Servings—6
Portion—2 tartlettes

12 pre-baked tartlette shells

6 ounces (180 g) cream cheese, room temperature

3 tablespoons (45g) 10-X sugar

1 cup (225 g) peanut butter

2 cups (½ L) whipped cream

3 peaches, peeled, pitted, and sliced into small cubes

2 tablespoons (30 g) sugar

¾ cup (180 ml) pear brandy

For filling, whip cream cheese with sugar. Add peanut butter, and mix for 5 minutes. With wooden spoon, carefully fold in whipped cream. Refrigerate filling for 30 minutes prior to filling tartlette shells. Serve with coulis.

For coulis, combine peaches, sugar and pear brandy in small skillet, and simmer for 20 minutes. Remove from heat and chill.

THE BARCLAY CHICAGO

Menu

Chilled Cream of Green Split Pea
Garni Mint—Sour Cream

Grilled Sweetbreads with Wild Mushrooms

Belgian Endive with Fromage Chevre and Apples
Sherry Wine Vinaigrette

Walnut Breaded Fillet of Sole

Sweet Potato Flan
Roasted Zucchini

Peppermint Bavarian

The Barclay Chicago, downtown Chicago's only all-suite luxury hotel, stands in the heart of the city's renowned Magnificent Mile, a boulevard of Chicago's finest shopping and entertainment establishments. Hotel guests are welcomed to the "Barclay Club," a prestigious members-only dining club, with award winning meals.

Chilled Cream of Green Split Pea

Servings—6-8
Portion—8 ounces (250 ml)

8 cups (2 L) chicken stock
2 cups (450 g) green split peas
1 quart (1 L) heavy cream
Salt and pepper to taste

Soak split peas overnight in plain water in double boiler.

Bring chicken stock to boil, add split peas, and simmer until completely cooked—45 minutes to 1 hour.

Strain peas from stock, purée in food processor, and add back into stock. Add salt and pepper to taste. Chill mixture for at least 3 hours. Add heavy cream and adjust seasoning to taste.

Serve in chilled soup cups.

Garnish with a swirl of sour cream and top with mint sprig.

Grilled Sweetbreads with Wild Mushrooms

Servings—8
Portion—3 ounces (85g)

2 pounds (900 g) sweetbreads
½ pound (225 g) each morels, shiitake, cepes, and chanterelles mushrooms (or any locally available mushrooms that are of a comparable quality and consistency).
2 cups (½ L) veal glacé (see recipe below)
¼ cup (60 ml) cognac
8 quarts (7½ L) water
Salt and pepper to taste

Clean, peel, and soak sweetbreads for 2 hours in plain water.

Pat dry and cut into eight 3-ounce (85 g) portions. Grill each portion, preferably on a charcoal grill, to sear. Set each piece aside on an ovenproof plate as they are seared.

Slice mushrooms uniformly, and sauté for 5 minutes in peanut oil, deglaze with cognac, and add veal glacé. Salt

and pepper to taste.

Place sweetbreads in preheated 325°F (170°C) oven for 5 minutes. Transfer to serving plate, and cover with mushrooms.

Garnish with fresh rosemary sprigs.

Veal Glacé—

6 cups (1.5 L) water
2-3 pounds (900 g-1⅓ kg) veal bones
2 onions
4 celery stalks
4 carrots
2 tomatoes
2 leeks

Brown bones in hot oven until well done but not burnt.

Put all ingredients in a 4-gallon (15 L) stockpot and simmer 12-15 minutes. Do not let water level reduce.

Strain stock, place in smaller pot (6-quart (5¾ L) saucepan). At rolling boil, reduce to ½ to ⅔, depending on richness desired.

Walnut Breaded Fillet of Sole

Servings—6
Portion—3 2-ounce (60g) pieces

4 eggs
3 cups (¾ ml) water
2 cups (200 g) walnuts
6 cups (720 g) rice flour
2 cups (240 g) semolina flour
Salt and pepper to taste
18 2-ounce (60 g) sole fillets
1 cup (250 ml) safflower oil
6 lemon wedges

Make egg wash with eggs and water. Place sole fillets in egg wash set aside.

In food processor, coarsely grind walnuts, rice flour, semolina flour, and salt and pepper. Be careful not to overprocess the mixture, as the oil from the walnuts will make the mixture too moist and cause it to clump.

Dredge sole fillets in walnut/flour mixture. Heat safflower oil in sauté pan, and, when medium hot, sauté fillets for 2–3 minutes per side.

Garnish each serving with a lemon wedge.

Peppermint Bavarian

Servings—8–10
Portion—1 tulip glass

½ pound (225 g) cinnamon hots
2 cups (½ L) water
8 cups (2 L) heavy cream
4 egg yolks
2 cups (450 g) sugar
1 teaspoon (5 ml) vanilla
2 tablespoons (30 ml) peppermint oil
6–8 fresh mint leaves
1 pound (450 g) red and white mints

Melt cinnamon hots in 2 cups water in small saucepan. Set aside.

Warm 4 cups (1 L) heavy cream to scald (bring to boil, but do not boil). Separate eggs and place yolks in double boiler with sugar. Whip until it reaches ribbon-like consistency. Slowly add warm cream, stirring constantly. Warm over medium heat to form custard. Slowly add vanilla and peppermint oil as custard is formed—about 20 minutes.

Let custard cool.

In a mixer, whip remaining cream to form high peaks.

In a food processor, grind mints to medium-fine granules.

Fold whipped cream and mint granules into custard mixture. Swirl cinnamon hots mixture around inside of an 8-ounce (¼ L) tulip champagne glass.

Pipe mixture into tulip glasses with number 1 star tip on pastry bag. Chill.

Garnish with fresh mint leaf.

OAK BROOK HILLS
HOTEL & CONFERENCE CENTER

Menu

Shrimp Sausage
with Lemon Cognac Sauce

Escargot Soup

Foie Gras Salad

Lamb Loin in Phyllo Dough
with Beurre Roux with Sun-Dried Tomatoes

Braised Lettuce with Grapes

Apple Pudding

Oak Brook Hills Hotel, located on 150 acres of wooded countryside, offers a unique dining experience. "Waterford", the specialty dining room, is elegant and intimate. Haute cuisine is served with impeccable service in a setting of rich wood, soft colors and imported Waterford crystal chandeliers.

Shrimp Sausage with Lemon Cognac Sauce

Servings—6
Portion—3 sausages

Shrimp Sausage—
- 1½ pounds (675 g) clean raw shrimp
- ½ cup (120 ml) heavy cream
- 4 egg whites
- 1 teaspoon (5 g) red pepper
- 1 teaspoon (5 g) salt
- 1 teaspoon (5 g) white pepper
- 1 teaspoon (5 ml) granulated garlic
- 1 sprig oregano, chopped
- 1 stem thyme, chopped
- Sausage skin

Place 1 pound (450 g) of raw shrimp in food processor along with all spices. Process on high and blend to a paste. Add cream and eggs, processing on slow until mixture is a thick mousse, about 15 seconds.

Take the last ½ pound (225 g) of shrimp and chop into ¼ inch (.6 cm) pieces.

Remove mousse from processor, and add to chopped shrimp. Mix well. Place all of mousse in a sausage stuffer. Grease tube before you place on sausage skin. Cut sausage skin about 2 inches (5 cm) longer than you need (to tie knot). Try to keep sausages as tight as possible. After you have piped all filling into skins and tied them, bring 1 gallon (3¾ L) of salted water to boil. Boil sausage for 7 minutes.

Lemon Cognac Sauce—
- 3 ounces (75 ml) cognac
- ½ cup (120 ml) heavy cream
- 1 lemon
- Salt and pepper to taste
- 2 tablespoons (30 g) butter

Place cognac in a 1-quart (1 L) saucepan over high heat; let flame. When flame is gone, add cream, and turn heat down to low. Squeeze in juice of one lemon. Let cook until cream thickens. Add salt and pepper to taste. Whisk in butter.

Place sausage in sauce in center of plate. Sausage should be cut into 1" (2.5 cm) segments, three per serving. Garnish with fresh rosemary sprigs and tomato rose.

Escargot Soup

Servings—6
Portion—¾ cup (180 ml)

- 1½ cups (375 g) canned French escargot
- 1 quart (1 L) heavy cream
- ½ cup (120 ml) white wine
- 2 garlic cloves, chopped
- ¼ cup (60 g) shallots, chopped
- 2 tablespoons (30 g) fresh chives, chopped
- 3 stems of thyme, chopped
- 3 sprigs rosemary, chopped
- 3 stems tarragon, chopped
- 6 leafs basil, chopped
- Salt and pepper to taste
- 1 cup (225 g) butter
- 6 slices seedless rye bread, cubed

Coarsely chop escargots and sauté in a little butter. Add shallots and all herbs (except salt and pepper). Sauté for about 2 minutes.

Add wine and flambé. Add heavy cream and cook slowly for about 5 minutes. Add salt and pepper to taste. Cook approximately 5 more minutes at a slow boil. Add remaining butter.

Cook rye bread cubes in oven at 350°F (180°C) until crisp.

Serve with rye cubes and a few chopped chives on top.

Lamb Loin in Phyllo Dough

Servings—6
Portion—6 ounces (180 g)

1 3-pound (1⅓ kg) lamb loin, untrimmed
½ pound (225 g) fresh spinach, stems removed
2 cloves garlic, chopped
6 sheets phyllo dough
Salt and pepper to taste
1 teaspoon butter
2 eggs

Trim all fat off lamb loin. Cut into 6-ounce (180 g) portions.

Pour a little olive oil in a sauté pan, and place over high heat. Salt and pepper each portion of lamb, and sauté rapidly on both sides, approximately 20 seconds on each side. Let cool.

Sauté spinach and garlic with a little salt and pepper. Blot any excess oil. Wrap spinach around lamb loins. Cover all the lamb.

Preheat oven to 350°F (180°C).

Lay out one sheet of phyllo dough (work quickly with dough.) Place lamb in center. Fold sheet over the top, so you have two layers on top. Cut off any excess from open ends, and tuck the rest under. Wrap in plastic. Wrap each loin in this manner.

When ready to cook, remove plastic and place on a buttered sheet pan. Beat egg and cover each one with egg wash.

Cook 10 minutes (medium-rare); 15 minutes (medium); 20 minutes (well-done).

Cut in half (across grain of lamb), and serve open-faced with beurre roux and sun-dried tomato sauce.

Beurre Roux with Sun-Dried Tomatoes

Servings—6
Portion—1 Tablespoon (15 g)

1 ounce (30 g) chopped shallots
¼ cup (60 g) chopped sun-dried tomatoes
½ cup (120 ml) red wine
½ cup (120 ml) heavy cream
1 cup (225 g) unsalted butter, room temperature
Salt and white pepper to taste

Place shallots, tomatoes, and red wine in heavy saucepan over medium heat. Reduce by half.

Add heavy cream. Let reduce by half. Remove from heat. Whip in butter.

Sauce may be held at warm temperature.

Apple Pudding

Servings—6
Portion—⅙

1 cup (225 g) flour
⅛ teaspoon (.6 ml) salt
3 eggs
1¼ cups (275 ml) milk
¼ cup (60 g) sugar
1½ pounds (675 g) apples, peeled, cored, and cut into ¼ inch (.6 cm) slices
¼ cup (60 g) sugar

For batter, mix flour and salt in bowl. Beat in eggs one at a time. Then beat in milk until smooth. Whip in sugar.

Preheat oven to 350°F (180°C).

Butter 6-cup (1½ L) soufflé dish and place apples in layer on bottom. Sprinkle with ¼ cup (60 g) sugar. Pour batter over apples.

Bake 40 minutes until cake tester comes out clean. Serve warm with whipped cream, flavored with 2 tablespoons (30 ml) Calvados.

THE CINCINNATIAN

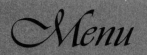

Menu

Minnesota Wild Rice Soup

Roast Loin of Veal
with Salmon and Spinach

Citrus Sorbet

Romaine Leaves Filled with Shrimp, Artichoke Hearts
and Sweet Red Pepper Pasta, Finished with Fresh
Basil, Tomatoes and Mustard Cream

Chocolate Peanut Butter Banana Tart

The newly restored Cincinnatian Hotel, opened in 1882 as The Palace, is one of the oldest existing hotels in the United States. Included in the National Register of Historic Places, The Cincinnatian's dining room, aptly renamed "The Palace," features New American cuisine, emphasizing regional menu items with each change of season.

Minnesota Wild Rice Soup

Servings—8
Portion—8 ounces (250 ml)

1 cup (200 g) uncooked wild rice
3 cups (¾ L) chicken broth
4 cups (2 L) heavy cream
3 cups (¾ L) demi glaze
3 cups (185 g) bacon, diced
3 cups (185 g) smoked ham, finely diced
¾ cup (185 g) carrots, finely diced
¾ cup (185 g) onion, finely diced
¾ cup (185 g) celery, finely diced
1 cup (225 g) clarified butter
1¼ cups (280 g) flour
Worcestershire sauce, Tabasco sauce
Salt and pepper to taste

Cook the rice in chicken broth. The rice should be slightly undercooked when finished.

In a 2-quart (2 L) saucepot, sauté bacon 2–3 minutes in the clarified butter, add vegetables, and sauté another 3–4 minutes. Add flour to make a roux. Add heavy cream and demi-glaze. Reduce at a simmer for 10 minutes on low heat.

Add rice and stir continuously for 15 minutes. Season to taste. Simmer another 10 minutes.

Roast Loin of Veal with Salmon and Spinach

Servings—8
Portion—6 ounces (180 g)

2 pounds (900 g) veal strip loin, trimmed of all fat and sinew
¾ pound (340 g) fresh salmon, boneless
1 cup (250 g) fresh spinach, blanched

Seasoning Mixture—

¾ cup (200 ml) olive oil
1 tablespoon (15 g) paprika
1 tablespoon (15 g) cayenne pepper
1 tablespoon (15 g) dry thyme
2 tablespoons (30 g) pommeray mustard
1 tablespoon (15 g) garlic, mashed
1 tablespoon (15 g) shallots, mashed

Butterfly the veal lengthwise almost in half, leaving 1 inch (2.54 cm) of meat to act as a hinge when opening up the veal strip loin. Cover the entire strip with plastic wrap. Pound with a meat mallet until ½ inch (1.3 cm) thick.

Cut the salmon into three 4-ounce (115 g) fillets, using same method of pounding as for veal. Flatten salmon fillets until ½ inch (1.3 cm) thick. Place salmon on top of veal strip loin, to evenly cover veal.

Thoroughly wash and remove all stems from spinach. In an 8-quart (7½ L) saucepan with lid, place cleaned spinach leaves along with 1 cup (250 ml) of water and bring to a boil. Remove pan from heat immediately and drain spinach completely through a colander; let cool. Spread spinach evenly over veal and salmon. Season with salt and pepper.

Roll entire veal strip loin lengthwise

and place the seam on the bottom. Tie loin with kitchen twine in three parts. Mix seasonings together and rub over entire roast. Heat ½ cup (120 ml) olive oil, in a sauté pan to very hot. Sear the roast on all sides. Transfer to a large baking dish and pour remaining seasoning mixture over roast. Place in a 350°F (180°C) oven for 20–30 minutes. Let rest for 20 minutes before slicing portions. Place small amount of veal juice under each serving portion.

Chocolate Peanut Butter Banana Tart

Servings—8
Portion—⅛ tart

Chocolate Short Dough—
   1½ cups (340 g) butter
   ½ cup (115 g) sugar
   1 egg
   1 tablespoon (15 ml) vanilla
   2 cups (240 g) cake flour
   6 tablespoons (90 g) cocoa powder

Cream sugar and butter together. Add vanilla and egg; whip until smooth. Sift cocoa and cake flour and then add to mix. Whip until smooth; let rest for 1 hour in refrigerator.

Pastry Cream—
   4 cups (1 L) milk
   15 egg yolks
   1½ cups (340 g) all-purpose flour
   ¼ cup (30 g) corn starch

Heat milk to slow boil. In separate bowl, mix egg yolks and sugar until well-blended. Add flour and corn starch; mix well. Add entire mixture to milk, mixing well until just thickened. Pour into container and allow to cool.

Chocolate Tart—
   ⅓ cup (75 g) sugar
   1 banana

Butter a 10″ (25 cm) tart tin (3″ (7.6 cm) deep. Roll chocolate short dough to ⅛″ (.3 cm) thick. Place evenly into tin. Perforate lightly with fork and

sprinkle with ⅓ cup (75 g) sugar. Bake at 375°F (190°C) in a preheated oven 12–15 minutes until sugar begins to dissolve. Remove and allow to cool. Slice banana into ¼ inch (6 cm) slices into bottom of cooled tart.

Pastry Cream Sauce—
   4 cups (1 L) pastry cream (above)
   1 cup (250 g) peanut butter
   2 packets gelatin (soften according to directions)
   4 cups (1 L) heavy cream (lightly whipped)

Mix pastry cream and peanut butter until smooth. Add softened gelatin to mixture. Mix well; fold whipped cream into mixture. Pour into tart shell and chill for ½ hour.

After chilled, fan-slice bananas on top. Melt 1 pound (450 g) of semi-sweet chocolate in a double boiler, pour over tart, and allow to cool before serving.

Excelsior Hotel Ernst

Menu

Terrine of Quails

Consommé of Truffles with Dumplings

Escalope of Salmon in Sorrel Cream

Baron of Lamb with Spices in a Savoy Coat
with String Beans and Gratinated Potatoes

Hazel-nut Parfait with Morello Cherries

Opposite the world famous cathedral and in the very center of the city is situated Cologne's leading luxury hotel. Cologne is recognized as one of the most important German centers for trade and industry, the third largest town in West Germany, the world's gathering point for the "Photokina" and organizer of the famous art fairs.

Terrine of Quails

Servings—4
Portion—4 slices

- **8 fresh quail**
- **½ fresh chicken**
- **½ cup (115 g) fillet of veal**
- **⅓ cup (80 g) butter**
- **½ cup (115 g) goose liver**
- **1¾ tablespoons (25 g) pistachio nuts**
- **1¾ tablespoons (25 g) dried morels**
- **1¾ tablespoons (25 g) fresh truffles**
- **2 tablespoons (30 ml) each, cognac, port, gin**
- **2 eggs**
- **Salt and pepper to taste**
- **Thin slices of bacon**

Marinate the meat of quail, chicken, and veal in cognac, port, and gin for 2 days. Soak morels in water until they are tender.

Sauté the marinated veal for a short time in butter, add a dash of cognac. Remove the meat from the frying pan, allow to cool. Mince all the meats and mix into a mousse. Add 2 tablespoons (30 g) goose liver, eggs, butter, salt and pepper to the mousse.

Line terrine form with thin slices of bacon. Pour in half of the mousse and top with the slices of truffles, pistachios, and morrels.

Fill the breast of quails with remaining goose liver, and place on top of the mousse. Pour in remaining mousse, and finish with bacon slices.

Heat oven to 170°F (75°C). Place terrine in a water bath and bake for about 1½ hours. Remove and cool. Unmold and slice.

Consommé of Truffles with Dumplings

Servings—4
Portion—1 cup (¼ L)

Consommé of Truffles—

- **4 cups (1 L) strong, skimmed chicken broth**
- **2 cups (½ L) truffle-jus**
- **12 slices fresh truffles**
- **Madeira wine, to taste**
- **Finely diced carrot, leek, and celery**

Bring the chicken broth and truffle-jus to a boil. Add Madeira and diced vegetables and simmer.

Dumplings—

- **¼ cup (60 g) meat of poulard**
- **¼ cup (60 g) marinated mousse of goose liver**
- **1 teaspoon (5 g) truffles**
- **2 tablespoons (30 ml) of double cream**
- **Salt and pepper**

Mix the meat of poulard in a mixer, add cream, truffles, and mousse of goose liver. Salt and pepper to taste. Boil some water in a pot adding salt. Scoop the mousse with a tablespoon and place in a pot of boiling, salted water for about 6 minutes.

Serve the consommé, dumplings, and slices of truffles in hot bowls.

Escalope of Salmon in Sorrel Cream

Servings—4
Portion—1 fillet

1⅓ pounds (600 g) fresh salmon
2 tablespoons (30 ml) vermouth
4 tablespoons (60 ml) dry white wine
2 shallots
⅔ cup (140 g) fresh sorrel
3 tablespoons (45 g) butter
Dash double cream
½ lemon
Salt and pepper to taste

Remove the fish bones, skin and cut into equal-size fillets. Boil the fish bones, skim fat, add spices, and boil for 10 minutes. Remove the fish bones and reduce the stock.

Add shallots, white wine, and vermouth to the stock, reduce and mix with butter in a mixer. Keep the sauce warm.

Wash the sorrel and remove stems, cut half in fine slices. Mix the other half with water. Reduce the sauce; add salt, pepper, and lemon juice. Add the sorrel purée, and keep the sauce warm. Do not boil again.

Mix some white wine and shallots in a pan, and add salted fillets. Sauté each side for about 1½ minutes.

To serve, top each fillet with one leaf of sorrel on a hot plate. Add the sauce. Serve immediately.

Baron of Lamb with Spices in a Savoy Coat with String Beans and Gratinated Potatoes

Servings—4
Portion—1 fillet

Saddle of Lamb—

2 pounds (900 g) saddle of lamb fillets
Olive oil
Salt, pepper, thyme, basil, tarragon, rosemary to taste

Sauté the lamb fillets on each side quickly in very hot olive oil and spices. Remove from frying pan, and set aside.

Sauce—

Lamb bones
Carrots, celery, shallots

Garlic, laurel leaf
1 cup (250 ml) red wine
2 tablespoons (30 g) butter
Thyme
Brown lamb sauce

Sauté the bones in frying pan until they become brown. Add the vegetables and garlic, and heat slowly. Add red wine and reduce. Add the lamb sauce, allow to reduce again; then strain.

String Beans/Gratineed Potatoes—

1⅛ cups (250 g) string beans
2 tablespoons (30 g) butter
Salt and pepper to taste
1 pound (450 g) potatoes
2 cups (½ L) cream

Cook string beans in salted water, plunge in cold water. Drain, add butter, salt and pepper to beans.

Peel potatoes and cut in slices. Rub an ovenproof dish with garlic, and layer potatoes in dish. Add cream, salt, and pepper. Bake in a 425F (220C) oven for about 90 minutes. Just before serving, brown the top under the broiler.

Menu

Grilled Corn and Smoked Chicken Soup

House Smoked Salmon

Sonoma Baby Lamb
with Roasted Garlic-Shallot Sauce and Pesto

Field Green Salad
with Warm Marinated Texas Goat Cheese

Blueberry Cheesecake with Oatmeal Crust
and Orange Yogurt Sauce

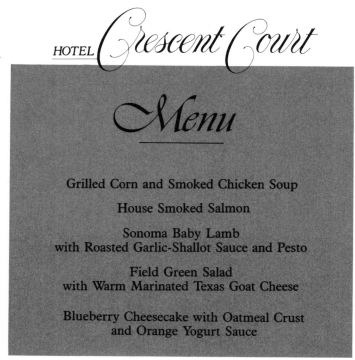

Overlooking downtown Dallas, Rosewood's landmark Hotel Crescent Court is the centerpiece of the Crescent Complex, offering guests luxury accommodations with European charm. Nestled inside is the famous "Beau Nash Restaurant," featuring Italian cuisine blended with a California flair.

Grilled Corn and Smoked Chicken Soup

Servings—6
Portion—1 cup (250 ml)

8 cups (2 L) chicken stock

6 tablespoons (85 g) apple-smoked bacon, diced ⅛″ (.3 cm)

¾ cup (180 g) smoked chicken breast, diced ⅛″ (.3 cm)

¾ cup (180 g) grilled corn (approximately 3 ears)

¾ cup (180 g) red onion, finely chopped

½ cup (115 g) cilantro leaves

½ cup (115 g) roma tomatoes, peeled, seeded and diced ⅛″ (.3 cm)

2 jalapeños, diced with seeds

6 wedges of lime

1 ripe avocado, cut into 6 wedges

1½ cups (340 g) tortilla strips ⅛″ (.3 cm), fried crisp

1½ cup (350 ml) sour cream

Bring chicken stock to a boil and reduce to a simmer. Cut corn off the cobs and add cobs only to chicken stock. Cook for 10 minutes and remove.

Brown bacon until crisp. Add bacon, chicken, red onion, tomato, corn, and jalapeños to chicken stock. Cook for 5 minutes; then add cilantro.

Divide the tortilla strips equally among the serving bowls. Place a wedge of lime and avocado in each bowl, ladle soup. Serve with sour cream on the side.

House Smoked Salmon

Servings—6–8
Portion—1 slice

1 cup (250 g) smoked salmon

1 cup (250 ml) sour cream

1 cup (250 g) bacon

1 bunch chives

½ cup (120 ml) chicken stock

½ cup (115 g) golden caviar

2 large potatoes

1 ½ cups (350 ml) cream

3 peeled shallots, finely chopped

2 tablespoons (30 g) butter

Salt and white pepper to taste

Peel potatoes and slice very thin—1/16″ (.15 cm). Cook briefly in boiling salted water (approximately 2 minutes). Drain and reserve. Melt butter in a saucepan, add shallots and bacon, cook until lightly browned. Add chicken stock and reduce by half. Add cream and reduce until very thick—about ⅓ the original volume. Stir in ¾ cup (200 ml) of the sour cream. Place potatoes in sauce and cook for 1 minute. Divide onto serving plates, making sure that each has an equal amount of potatoes. Place plates underneath preheated broiler and brown. (Use ovenproof plates only.) Broil until golden brown and bubbly. Remove plates and top with 1 slice of salmon, (approximately 1 ounce (30 g)). Top with a dollop of sour cream and golden caviar. Sprinkle with chives and serve immediately.

Sonoma Baby Lamb with Roasted Garlic-Shallot Sauce and Pesto

Servings—4
Portion—1 lamb rack

- 4 baby lamb racks
- 4 cups (1 L) lamb stock
- 2 large-head garlic cloves, peeled
- 12 shallots, peeled
- 2 medium zucchini
- 2 medium carrots
- 1 medium red onion
- 2 medium yellow squash
- 1 medium red pepper
- ½ cup (115 g) shiitake mushrooms
- 1 bunch rosemary
- 6 tablespoons (85 g) butter

Preheat oven to 500°F (260°C). Cut zucchini, carrot, red onions, mushrooms, and red peppers into fine julienne strips all the same size. Place 3 tablespoons (45 ml) olive oil in a large roasting pan and heat on stovetop until very hot. Season the lamb racks with rosemary, salt, and black pepper. Place fat side down and brown. Flip racks over and place roasting pan with lamb into oven. Add whole shallots and garlic cloves. Cook at 500°F (260°C) for 8–10 minutes. Remove from oven and place lamb on warm platter to rest for 10 minutes before cutting into chops.

To make sauce: heat lamb stock in saucepan, and add 1 branch rosemary, roasted garlic, and shallots. Reduce and swirl in 4 tablespoons (60 g) butter. Cook vegetables in butter. Add salt and pepper. Place vegetables in a mound on serving plate. Lean the chops against the vegetables and pour sauce over the chops. Serve immediately.

Lamb Stock—

- 5 pounds (2¼ kg) lamb bones
- 1 medium carrot, sliced
- 1 medium onion, split
- 1 rib celery, chopped
- 1 bunch thyme
- 1 teaspoon (5 ml) tomato paste

In a 400°F (200°C) oven, brown bones in roasting pan. Brown carrots, onion, and celery in 3 tablespoons (30 ml) olive oil. Place bones in large 12-quart (11 L) saucepan and immerse in water.

Add thyme, tomato paste, and vegetables. Bring to a boil. Reduce to light simmer and cook 3–4 hours, stirring frequently. Strain.

Pesto Sauce—

- 2 cups (500 g) basil leaves
- ¼ cup (25 g) pine nuts, roasted
- 4 garlic cloves
- ¼ cup (60 ml) olive oil
- ½ cup (60 g) Parmesan cheese, grated
- 1 teaspoon (5 g) black pepper, cracked
- 1 teaspoon (5 g) salt

Place all ingredients in food processor with steel blade. Using "pulse" technique, reduce mixture to a chunky texture (approximately 20–30 seconds of processor action).

Blueberry Cheesecake with Oatmeal Crust and Orange Yogurt Sauce

Servings—8
Portion—⅛" (3 mm) slice

Filling—

- 1¾ cups (400 g) cream cheese
- 6 tablespoons (85 g) granulated sugar
- 2 eggs
- 1 tablespoon (15 ml) vanilla extract
- 2 cups (500 g) fresh blueberries

Cream the cream cheese, and slowly add sugar. Add eggs, one at a time, mixing until smooth. Add vanilla. Fold in blueberries.

Oatmeal Crust—

- ½ cup (115 g) butter
- 1 cup (250 g) oatmeal
- ½ cup (115 g) flour
- ½ cup (100 g) brown sugar

Melt butter. Combine dry ingredients, and stir into melted butter. Place in 9 inch (23 cm) high-side ring pan. Bake 35 minutes at 350°F (180°C). Serve with orange yogurt sauce.

Orange Yogurt Sauce—

- ¾ cup (200 ml) plain yogurt
- 3⅓ tablespoons (50 ml) orange juice
- Grated zest of 1 orange

Combine all ingredients. Whisk until smooth.

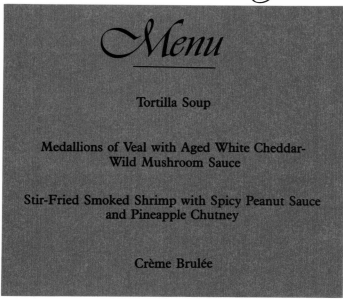

the Mansion on Turtle Creek

Menu

Tortilla Soup

Medallions of Veal with Aged White Cheddar-Wild Mushroom Sauce

Stir-Fried Smoked Shrimp with Spicy Peanut Sauce and Pineapple Chutney

Crème Brulée

The magnificent original dining room, now the Cocktail Lounge of the "Mansion on Turtle Creek Restaurant," was designed by the great French architect, M. Jacques Caree. The room has an inlaid ceiling composed of 2,400 separate pieces of wood. The fireplace in this room is a reproduction of one in the Bromley Castle in England.

Medallions of Veal with Aged White Cheddar-Wild Mushroom Sauce

Servings—4
Portion—2 medallions

    8 2½-ounce (70 g) veal loin fillets,
        about ½-inch (1 cm) thick
    4 tablespoons (60 ml) peanut oil
    Salt to taste
    Aged white cheddar and wild
        mushroom sauce
    Asparagus-leek compote

Heat oil in large sauté pan over medium heat. Season fillets with salt to taste and quickly sauté veal for about 3 minutes on one side. Turn medallions and brown for 2 minutes. Do not crowd pan. Remove from pan and keep warm.

Ladle aged white cheddar and wild mushroom sauce over bottom plates. Place 2 medallions of veal on each plate. Garnish with equal portions of asparagus-leek compote, and serve immediately.

Aged White Cheddar-Wild Mushroom Sauce—

    ½ pound (225 g) veal bones, cut into
        small pieces
    1 tablespoon (15 ml) peanut oil
    2 large white mushrooms, wiped
        clean and thinly sliced
    2 large shallots, peeled and chopped
    1 clove garlic, peeled and chopped
    2 sprigs fresh thyme
    2 cups chicken stock
    1 cup (250 ml) heavy cream
    ½ cup (60 g) aged white cheddar
        cheese, grated
    1 tablespoon (15 g) unsalted butter
    1½ cups (340 g) assorted wild mush-
        rooms (such as shiitake, chan-
        terelles, pleurotes), julienned
    Salt to taste
    Juice of ½ lemon or to taste

Preheat oven to 400°F (200°C).

Ask butcher to cut bones into pieces. Place veal bones on a baking sheet and roast for about 12–15 minutes or until brown. Be careful not to burn or blacken.

Heat peanut oil over medium heat. Add white mushrooms and sauté for 1 minute. Add shallots and garlic; sauté for 1 minute. Add browned veal bones, thyme, and chicken stock. Bring to a boil, then simmer for 20 minutes.

Add cream and return liquid to a boil. Lower heat and simmer for about 15 minutes or until liquid is reduced by about ¼ or is thick enough to coat the back of a spoon. Remove bones from sauce. Pour sauce into a food processor or blender along with cheese. Process until smooth. Strain and keep warm.

Melt butter over medium heat, then add mushrooms. Sauté mushrooms for 2 minutes. Season lightly with salt. Fold cooked mushrooms into sauce. Adjust seasoning with salt and lemon juice.

Crème Brulée

Servings—6
Portion—1 pastry
Puff Pastry—
   2 cups (450 g) flour
   Pinch of salt
   1 cup (225 g) unsalted butter
   ½ cup (120 ml) ice water
   1 teaspoon (5 ml) lemon juice

Combine flour, salt, and 3 tablespoons (45 g) butter. Cut butter into flour using a pastry cutter or food processor.

Combine water and lemon juice. Add to flour, mixing to form a pliable dough. Knead by hand 2–3 minutes, or process in a food processor until dough forms a ball.

Roll dough on lightly floured chilled surface, preferably a marble slab. Surface *must* be chilled. Roll dough to an 8 × 12-inch (20 × 30 cm) rectangle. Butter should be cool but malleable. Place pastry with short side facing you. Place butter in center of rectangle and fold third of pastry in toward center. Repeat with far third of pastry in toward center. Repeat with far third of pastry to form three layers. Press edges of pastry lightly with rolling pin to seal. Give pastry a quarter turn and roll again into a rectangle; fold and seal as before. Be careful to ensure that butter does not break through during rolling. If it does, immediately lightly dust with flour and roll again. Wrap and chill at least 15 minutes.

Repeat rolling, folding, and chilling 5 more times, chilling 30 minutes each time. Chill 1 hour after final rolling.

Preheat oven to 350°F (180°C).

When well-chilled, roll out as thin as possible on lightly floured, *chilled* surface. Cut out six 6-inch (15 cm) rounds. Using rounds, line the ungreased cups of muffin pan (3½ inches × 1½ inches (8 × 3 cm)). Press evenly into cups and trim edges. Line with a small coffee filter or parchment paper and fill to the top with dried beans (or commercial pastry weights).

Place in preheated oven and bake for 20–30 minutes or until pastry is crisp and golden. Remove beans (or weights) and allow shells to cool to room temperature.

Crème Brulée
   6 extra large egg yolks
   1¼ cups (285 g) sugar
   3 cups (675 ml) heavy cream
   1 vanilla bean, split
   1 cup (250 g) raspberries
   Puff pastry (see above)
   Raspberry sauce (see below)

Combine yolks and ½ cup (115 g) sugar in top half of a double boiler over very hot water. Whisk (or beat with a hand mixer) until lemon-colored and the consistency of mousse. Remove from heat and set aside.

Place cream and vanilla bean in a heavy saucepan over medium heat. Bring to a boil and immediately remove from heat. Strain through a fine sieve. Slowly pour into egg yolks, whisking rapidly.

Return double boiler to heat and cook, stirring constantly, for about 10 minutes or until quite thick. Remove top half from double boiler and place in a bowl of ice. Stir occasionally while mixture cools and reaches the consistency of very thick custard.

Scatter a single layer of fresh raspberries into baked pastry shells. Pour cooled crème over raspberries to top of shell. Refrigerate for at least 3 hours (or up to 12 hours). When chilled, sprinkle 2 tablespoons (30 g) sugar over each filled shell and place about 6 inches (15 cm) away from broiler flame for about 3 minutes or until sugar caramelizes. Do not overbroil, or crème will melt.

Immediately remove from heat. Pour raspberry sauce over the bottom of dessert plates. Place a crème brulée in center and serve immediately.

Raspberry Sauce—
   1 cup (225 g) fresh raspberries
   ¼ cup (60 ml) simple syrup

Purée raspberries in a blender or food processor. When smooth, strain through an extra fine sieve to remove all seeds. Stir simple syrup into raspberry purée until well blended.

The Brown Palace Hotel

Menu

Smoked Salmon Terrine
with Watercress Sauce

Filet of Dover Sole
with a Scallop Mousse and Saffron Cream

Warm Foie Gras with Field Greens

Grilled Rack of Lamb
with Black Truffle Sauce

Surprise Du Poire, Massenez

The Brown Palace Hotel, a near-century-old national historic land-mark, is conveniently located in the heart of downtown Denver. "The Palace Arms Restaurant" is internationally acclaimed for award-winning cuisine and elegant atmosphere. The formal dining room is enriched by historic stained glass and genuine antiques.

Smoked Salmon Terrine with Watercress Sauce

Servings—6
Portion—3 ounce (85 g) slice

Terrine—
  1½ cups (340 g) cream cheese
  ¼ cup (60 g) fresh dill
  ¼ cup (60 g) salmon caviar
  Salt and pepper to taste
  ½ pound (225 g) thinly sliced smoked salmon

Whip cream cheese until soft. Fold in the dill and salmon caviar. Season to taste.

To assemble the terrine, line a small loaf pan or terrine mold with plastic wrap, extending wrap well over sides. Line the bottom and sides with the sliced smoked salmon overlapping slices lightly. Spread a ¼ inch (.6 cm) thick layer of the filling in the bottom of the terrine. Layer smoked salmon on filling. Repeat the layers of filling and salmon to the top of the terrine, ending

with salmon. Fold the ends of the salmon from the pan liner over the top layer of salmon. Wrap top with plastic wrap and refrigerate overnight.

Sauce—
  1 bunch watercress
  1 cup (250 ml) sour cream
  ¼ cup (60 ml) heavy cream
  Salt and pepper to taste

Wash and finely chop watercress leaves. Mix watercress, sour cream, and heavy cream well. Season to taste.

Unmold and unwrap terrine. Place sauce on the lower third of each serving plate. Slice terrine with a hot wet knife. Place each slice on plate partially on the sauce.

To garnish, place 1 tablespoon (15 g) each of Beluga and golden caviars at lower corner of slice so that they form petals (a "V"). Between the caviars, place a small sprig of fresh dill.

Grilled Rack of Lamb with Black Truffle Sauce

Servings—6
Portion—3 chops

Lamb—
  18 French rib chops
  Salt and pepper to season

Lamb chops should have a 2½-inch (6 cm) French rib bone and ½-inch (1.3 cm) of tail meat from the eye of the chop. Season each chop with salt and pepper just before cooking. Preheat the broiler oven to 550°F (275°C). Place chops on broiler and cook 4–5 minutes on each side to desired doneness.

Black Truffle Sauce—
  ½ cup (125 g) shallots, peeled and coarsely chopped
  3⅓ tablespoons (50 ml) Madeira wine
  3⅓ tablespoons (50 ml) brandy
  1¼ cups (275 ml) brown sauce

2 tablespoons (30 g) truffle peelings
4 tablespoons (60 g) unsalted butter

Peel and coarsely chop the shallots. Add Madeira, brandy, and shallots to saucepan. Bring to a boil and reduce liquid by ½. Add brown sauce. Bring to a boil and reduce heat to simmer 10 minutes. Check seasoning. Strain sauce into another saucepot. Add truffle peelings and whip in butter. Keep sauce hot until ready to serve.

Brown Sauce—

Brown lamb bones and trim in saucepot with basic mirepoix (onions, celery, carrots). Add garlic, rosemary, and a tomato product. Add water to cover. Bring to a boil; then simmer for 1–2 hours. Strain liquid.

To serve, heat dinner plates. Ladle ¼ cup (60 ml) of sauce on the lower half of plate. Arrange a selection of fresh cooked vegetables across the top half of plate. Shingle three lamb chops across the sauce with the rib bones leaning against the vegetables. Garnish with sprig of fresh rosemary.

Surprise Du Poire, Massenez

Servings—6
Portion—1 pear

Pears—

6 red bosc pears
12 cups (2¾ L) water
2 cups (450 g) sugar
3 tablespoons (45 ml) lemon juice
⅓ cups (75 ml) pear liqueur

Using a lemon zester, stripe the outside skin of each pear in a spiral pattern from top to bottom. Combine the liquid ingredients in a saucepan and bring to a boil. Reduce heat and simmer pears in the syrup. Poach approximately 20–30 minutes until tender (test with a knife). Remove pears from liquid when done, and chill quickly.

Vanilla Sauce—

1 cup (250 ml) milk
3 tablespoons (45 g) sugar
½ cup (120 ml) heavy cream
2 teaspoons (10 ml) vanilla extract
4 egg yolks

Heat milk and sugar in saucepan until it simmers. In a separate bowl, combine remaining ingredients and mix well. Add yolk mixture to hot milk. Stir constantly and cook 3–4 minutes until sauce starts to thicken. *Do not boil.* Remove from heat and continue stirring an additional 2 minutes. Chill immediately.

Chocolate Sabayon Filling—

4 egg yolks
2 teaspoons (10 g) sugar
2 teaspoons (10 ml) Marsala
3 tablespoons (30 g) burgundy chocolate
1 cup (250 ml) whipped cream
¼ tablespoon (4 g) gelatin powder

In a double boiler, whip egg yolks, sugar, gelatin powder, and Marsala until the mixture forms stiff peaks. Cool mixture, stirring occasionally. Melt burgundy chocolate. Whip heavy cream to soft peaks. Add melted chocolate to egg yolk mixture and mix lightly. Gently fold whipped cream to yolk chocolate mixture. Refrigerate filling.

To serve, remove the core of the pear from the flower end, up through the middle of the pear, leaving the stem end intact. Fill a pastry bag with the chocolate filling and fill the cavity made in the pears. Chill plates. Ladle vanilla sauce on the center of each plate. Place the filled pear on the center of plate. Garnish with either a pulled sugar rose or strawberry flower.

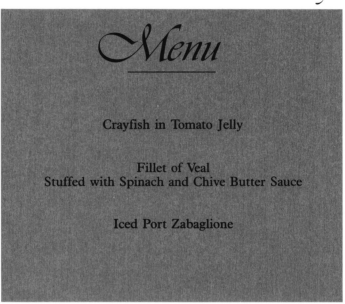

Breidenbacher Hof

Menu

Crayfish in Tomato Jelly

Fillet of Veal
Stuffed with Spinach and Chive Butter Sauce

Iced Port Zabaglione

The Breidenbacher Hof represents a tradition which dates back 175 years. The hotel's signature restaurant, the "Grill Royal", has always been the social focal point of Nordrhine-Westphalia. The fine cuisine and select wine list match the works of art which decorate this elegant and exclusive restaurant.

Crayfish in Tomato Jelly

Servings—4
Portions—1 mold

> **12 crayfish**
> **4½ pounds (2 kg) Italian tomatoes**
> **2 quail eggs**
> **1 cup (250 ml) heavy cream**
> **⅓ cup (80 g) caviar**
> **Salt, pepper and sugar to taste**
> **Lemon juice**
> **Lamb's lettuce**
> **Juniper berries**
> **Caraway seeds**
> **Bay leaf**
> **Gelatin**

Quarter the tomatoes, mix briefly and add salt and sugar. Drain tomatoes in cheesecloth, and save tomato juice. Soak gelatin. Boil quail eggs. Season crayfish with greens, caraway seeds, bay leaf, juniper berries, salt, and pepper and boil for 2 minutes.

Dissolve gelatin in tomato juice; season to taste with salt and pepper.

Follow this pattern to fill each small mold:

1st layer—½ quail egg with egg yolk facing the bottom; add tepid juice and let cool.
2nd layer—crayfish and tepid juice; let cool.
3rd layer—lamb's lettuce and tepid juice; let cool.

It is very important to allow each layer to cool before adding the next layer. Unmold when set.

Whisk heavy cream. Season with salt, pepper and lemon juice. Top each mold with cream and add caviar carefully.

Fillet of Veal

Servings—4
Portion—1 fillet

> **1⅓ pounds (600 g) fillet of veal**
> **2 cups (500 g) spinach**
> **7 tablespoons (100 g) leek**
> **2 cups (425 ml) broth**
> **1 cup (250 ml) white wine**
> **⅔ cup (150 g) butter**
> **2 cups (500 g) potatoes**
> **24 asparagus tips**

Scoop out the middle piece of fillet and stuff with boiled and seasoned spinach. Season fillet with salt and pepper, and roast for approximately 10–12 minutes. Turn frequently to roast all sides.

Chive Butter—

Reduce broth and white wine, add butter, and boil. Brown shallots and add gravy; boil again briefly. Drain and mix. Add the chive and season to taste.

Garnish each fillet with cherry tomato, chervil and truffle julienne.

Iced Port Zabaglione

Servings—3
Portion—½ melon

3 egg yolks
¼ cup (60 g) sugar
⅓ cup (75 ml) red port
1 cup (250 ml) fresh cream
Melon balls and melon purée

Whisk egg yolk with one-half of the sugar. Boil other half of sugar with port and cold egg yolks. Stir until cool. Add fresh cream and freeze.

Cut melon balls out of one-half of the melon. Purée other half of the melon, and garnish plate. Place frozen slice of zabaglione on the lower part of the plate, and garnish upper part of the plate with melon balls.

Pier 66
HOTEL AND MARINA

Menu

Everglades Pâté

Lobster & Kiwi Mussel Salad

Indian River Grapefruit Sorbet

Veal Tenderloin

Fresh Strawberry Mousse

Kiwi and Key Lime Coulis

The Pier 66 Hotel and Marina offers the best of both a luxury conference and resort hotel. Guests can relish the ultimate in nouvelle cuisine at the elegant, internationally-acclaimed "Windows on the Green." Cocktails are served 17 stories above the ocean and the Intracoastal Waterway in the famous "Pier Top Lounge."

Everglades Pâté

Servings—40
Portion—1 slice

- 1 pound (450 g) boneless lean veal, ½ cut into thin strips; ½ diced
- 1 pound (450 g) pork belly lean meat diced; fat chopped
- 1 pound (450 g) venison, ½ cut into thin strips; ½ diced
- 1 pound (450 g) duck breast, ½ cut into thin strips; ½ diced
- ½ pound (225 g) chicken livers, trimmed and ground
- ½ pound (225 g) goose/duck livers, trimmed and ground
- ½ cup (120 ml) brandy
- 1 cup (250 ml) white wine
- 3 eggs
- ¾ pound (340 g) fresh pork fatback, sliced into strips
- Salt and pepper to taste
- 1 whole truffle, sliced
- ¾ cup (180 g) flour
- 1 onion, thinly chopped
- ½ teaspoon (2.5 g) basil

- ½ teaspoon (2.5 g) thyme
- 6 tablespoons (85 g) melted lard

Place diced meats, chopped fat, chicken liver, onion, wine, brandy, and seasonings in a bowl; marinate 24 hours. Knead eggs and flour into marinade, brown. Line a 3-quart (2¾ L) terrine with mold strips of fatback, place a layer of mixture, a layer of veal strips, layer of mixture, and so on, until mold is ¾ full. Put in sliced duck liver and truffles. Continue to layer mixture until full. Cover terrine with strips of fatback, cook in water bath in a preheated 325° (170°C) oven for 3½ hours.

When cool, cover surface with melted lard.

Lobster and Kiwi Mussel Salad

Servings—2
Portion—½ salad

- 1 Maine lobster
- 6 kiwi mussels

- 4 leaves Bibb lettuce
- 2 leaves radicchio
- 4 leaves Belgian endive
- 10 snow peas
- 2 bunches mint leaves
- 2 black chanterelles

Dijon Mustard Dressing—

- 1 cup (250 ml) salad oil
- 1 cup (225 g) sugar
- 1 quart (1 L) red wine vinegar
- ¼ cup (60 g) steel-cut black pepper
- 4 cups (900 kg) Dijon mustard

Poach lobster; when cooked, chill. Crack lobster pinchers and pull out meat. Then crack open shell of tail and pull out meat. Slice tail meat into medallions. Pull kiwi mussels from shell. Arrange lobster slices on top of lettuces and arrange mussels, on the side.

Mix Dijon mustard, sugar and pepper. Gently blend in oil. Add vinegar to taste.

Veal Tenderloin

Servings—2
Portion—1 tenderloin

**2 trimmed and cleaned veal
    tenderloin**
½ cup (115 g) shallots
Bourbon to taste
¼ cup (60 g) Dijon mustard
Heavy cream
Salt and pepper to taste
2 large baking potatoes
4 miniature eggplants
4 miniature yellow squash
4 miniature carrots
4 tablespoons (55 g) butter
**1 Granny Smith apple (peeled, cored,
    and wedged)**

Season whole tenderloins and sear with
melted butter. When brown on all
sides, remove from pan. Add shallots
and sauté until golden brown. Splash in
bourbon (to desired taste). When liquid
boils, using a wooden spoon, scrape off
deposits from pan. Deglaze the pan;
add Dijon mustard, again to desired
taste.

When liquid and shallots are blended
with mustard, add heavy cream. The
amount will vary on amount of sauce
required.

Stir the cream and deglazing liquid together. When sauce is blended together,
boil for a few minutes. Pass sauce
through a strainer and return to heat
for 1-2 minutes, until it thickens
enough to coat spoon.

Peel potatoes; use ball cutter to make
potato balls. Soak the potato balls in
water. Lightly poach in salted water until ¾ cooked. In a hot buttered sauté
pan, drop in potato balls and brown
them.

Trim and poach vegetables in salted
water. Lightly poach apple in sugar
water.

To serve: Slice the tenderloin on a bias.
Pour sauce on the plate. Place tenderloin on top of sauce. Arrange the
poached apples and vegetables onto the
plate. Place the potatoes in the center,
garnish with fresh leaves and nastur-
tiums.

Kiwi and Key Lime Coulis

Servings—4
Portion—1 plate

4 kiwi fruit, sliced
1 tablespoon (15 ml) Key lime juice
Sugar to taste

Peel and dice kiwi. Place into blender
with lime juice and blend together.

Place coulis on base of plate, place
sugar shell basket with strawberry
mousse in center. Chill and serve.

Hotel NASSAUER HOF

Menu

Lentil Soup with Pheasant and Sherry

Parfait of Smoked Salmon and Trout

Fillet of Pike-Perch "Baden" Style
in a Cream and Mushroom Sauce

Saddle of Venison in Juniper Crust

Vacherin with Corn Salad and Nut Bread

Quark Gratin with Vineyard Peaches

The Nassauer Hof, with its luxuriously furnished guest accommodations, is located in downtown Wiesbaden opposite the Gambling Casino, the park and the Opera House and only 20 minutes from the Frankfurt airport. The friendly, elegant hotel restaurant, with apéritif bar and terrace, serves regional specialties.

Lentil Soup with Pheasant and Sherry

Servings—10
Portion—½ cup

Stock—

1 pheasant
1 bayleaf
2 cloves
1 onion
½ leek
1 carrot

Soup—

¼ cup (60 g) onions
½ cup (115 g) bacon
½ cup (60 g) carrots
½ cup (60 g) celery
2 tablespoons (30 g) tomato purée
2 cups (300 g) lentils, soaked
1 teaspoon (5 g) mustard
2 tablespoons (30 ml) red wine
1 tablespoon (15 ml) sherry
2-3 tablespoons (30–45 ml) balsamic vinegar
Salt, pepper, nutmeg, chives

Boil the pheasant, vegetables, bay leaf, and cloves in 4 quarts (3¾ L) of water until the pheasant is soft and the liquid has reduced to a strong stock. Skin the pheasant while warm.

Finely dice onions, bacon, carrots, and celery. Simmer in 1 tablespoon (15 ml) lard, add the tomato purée and sauté until slightly brown.

Stir in red wine, add 2 quarts (2 L) of pheasant stock, and boil lentils until soft.,

Remove pheasant meat from bones and cut into strips.

Add sherry, vinegar, mustard, and spices to give the lentil soup a sweet-sour flavor. Add pheasant meat.

Garnish with chives and strips of crisply fried bacon.

Parfait of Smoked Salmon and Trout

Servings—10
Portion—1 slice

Trout—

½ pound (225 g) smoked trout fillet
½ cup (120 ml) fish stock
½ cup (120 ml) Riesling wine
2 tablespoons (30 ml) Noilly Prat
1 teaspoon (5 g) cornstarch
4 leaves gelatin, dissolved
2 tablespoons (30 ml) whipped cream
Lemon juice, cayenne, pepper, salt

Salmon—

1 pound (450 g) smoked salmon
1 tablespoon (15 ml) smoked salmon stock
1 tablespoon (15 ml) Riesling wine
1 teaspoon (5 g) cornstarch
4 leaves gelatin
1⅓ cups (300 ml) whipped cream

Bring fish stock and Riesling to a boil and thicken with cornstarch and Noilly Prat. Cool and blend with trout. Whip cream, add dissolved gelatin, and carefully fold into the trout mixture. Season with salt, cayenne pepper, and lemon juice.

Prepare the salmon mixture as above. Fill a ring mold with alternate sections of the two mixtures and marble carefully with a fork. Refrigerate for 12 hours before unmolding.

Arrange a slice on a plate and garnish with black trout caviar, red salmon caviar, crème fraîche, and seaweed. Serve with beanshoot cakes.

Saddle of Venison in Juniper Crust

Servings—10
Portion—2 slices

- 2½ pounds (1¼ kg) saddle of vension (fillet; save bones and sinews)
- 10 tablespoons (100 g) freshly grated white bread (without crust)
- ¾ cup (160 g) salted butter

- ¼ cup (60 g) fresh green juniper berries
- 1 shallot
- ¼ cup (60 g) celery, chopped
- Salt and pepper
- Juice of ½ lemon

Sauce—

- 2 cups (½ L) venison stock
- ½ cup (120 ml) red wine
- 2 tablespoons (30 g) cranberries
- ¼ cup (60 ml) gin
- 1 sprig of thyme
- 1 cup (250 ml) cream
- 2 tablespoons (30 g) butter
- 10 juniper berries
- 1 bayleaf
- 10 peppercorns

Chop venison sinews and bones finely, sauté briefly with shallot, chopped celery, carrot, juniper berries, thyme, and bay leaf. Stir in red wine and gin, add venison stock, and reduce. Sieve, add cream, and reduce. Add cranberries, and enrich with butter.

To make crust, purée the fresh juniper berries with butter and freshly grated white bread and season.

Season the venison fillet, brown quickly on all sides, and remove from pan to cool. Coat with crust and bake in 400F (200C) oven for 15 minutes.

Serve with handmade "Spätzle" noodles, purée of parsley root (recipes follow), and cranberries.

Purée of Parsley Roots—

- 1¾ pounds (800 g) parsley roots with green
- 2½ cups (⅜ L) cream
- 4 tablespoons (50 g) butter
- Salt, pepper, nutmeg

Peel parsley roots and remove green. Pick leaves from stalks. Cut roots into small pieces and simmer in cream until soft. Add parsley leaves and blend finely. Season and enrich with butter.

"Spätzle" Noodles—

- 1½ cups (350 g) flour
- 5 eggs
- 1 tablespoon (15 ml) oil
- ½ cup (120 ml) water
- Salt to taste

Blend ingredients to a smooth dough that forms bubbles.

Immerse a wooden board in boiling, salted water with a little oil. Slice thin strips of dough into the boiling water with a palette knife to cover the board. The noodles float to the surface when done. Remove with a slotted spoon, plunge in cold water and drain. Toss briefly in melted butter before serving.

To serve, pour a little sauce on the front of the plate and arrange two slices of meat on top. At the upper edge of the plate, spoon some puréed parsley roots and a spoonful of cranberries. Pass the handmade "Spätzle" noodles separately.

The Peninsula

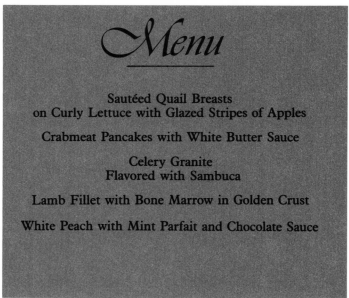

Menu

Sautéed Quail Breasts
on Curly Lettuce with Glazed Stripes of Apples

Crabmeat Pancakes with White Butter Sauce

Celery Granite
Flavored with Sambuca

Lamb Fillet with Bone Marrow in Golden Crust

White Peach with Mint Parfait and Chocolate Sauce

The Peninsula features one of the finest French restaurants in Hong Kong, "Gaddi's." Gourmet cuisine, impeccable service, and an opulent decor are some of the qualities that have sustained "Gaddi's" place in the ranks of the world's top restaurants.

Lamb Fillet with Bone Marrow in Golden Crust

Servings—4
Portion—1 loin

   4–¼ pound (120 g) lamb loins
   ¼ pound (120 g) black mushrooms
   ¼ pound (120 g) champignons
   1 tablespoon (20 g) butter
   2 egg yolks
   2 tablespoons (40 g) parsley
   5 tablespoons (160 g) bone marrow
   Several fresh spinach leaves
   1 cup (200 g) prepared puff pastry
   ⅓ cup (80 g) gravy

Chop the mushrooms and sauté in the butter until dry. Add the gravy and reduce. Lower heat and add parsley and egg yolk, mixing well. Chill mixture until required to coat loins.

Wrap the marrow with the spinach leaves, making four round 4-inch (1 cm) diameter long pieces, then freeze.

Trim fat, joints and bones from loins,

but do not remove the end bone. Keep trimmings to prepare gravy. Season and roast the loins until rare. Make a hole lengthwise through the loins with a thin knife and push the marrow stick inside. Cover the loins with the mushroom mixture on all sides.

Roll out the pastry to four ⅛ inch (2 mm) thick pieces and cover each loin with one piece. Use the endcuts for garnish. Allow the pastry covered loins to stand for 30 minutes. Roast in 320°F (160°C) oven for 8 minutes, then at 425° (220°C) for 2 minutes.

Slice the lamb loins into three pieces and arrange on serving plates. Garnish with a mint leaf and a boiled Chinese mushroom. Sautéed carrots, Italian squash, cubed potatoes, and brunoise of red peppers add a touch of color to this dish.

Prepare gravy and serve separately.

Crabmeat Pancakes with White Butter Sauce

Servings—10
Portion—2 pancakes

   ½ cup (80 g) flour
   ⅔ tablespoons (10 ml) oil
   1 egg
   ¾ cup (200 ml) milk
   5½ pounds (2½ kg) blue swimmer crabs
   4 tablespoons (60 g) butter
   1 teaspoon (10 g) chopped garlic
   2½ cups (550 ml) fish stock
   1 cup (250 ml) dry white wine
   3 tablespoons (40 g) chopped shallots
   ½ bay leaf
   1¾ cup (400 ml) fresh cream
   1 cup (200 g) soft butter
   Salt and pepper to taste
   Dash lemon juice
   20 small black truffles
   20 puff pastry half moons

Thoroughly mix flour, oil, egg, milk and salt together for pancake mixture.

Set aside. Prepare the pancakes after the butter sauce is finished.

Boil crabs in water for 15 minutes. Break crabs open and remove meat.

Pour fish stock, white wine, shallots and bay leaf into a saucepan, and boil to reduce mixture to one-third. Add cream and reduce again until ⅔ cup (150 ml) remains. Pour this sauce into a blender to mix, adding the soft butter slowly. Season with salt, pepper and a dash of lemon juice.

Sauté crabmeat in butter with garlic, adding a little of the butter sauce. Mix lightly, then pour the mixture on the prepared pancakes. Fold each pancake over and place on a serving plate. Pour the remaining sauce over the pancakes.

Decorate each serving plate with the truffles and puff pastry half moons.

Celery Granite Flavored with Sambuca

Servings—10
Portion—½ cup (115 g)

1¾ pounds (800 g) celery
½ cup (120 ml) white port
¼ cup (60 ml) sambuca

Produce celery juice from the celery stalks. Mix the port and sambuca with the celery juice. Freeze mixture in an ice tray. Stir occasionally with a whisk to prevent a solid ice block of the mixture. This dish should be served as fine crushed ice.

White Peach with Mint Parfait and Chocolate Sauce

Servings—10
Portion—1 peach half

Mint Parfait—
2 tablespoons (30 g) egg yolk
2 egg whites, separated
1 teaspoon (8 g) honey
1½ tablespoons (20 g) sugar
½ cup (100 g) whipped cream
1 tablespoon (15 g) dark chocolate
Dark Chocolate Sauce—
6 tablespoons (90 g) sugar
¾ cup (180 g) couverture

¾ cup (180 ml) cream
¼ cup (90 ml) water
Creme de Menthe Sauce—
⅓ cup (80 ml) mint liqueur
5½ tablespoons (90 ml) cream
2 tablespoons (20 g) sugar
10 white peach halves
40 raspberries

To prepare mint parfait; mix ingredients in top half of double boiler and beat over moderate heat until mixture thickens. Remove from heat and continue beating until mixture is cool.

Beat second egg white and mix with coarsely chopped chocolate and whipped cream. Combine this mixture with the cooled parfait mixture and pour into a 1 inch (2 cm) dish and freeze.

To prepare chocolate sauce; mix all ingredients together and warm slightly.

To prepare Creme de Menthe Sauce, beat egg yolks and sugar together in double boiler. Add cream and liqueur. Pour dark chocolate sauce on serving plates. Pour the creme de menthe sauce in a ring shape in the middle of the chocolate sauce. Put a spoonful of mint parfait in this ring and top with a peach half. Decorate each plate with some mint leaves and 3 to 4 raspberries.

Menu

New Potato Salad with a Sauce of Sevruga Caviar

Broiled Opakapaka with Black Olives
in a Seafood Sauce

Stewed Breast of Duck
with Wild Mushrooms and Chervil

Strawberry Sunburst with Almond Cream
and Fresh Mint

"St. Remon" Chocolate Cake with Vanilla Sauce

Halekulani, an oasis of refinement on Waikiki Beach, offers elegantly appointed interiors, lush gardens and personalized service. "La Mer" is named for its spectacular oceanfront setting enhanced by the distinctive, Orient-inspired decor, romantic ambiance and exquisite French haute cuisine.

Broiled Opakapaka Filled with Black Olives in a Light Seafood Sauce

Servings—4
Portion—1 fillet

   4 fillets–½ pound (225 g) opakapaka (pink snapper) cleaned, scaled and boned

   8 black olives, pitted and quartered

   ¼ cup (60 ml) olive oil

Nage of Aromatics—

   2 cups (½ L) white wine

   1 cup (250 ml) water

   ½ cup (115 g) carrots, chopped

   ½ cup (115 g) onions, chopped

   ¼ cup (60 g) shallots, chopped

   ¼ cup (60 g) celery with leaves, chopped

   2 whole cloves of garlic

   2 whole cloves

   1 bouquet of herbs: (bay leaf, parsley, thyme)

   ½ lemon, juiced

   1 tablespoon (15 g) salt

   Dash of white pepper, with a pinch of cayenne pepper

Seafood Sauce—

   1 cup (250 ml) finished nage of aromatics

   ¼ cup (60 ml) olive oil

   ¼ cup (60 g) shallots, chopped

   5 medium tomatoes

   ¾ cup (180 g) chopped herbs (chives, tarragon, chervil, seaweed, parsley)

   ¼ cup (60 g) butter

   1 lemon, juiced

   Salt & pepper to taste

Nage of Aromatics—

Bring water and wine to a boil. Add chopped vegetables, aromatic herbs and lemon juice. Continue to boil for 30 minutes; halfway through, add salt and pepper.

Strain the mixture through a fine sieve. Set the clear liquid aside to cool, and discard rest of ingredients.

Seafood Sauce—

Blanch tomatoes and cut fine lines from top to bottom just deep enough to cut skin. Drop tomatoes in rapidly boiling water. Drain after 30 seconds and run under cold water, until tomatoes are cool enough to handle. Peel skin, cut in half and remove seeds, dice.

Combine diced tomatoes, chopped shallots and olive oil in a frying pan. Simmer about 5 minutes, until shallots are transparent. Add the nage of aromatics, lemon juice, butter and mixed herbs. Whisk and continue to simmer for 5 minutes over medium heat. Season to taste. Remove from heat and set aside.

Preheat oven to 500°F (260°C). Pierce 8 holes in each fillet and stuff with olive quarters. Coat both sides of fillets with olive oil and broil for 3–5 minutes. Place fillet on large dinner plate, pour ½ cup (120 ml) seafood sauce over, and serve hot.

Stewed Breast of Duck with Wild Mushrooms and Chervil

Servings—4
Portion—½ breast

- 2 4–5 pounds (1¾ g–2¼ g) whole ducks
- ½ cup (115 g) butter
- 12 cups (2¾ L) water
- 2 small onions, chopped
- 1 large stalk celery, chopped
- 1 large leek, chopped
- 2 tablespoons (30 g) 1 large carrot, chopped
- Chervil, chopped
- 1 bouquet of herbs (thyme, parsley, bay leaf)
- Salt & pepper to taste
- 1 pound (450 g) wild mushrooms (shiitake, chanterelle, morel, oyster)

Remove duck legs and wings, cutting at the joints. Next, remove the wishbone, then the skin and fat. Place the duck breast side up, and begin carving the breast meat away from the backbone and ribcage, in one whole piece. Continue on other side. Cut carcasses into small pieces to make stock.

Place bones in a pan and brown them completely in a very hot oven, 500°F (260°C). Toss often, until dark brown, about 20–30 minutes. While bones are browning. Simmer the chopped carrots, onions, celery and leeks in ¼ cup (60 g) butter in a large pot, stirring often. When the bones are brown, add them to the vegetables, water, and the bouquet of herbs. Simmer for 1 hour. Strain the stock and reduce clear stock to ½ cup (120 ml). Remove from heat. Whip in 2 tablespoons (30 g) butter, add chopped chervil.

Slice each breast diagonally into 6 pieces. Sauté the breasts in 1 tablespoon (15 g) butter for 2 minutes on each side. Remove from heat and set aside. In another pan, sauté wild mushrooms in 1 tablespoon (15 g) butter, for 5 minutes. Set aside.

Place the duck breast on a warmed plate, garnish with wild mushrooms. Pour 2 tablespoons (30 ml) of stock over duck and mushrooms. Serve hot.

Strawberry Sunburst with Almond Cream and Fresh Mint

Servings—8
Portion—1 plate

Pastry Cream—

- ⅔ cup (150 ml) milk
- 2 egg yolks
- 2 tablespoons (30 g) sugar
- 1 tablespoon (5 g) cornstarch

Almond Cream—

- ½ cup (115 g) butter (soft)
- ½ cup (115 g) almond meal
- ½ cup (115 g) sugar
- 1 egg
- 2 tablespoons (30 ml) Amaretto

Strawberry Sauce—

- 2 cups (450 g) fresh strawberries
- ¼ cup (60 g) sugar
- 1 lemon, juiced

Garnish—

- 3 pounds (1⅓ kg) fresh strawberries
- 1 bunch fresh mint leaves

Pastry Cream—Bring milk to boil. Mix together 2 egg yolks, sugar and cornstarch. Whisk until smooth. Add mixture to boiling milk and continue to whip until cooked, approximately 2 minutes. Remove from heat and pour pastry cream into a shallow pan, to cool the cream as quickly as possible. Continue to stir until completely cold. Refrigerate.

Almond Cream—Combine butter, almond meal and sugar. Whip briskly. Add the egg and moisten with Amaretto. Mix with cold pastry cream.

Strawberry Sauce—Purée stemmed and washed strawberries in a food processor. Add sugar and lemon juice, mix well. Strain mixture, saving the liquid and discarding the rest.

Prepare the plates: Wash and stem whole strawberries. Set 8 aside. Cut the rest into quarters, lengthwise. With a spatula, spread the almond cream to cover ⅔ of the bottom of a dinner plate. Arrange sliced strawberries on top of cream in a sunburst design, fanning from the rim of the plate inward. Top the center with 1 whole strawberry.

Preheat broiler. Heat plates under broiler for 5 minutes. Finely chop the mint leaves, saving a few whole leaves. Remove plates from oven and carefully pour a small amount of sauce around edges of dessert. Sprinkle chopped mint over dessert. Garnish center with whole mint leaves.

The Warwick

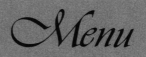

Menu

Escargots in Phyllo

Baked Shrimp with Spinach and Scallop Mousse
with Saffron Sauce

Asparagus Consommé

Stuffed Veal Cutlet "Warwick" with
Sour Banana Pepper Sauce

Glazed Berries with Kahlua Sabayon

"The Hunt Room" is as pleasing to the eye as the succulent menu selections are delightful to the taste. Traditional trappings of the hunt appear as accessories...a massive marble fireplace, a handsome bar and dining tables of oak with gleaming black leather companion chairs contrast richly with the red Brussels carpeting.

Baked Shrimp with Spinach and Scallop Mousse with Saffron Sauce

Servings—6
Portion—3 shrimp

18 shrimp
20 spinach leaves
2½ cups (500 g) sea scallops
1 egg
2⅓ cups (550 ml) heavy cream
1 pinch saffron
1 tablespoon (15 g) shallots, finely chopped
Salt and white pepper to taste
½ cup (120 ml) Noilly Prat

To make scallop mousse, place Noilly Prat and shallots into a saucepan. Boil and reduce until it becomes ¼ cup (60 ml) of liquid. Cool.

In another saucepan, add 1 cup (250 ml) heavy cream and pinch of saffron. Bring to a rolling boil and reduce to one-third. Cool.

Remove the muscles from scallops, and place the scallops and the two mixtures in blender. Add the seasonings and blend, slowly adding ⅓ cup (75 ml) heavy cream, until the mixture turns to a paste consistency.

Butterfly shrimp and season. Cover each shrimp with a slightly blanched and dried spinach leaf. Spread with the scallop mousse, then roll into the spinach leaf.

Saffron Sauce—

½ cup (120 ml) white wine
¾ cup (200 ml) chicken stock
1 tablespoon (15 g) shallots, finely chopped
½ cup (120 ml) heavy cream
1 pinch saffron
⅔ cup (140 g) unsalted butter
Bay leaves
Lemon

Bring the wine, chicken stock, and shallots to a boil. Lower heat, and reduce to one-half. While the sauce is re-

ducing, coat the bottom of a sheet pan with butter and some chopped shallots, a few bay leaves, and some thinly sliced lemon. Add the rolled shrimp and a dash of wine for moisture. Cover with aluminum foil and bake in a 375°F (190°C) oven for about 10–12 minutes.

When the rolled shrimp have baked, drain the liquid from the baking pan and add to the sauce. Reduce to ½ cup (120 ml) of liquid. Remove from heat and slowly add butter, while whisking. Season to taste; then strain through a china cap.

Stuffed Veal Cutlet "Warwick" with Sour Banana Pepper Sauce

Servings—6
Portion—1 cutlet

6 veal cutlets, 6½–7 ounces (180-200 g) each
⅔ cup (140 g) smoked sausage
2½ tablespoons (50 g) pecans, chopped

2½ tablespoons (50 g) celery, chopped

1 apple, chopped

1 tablespoon (15 g) parsley, chopped

½ tablespoon (7.5 g) shallots, chopped

½ cup (120 ml) heavy cream

½ cup (120 g) fresh breadcrumbs

1 egg, well-beaten

1 pinch marjoram

Make a slit in the side of each veal cutlet to form a pocket for stuffing.

Sauté the shallots in fresh butter with celery and apple. Cool and add remaining ingredients. Mix well and stuff into the cutlets.

Combine butter and salad oil in a 1:1 ratio. Sauté veal cutlets in this mixture until brown. Finish cooking in a moderate oven.

Sour Banana Pepper Sauce—

1 teaspoon (5 g) shallots

1 cup (250 ml) white wine

½ cup (120 ml) veal juice

4 banana peppers

Sauté the shallots in butter until soft. Add white wine and reduce to one-third. Add veal juice, and reduce to one-half. Cut the banana peppers into 1½ inch (4 cm) julienne strips and blanch in white vinegar. Add to sauce and heat for 1 minute until warm.

To serve, cover the veal cutlet with the sauce.

Escargots in Phyllo

Servings—6
Portion—8 escargots

48 escargots

½ package phyllo dough

1½ pounds (675 g) butter

½ cup (115 g) fresh garlic, finely chopped

2 teaspoons (10 g) shallots, finely chopped

Pinch of parsley

Tarragon Butter—

2 tablespoons (30 g) soft butter

1 tablespoon (15 g) tarragon

2 teaspoons (10 g) chopped shallots

Wash the escargots and dry thoroughly. Sauté the shallots in butter. When they are half-cooked, add the garlic, escargots, and parsley. Flambé with Pernod and let cool.

Spread 1 sheet of phyllo dough on a wooden board and cut into 2½ inch × 2½ inch (6 cm × 6 cm) squares. Brush lightly with butter. Take a second 2½ inch × 2½ inch (6 cm × 6 cm) sheet of dough, place it over the first, and brush lightly with butter.

Place ¼ tablespoon (3 g) tarragon butter in the center of a phyllo square, and place an escargot on top. Fold the four points to the center. Bake in a 375°–400°F (190–200°C) oven until brown and crispy.

Glazed Berries with Kahlua Sabayon

Servings—6
Portion—1 plate

Sabayon Sauce—

3 egg yolks

⅓ cup (90 ml) white wine

3⅓ tablespoons (50 ml) Kahlua

1½ teaspoons (10 g) sugar

Strawberries, raspberries, blueberries, blackberries or other berries in season

Cook all ingredients (except berries) in a double boiler until fluffy and creamy.

Starting from the center, arrange berries in a circular pattern on a dinner plate.

Cover the fruit with a thin layer of sabayon sauce, and place in the oven at 325°F(160°C) until glazed.

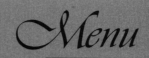

Menu

Marinated Fresh Tuna
on Red Onion Slices and Avocado
with Cilantro-Soy Marinade

Beef Consommé with Lobster Ravioli

Sorbet

Baked Pork Tenderloin "Heartland"
with Rosemary Currant Sauce

Warm Goat Cheese on Seasonal Greens
Hazelnut Dressing

Fresh Raspberries with Lemon Curd

"Beaulieu" is a remarkable restaurant at The Canterbury Hotel with mahogany panelled walls adorned with the works of post-impressionist masters. Our European Chef combines classical and house specialties with a daily changing prix fixe menu. The extensive wine list offers a selection of California wines and excellent French vintages.

Beef Consommé

Servings—6
Portion—2 cups (½ l)

   4 quarts cold water
   2 pounds (900 g) ground beef trimmings
   1 large carrot, cut into 1-inch (2.5 cm) chunks
   2 cloves garlic, halved
   4–5 sprigs parsley
   1 small onion, cut in half crosswise and blackened
   ½ teaspoon (2.5 ml) cracked black pepper
   Salt to taste

Combine beef trimmings, carrot, celery, parsley, garlic, and spices. Mix well, add water, and bring to a boil. When stock boils at a simmer remove excess foam and add onion. Simmer for at least 1 hour. Turn off heat and let rest for a few minutes. Strain slowly through cheesecloth to remove impurities.

Lobster Ravioli

Servings—6
Portion—5 ravioli

   Dough—
   2⅓ cups (300 dl) semolina flour
   ½ teaspoon (2.5 g) salt
   3 beaten eggs
   ⅓ cup (75 ml) water
   1 teaspoon (2.5 ml) cooking oil

In a mixing bowl, add 2 cups (260 g) flour and salt. Make well in center. Combine eggs, water, and oil, and add to flour. Mix well. Sprinkle kneading surface with remaining flour, turn dough out of bowl, and knead until consistency is smooth and elastic (8-10 minutes). Cover; let rest.

   Filling—
   10 ounces (285 g) lobster meat, rinsed, drained, and chopped
   1 ounce (30 g) mushrooms, chopped
   2 green onions, sliced
   1 teaspoon (5 ml) soy sauce

   ½ teaspoon (2.5 g) grated fresh ginger root
   1 teaspoon (5 g) chopped parsley
   1 teaspoon (5 ml) sesame oil

Combine lobster, mushroom, onion, and other ingredients. Sauté for 1 minute and allow to cool.

Cut dough in half and roll both pieces with rolling pin to approximately ¹⁄₁₆″ (.16 cm) thickness. Lay piece on cutting board and portion 1 teaspoon (5 ml) filling on dough a little more than 2 inches (5 cm) apart. Brush edges of each portion with egg wash, and cover with second sheet. With 2-inch (5 cm) cookie cutter, cut each portion, keeping filling in center. Press outside of ravioli with fork to seal dough. Drop in boiling water, approximately 1 quart (1 L) with 2 tablespoons (30 ml) oil and a pinch of salt. Simmer until ravioli floats to the top (8-10 minutes). Rinse with cold water and store (until used) on moist cheesecloth or between wax paper.

Baked Pork Tenderloin "Heartland"

Servings—6
Portion—2 slices

2½ pounds (1¼ kg) pork tenderloin, fat and silverskin removed

1¼ cups (285 g) fresh corn

¼ cup (60 g) diced red peppers, blanched for 30 seconds

¼ cup (60 g) diced green peppers, blanched for 30 seconds

7 spring-fresh thyme leaves (removed from stem)

¾ cup (180 g) fresh spinach leaves, slightly blanched; stems removed

¼ cup (60 g) flour

2 tablespoons (30 g) butter

2 whole eggs; 1 egg white

Salt and pepper to taste

½ cup (120 ml) half-and-half

1 10″ × 15″ (25 × 40 cm) puff pastry dough sheet

Sear tenderloin quickly on all sides in hot oil, let cool. Prepare roux with flour and butter, add half-and-half, and cook, stirring to a smooth, creamy consistency. Add thyme, salt, pepper, and of remainder ingredients. Whip eggs and fold into mixture. Pack corn mixture over tenderloin, cover with spinach leaves, and wrap in thinly rolled puff pastry sheet. Brush with egg, and bake for 35 minutes in 350°F (180°C).

Rosemary Currant Sauce

Servings—1 cup (¼ l)
Portion—1 tablespoon (15 ml)

⅓ cup (75 ml) currant jelly

3 tablespoons (45 ml) Dijon mustard

¾ cup (180 ml) burgundy

¾ cup (180 ml) beef jus

½ teaspoon (2.5 g) fresh rosemary leaves

Reduce burgundy by ½. Combine rest of ingredients, and simmer until sauce begins to thicken.

Lemon Curd

Servings—6
Portion—2 tablespoons (40 ml)

Lemon juice of 3 lemons, and grated rind of 1 lemon

1½ cups (340 g) sugar

4 egg yolks

½ cup (115 g) butter

1 cup (250 ml) whipping cream

In a mixing bowl, combine lemon juice, rind, sugar, and egg yolks. Whip over double-boiler until mixture thickens and is smooth and creamy. Remove from heat and slowly whip in warm butter. Allow to cool.

In separate bowls whip cream until slightly thick. Fold in cooled egg mixture, and serve over berries.

Menu

Cream of Veal Soup with Wild Mushrooms

Lobster "Plaza" Thermidor

Potato Cocotte

Asparagus

Fresh Fruits with Butterscotch Sabayon

The award-winning Alameda Plaza's "Rooftop Restaurant," features exquisitely prepared, graciously served Continental cuisine; one of America's finest wine lists; an elegant, yet comfortable atmosphere; and a spectacular view of the famed Country Club Plaza, Kansas City's premier shopping and entertainment district.

Cream of Veal Soup with Wild Mushrooms

Servings—8
Portion—1 cup (250 ml)

2 quarts (2 L) rich veal stock
10 pounds (4½ kg) veal shank bones
3 onions
1¾ cups (400 g) carrots
1¾ cups (400 g) leeks
1¾ cups (400 g) celery
2 cups (425 ml) heavy cream
12 cloves
3 bay leaves
1 cup (250 ml) white wine
6 tablespoons (85 g) flour
⅔ cup (140 g) butter
¼ cup (60 g) shiitake mushrooms
¼ cup (60 g) cepes mushrooms
¼ cup (60 g) morels
Salt and black pepper to taste

In a 5-gallon (19 L) stockpot, plunge the veal shank bones into boiling water, and boil rapidly for 5 minutes, skimming as necessary. Remove the bones.

Clean the pan and return the bones and add onions. Add 4 gallons (15 L) of clean water, bring to a boil. Skim as necessary, for 6 hours. Strain the liquid.

Peel, cut and wash the remaining root vegetables. Sauté them in ¼ cup (60 g) melted butter.

Add the reduced veal stock, cloves, and bay leaves, bring to a boil, and simmer until the stock reduces to about 8 cups (2 L). Strain stock and reserve.

Melt the remaining butter, and sauté the finely sliced wild mushrooms until well-cooked. Remove the mushrooms and add the flour, stirring over a low heat for 1 minute. Gradually add the veal stock, constantly whipping, until smooth consistency is obtained.

Strain the soup and add the sautéed mushrooms and heavy cream. Cook slowly for 5 more minutes. Season with salt and pepper to taste.

Lobster "Plaza" Thermidor

Servings—8
Portion—1 lobster

8 lobsters (1½ pound (675 g) each), boiled
1 cup (225 g) shallots
½ cup (120 ml) white wine
¼ cup (60 g) Dijon mustard
1⅓ cups (300 ml) heavy cream
¼ cup (60 g) Parmesan cheese
¼ cup (60 ml) brandy
1 pound (450 g) blanched and seasoned strips of onion, celery, carrot, and leek
¼ cup (60 g) butter
Salt and small pinch of cayenne pepper to taste

Separate the claws and arms from the lobster, and remove the meat from the shells by cracking the shell with a nutcracker. Reserve the meat for later use.

Separate the tail from the body. Squeeze the edges of the lobster tail together, crushing the shell. Peel away the shell, section by section, until the lobster tail can be removed intact and in one piece. Discard the shell, but retain the tail piece for later decoration.

Remove the legs and lower part of the lobster body by pulling the top from the bottom. Using a teaspoon, scrape the creamy parts of the lobsters that remain in the upper shell into a bowl.

With a small, sharp knife, cut a line about ⅛-inch (.3 cm) deep along each of the back of the lobsters tails to reveal the waste intestine. Carefully remove this tissue and discard. Slice each tail into medallions about ⅜-inch (.95 cm) thickness, and reserve for later use.

Peel and dice the shallots. In a 10-inch (25 cm) skillet, melt half the butter, and sauté the diced shallots until transparent. Add brandy, and flame the pan. Add white wine and reduce until almost all of the liquor is evaporated. Add heavy cream, creamy parts of the lobster bodies, mustard, and Parmesan cheese. Reduce the sauce until it becomes a syrup. Strain.

Carefully arrange the sliced tails and the claws in a skillet, so that each medallion can be identified and placed in order to reassemble the tail. Carefully add the prepared sauce to the pan, and very gently heat the lobster meat in the sauce. Add a small pinch of cayenne pepper and salt to taste.

Heat the blanched stripped vegetables in the remaining butter, and season to taste.

Place about ¼ cup (60 g) of the prepared vegetables in a line down the center of a serving plate. Arrange the tail pieces in order on top of the vegetables, placing the claws at each side of the tail. Gently coat the medallions with the sauce. Place the tail piece of the shell on the plate so that the dish resembles a complete whole lobster.

Potato Cocotte

Servings—16
Portion—1 potato

16 potatoes, cocotte style
Butter, clarified
Parsley, chopped

Peel potatoes. Quarter the potatoes into a longish olive shape, about 2 inches (5 cm). Boil or steam (preferably steam).

Lightly glaze with clarified butter. Sprinkle with chopped parsley to garnish.

Fresh Fruits with Butterscotch Sabayon

Servings—8
Portion—¼ cup (60 g)

10 egg yolks
3 tablespoons (30 ml) white wine
2 tablespoons (30 g) sugar
3⅓ tablespoons (50 ml) butterscotch syrup
3 tablespoons (30 ml) melba sauce
½ cup (115 g) blueberries
½ cup (115 g) raspberries
½ cup (115 g) strawberries
½ cup (115 g) blackberries

Wash and drain fresh fruit.

In a double boiler, combine the sugar, white wine, and egg yolks and whip the mixture into a froth. Continue beating until froth becomes thick and creamy so that it will coat the back of a spoon. Add the warmed butterscotch syrup and blend it into the sabayon.

Pour a neat puddle of sauce on a warm serving plate about 5 inches (13 cm) in diameter. On two opposite sides of the plate, carefully place two nickel-size dots of melba sauce (two on each side) about 1½-inches (3.5 cm) apart. With a cocktail stick, scribe the melba sauce in an arc directly through each disc, so that the melba sauce will be pulled into two heart shapes elongated into each other. Repeat on the opposite side of the plate.

Arrange the fruit between the two decorative motifs. Serve.

KEYSTONE RESORT COLORADO

Menu

New Garden Vegetables Vinaigrette

Leek and Lentil Lamb Soup

Colors of Colorado Summer Salad

Strawberry Sorbet with a Crenshaw Melon Sauce

Lobster Saints John

Burnt Sugar Cream

The Keystone Lodge is a modern hotel, designed to take maximum advantage of mountain views and Colorado sunshine. "The Keystone Ranch," the resort's finest dining experience, is a skillfully restored 1930's log ranch residence. It resides in a pristine valley with views of 14,000 foot mountains and the Gore Mountain Range.

New Garden Vegetables Vinaigrette

Servings—6–8
Portions—4 ounces (115 g)

Tomato Vinaigrette—
- **1 cup (225 g) canned crushed tomato**
- **2 cups (425 ml) white wine vinegar**
- **1 quart (1 L) salad oil**
- **2 cups (½ L) olive oil**
- **2 teaspoons (10 g) salt**
- **1 teaspoon (5 g) black pepper**
- **dash Tabasco**
- **10 minced anchovies**
- **10 minced fresh basil leaves**
- **1 tablespoon (15 g) minced capers**
- **1 tablespoon (15 g) Dijon mustard**
- **2 teaspoons (10 ml) honey**
- **3 eggs**
- **1 teaspoon (5 ml) Worcestershire sauce**

Calypso dressing—
- **2 eggs**
- **2 cups (½ L) salad oil**
- **½ cup (120 ml) white wine vinegar**

- **½ teaspoon (2.5 g) white pepper**
- **dash Tabasco**
- **1 teaspoon (5 g) salt**
- **1 teaspoon (5 g) minced fresh ginger**
- **¼ cup (60 g) tomato paste**
- **½ cup (120 ml) cream**
- **2 tablespoons (30 ml) brandy**

Vegetables—
- **4 ounces (115 g) assorted blanched mini vegetables (see below)**

Mix ingredients thoroughly in a mixer with a wire whip for Tomato Vinaigrette dressing.

Using a blender, slowly pour in each of the ingredients for the Calypso dressing.

Coat serving plate with about 4 tablespoons (60 ml) of Tomato Vinaigrette. With a squeeze bottle (such as that commonly used for honey), draw lines on the Tomato Vinaigrette with the Calypso Dressing. Draw a knife through the dressings to complete the plate painting.

Artistically arrange lightly blanched vegetables and mini vegetables on the plate, being careful not to disturb or hide the plate painting. Vegetables often used include asparagus, baby carrots, mini globe carrots, mini beets, mini candystripe or yellow beets, strips of red pepper, haricot verts, mini zucchini, slices of pear tomatoes or tomatillos, and trumpet mushrooms.

Strawberry Sorbet with a Crenshaw Melon Sauce

Servings—8
Portions—1 glass

- **2 pints (1 L) of cleaned, very ripe strawberries**
- **Juice of 1 small lime**
- **Zest of 1 small lime**
- **1 tablespoon (15 ml) honey**
- **2 ounces Grand Marnier**

Sauce—
- **¾ cup (180 g) ripe Crenshaw melon meat**
- **¼ cup (60 ml) Sauterne wine**

In a food processor, purée all ingredients for the sorbet. Pour into a loaf pan and freeze overnight. Purée ingredients for sauce.

The following day, scrape the sorbet into balls, using a small ice cream scoop.

When ready to serve, spoon 2 tablespoons (30 ml) of sauce into the bottom of a champagne glass, and lay the scoop of sorbet on top. Garnish with mint.

Lobster Saints John

Servings—6
Portions—1 lobster tail

**6 lobster tails 6–8 ounces
  (180–225 g)**
1 cup (250 ml) Sauterne wine
Pinch saffron
Cornstarch to thicken
1 cup (225 g) sweet butter
Juice of ½ lime
Zest of ½ lime
Pinch salt

With poultry shears, shell the tails carefully down both sides on the bottom so that meat is not cut. Reserve fins. Skewer each tail with thin bamboo skewers (2 for each tail) so tails do not curl during cooking.

To prepare sauce: bring wine to a boil, let flame, and thicken to the consistency of heavy cream with cornstarch mixed with a little water. The cornstarch makes a clear sauce and stabilizes the butter. Add saffron, butter cut into small cubes, lime zest and juice, and salt; whisk the sauce to incorporate the butter. Set aside at room temperature until the lobster is prepared.

Bring a pot of lightly salted, lemon water to a boil, and simmer the tails just until firm. Remove the skewers, slice into medallions, and fan on a plate, garnishing with the tail fan.

Spoon sauce over the lobster medallions and serve. This entrée can be served with couscous molded into poached butter lettuce, asparagus in a puff pastry case, poached seaweed, and a crayfish garnish.

Burnt Sugar Cream

Servings—8
Portions—1 custard cup

4 egg yolks
1 cup (250 ml) heavy cream
1 cup (250 ml) half and half
¼ cup (60 g) granulated sugar
Zest of ¼ orange
2 tablespoons (30 ml) Grand Marnier
¼ cup (60 g) sugar for top of custard
Fruits for garnish

Mix yolks, cream, half and half, sugar, the zest, and Grand Marnier. Bake the mixture in shallow custard cups at 200°C (400°F) in a pan with a little water. When the custard is set (about 30 minutes), remove and refrigerate until serving time.

Garnish a base plate with seasonal fruits and pre-heat broiler. To save, spread the remaining sugar over the eight custards, covering them completely.

Set the custard cups under the broiler and watch them carefully. They should carmelize evenly. Remove from broiler and serve cups on garnished plate.

DESERT INN

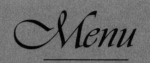

Menu

Crab Wellington with Dill Sauce

Cream of Avocado Soup

Chicken Marengo

Watercress and Endive with Hearts of Palm

Coupé Glacé de Marrons

Demitasse

The Desert Inn Hotel & Casino, Las Vegas, features epicurean delights from around the world. The "Monte Carlo Room" offers exquisite French cuisine. At the "Portofino," you'll find delicious Northern Italian specialties. And, for the flavors of Mandarin, Cantonese and Szechuan cooking, the "Ho Wan" beckons.

Crab Wellington with Dill Sauce

Servings—4
Portion—6 ounces (180 g)

- ¼ pound (115 g) crabmeat
- 6 ounces (185 g) white fish fillets
- 1½ teaspoon (10 ml) lemon juice
- 1 tablespoon (15 g) chopped pimiento
- 1 tablespoon (15 g) chives, chopped
- Pinch of parsley, chopped
- ¾ cup (75 g) Monterey Jack cheese, shredded
- 2 tablespoons (15 g) dry bread crumbs
- 2 eggs, slightly beaten
- Cayenne pepper and salt to taste
- Prepared puff pastry
- 2 teaspoons (10 g) butter, melted
- 1 tablespoon (15 g) eggwash
- Pinch dill weed, chopped
- 1 cup (250 ml) cream sauce

Combine the first ten ingredients, gently tossing together until thoroughly mixed. Shape into a loaf.

Roll puff pastry into a rectangle, brushing with melted butter. Place crab loaf in the center of the rectangle. Fold dough over loaf. Seal seams with eggwash. Place loaf seam-side down on baking sheet. If desired, roll out remaining dough trimmings and cut into shapes to garnish tops. Brush with eggwash.

Bake in 375°F (190°C) oven for 25 minutes or until golden brown. Heat cream sauce and add dill. Serve each portion topped with cream sauce.

Cream of Avocado Soup

Servings—6
Portion—6 ounces (180 g)

- 4 cups (1 L) chicken stock
- 2 large avocados, peeled, mashed, and sieved
- 1 cup (250 ml) whipping cream
- 1 teaspoon (5 g) chili powder
- 1 teaspoon (5 g) parsley, chopped
- 1 teaspoon (5 g) chopped cilantro
- Salt and pepper to taste

Bring chicken stock to a boil in double boiler. Stir in avocados and seasonings. Bring to boiling point again, adding cream slowly. Season with salt and pepper. Remove from heat and cool. Refrigerate and chill thoroughly. Garnish with slices of avocados or cucumbers and serve cold.

Chicken Marengo

Servings—4
Portion—1 breast

- 2 chicken breasts, skinned and cut in half
- 2 lobster tails (with end of tail or fan removed), cut into golf ball-sized pieces
- ½ cup (112 g) butter
- 2 tablespoons (30 ml) olive oil
- 1 tablespoon (85 ml) flour
- 1 teaspoon (5 g) parsley, chopped
- 1 teaspoon (5 g) chives, chopped
- 2 teaspoons (10 g) garlic, chopped
- 8 large mushrooms, sliced
- 6 stuffed green olives, sliced

¼ teaspoon (1.25 g) oregano

½ teaspoon (2. g) tarragon

1 bay leaf, crushed

2 slices green pepper

4 small tomatoes

2 tablespoon (30 g) tomato purée

4 tablespoons (60 ml) dry sherry

1 dash crème de banana

1 dash brandy

4 tablespoons (60 ml) chicken broth

1½ large onions, chopped fine

½ cup (120 ml) white wine

Salt and pepper to taste

Combine a dash of salt and pepper and flour in a paper bag. Shake the chicken inside the bag to coat. Remove the chicken and follow the same procedure with the lobster. Keep the chicken and lobster separate.

Melt butter and add olive oil. When sizzling, add chicken. Brown on both sides, then move chicken to side of pan and add lobster. Cook lobster until it begins to turn white. Mix chicken and lobster together. Add green pepper, onion, oregano, garlic, tarragon, and bay leaf. Stir to prevent sticking. Add

chicken broth, tomato purée, tomatoes, and mushrooms. Cook for 10 minutes, stirring constantly to prevent sticking. Add sherry, a dash of crème de banana and white wine. Cook for 15 minutes. Add brandy and flame.

Place in deep dish ovenware. Sprinkle with olives, parsley, and chives. Place in preheated 365°F (188°C) oven for 25 minutes.

Garnish with 1 fried egg on top of each serving.

Watercress and Endive with Hearts of Palm

Servings—4

Portion—1 salad

2 heads Bibb lettuce

2 bunches watercress

2 cups (450 g) hearts of palm

1 Belgian endive

1 cup (250 ml) Watercress and Bibb dressing

Place lettuce, watercress, hearts of palm, and endive in a bowl. Add dressing, toss well and serve.

Watercress and Bibb Dressing

Servings—1 cup

Portion—2 tablespoons (30 ml)

1 clove garlic

¼ teaspoon (1.25 ml) salt

¼ teaspoon (1.25 ml) fresh black pepper

1 teaspoon (5 ml) Worcestershire sauce

½ teaspoon (2.5 ml) Dijon mustard

¼ cup (60 ml) lemon juice

½ cup (120 ml) olive oil

Rub a wooden bowl with garlic, salt, and pepper until garlic disappears. Add Worcestershire sauce, mustard, and lemon juice, mixing well. Add olive oil gradually until mixture thickens.

Pour dressing over greens.

Coupé Glacé de Marrons

Servings—6

Portion—1 glass

2 cups (450 g) marrons (chestnuts)

2 cups (425 ml) whipping cream

2 tablespoons (30 ml) Kirschwasser

3 tablespoons (45 ml) maraschino liqueur

6 scoops ice cream

Drain syrup from marrons and set aside, saving 6. Chop marrons, add cherry liqueur, and stir well. Mash ingredients to make a sauce. Whip cream and add maraschino liqueur.

Place a scoop of ice cream in a champagne glass, cover with 1 tablespoon (15 ml) of sauce and 1 tablespoon (15 ml) of whipped cream and top with a marron.

The DORCHESTER

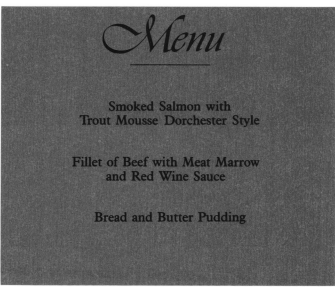

Menu

Smoked Salmon with
Trout Mousse Dorchester Style

Fillet of Beef with Meat Marrow
and Red Wine Sauce

Bread and Butter Pudding

The Dorchester "Grill Room" is proud of its tradition of serving the best of British food. Here, amid the Spanish style decor and walls hung with 18th-century tapestries, you can enjoy roast beef and Yorkshire Pudding. It is guaranteed that everything on the menu has been grown or bred in the British Isles or the Channel Islands.

Smoked Salmon with Trout Mousse Dorchester Style

Servings—4
Portion—2 slices

- **8 slices Scottish smoked salmon, finely cut**
- **4½ ounces (120 g) smoked trout fillet**
- **2 leaves of gelatin, soaked in cold water and dissolved in 1½ tablespoons (1.5 ml) of warm water**
- **¾ cup (200 ml) whipped cream**
- **1½ tablespoons (20 ml) sherry**
- **1 tablespoon (15 ml) cognac**
- **Fresh horseradish, finely grated**
- **Salt, freshly ground pepper to taste**

Garnish:

- **4 lettuce leaves**
- **4 red chicory leaves**
- **4 half slices of cucumber**
- **4 slices of hard-boiled egg**
- **4 tomato slices**
- **4 slices of truffle**
- **4 sprigs of parsley**

Arrange the finely cut slices of salmon on small glass dishes, overlapping the sides. Refrigerate.

Purée the smoked trout fillet.

Add the dissolved gelatin. Fold in the whipped cream; add sherry and cognac. Season with the finely grated horseradish, salt, and pepper. Place carefully on top of the salmon slices. Fold the salmon sides back over the mousse. Refrigerate for about ½ hour.

Serve on a plate decorated with the lettuce and red chicory leaves. Garnish with the slices of cucumber, egg, tomato, truffles, and sprigs of parsley.

Fillet of Beef with Meat Marrow and Red Wine Sauce

Servings—4
Portion—1 tournedo

- **4 5½ ounce (160 g) tournedos**
- **Salt and freshly ground pepper to taste**
- **1 tablespoon (15 ml) peanut oil**

Garnish:

- **¼ pound (105 g) beef marrow, diced sprinkling of chopped parsley**
- **1 teaspoon (10 g) white breadcrumbs**
- **¼ cup (60 ml) white wine**
- **4 ½-inch (1 cm) high blanched marrow bones**

Season the well-trimmed tournedos and grill according to taste. Keep warm.

Thoroughly mix the beef marrow, parsley, breadcrumbs, and white wine.

Arrange the garnish on the tournedos, and broil for 6–7 minutes.

Arrange the tournedos on the marrow bones and serve with red wine sauce.

Serving the tournedos on the marrow bones is not only original, but it also prevents the meat from becoming overcooked on a hot serving dish.

Red Wine Sauce

Servings—4
Portion—for tournedos

- 1 teaspoon (10 g) finely chopped shallot
- 1 cup (250 ml) red wine
- Pinch thyme
- 1 cup (250 ml) brown veal stock
- 2 tablespoons (50 g) butter
- Freshly ground white pepper

Sweat the finely chopped shallot carefully in butter, without allowing it to color. Add the red wine and the thyme, and reduce to half the original volume. Add the veal stock and reduce again. Season with salt, pepper, and butter.

Bread and Butter Pudding

Servings—4
Portion—¼ dish

- 1 cup (250 ml) milk
- 1 cup (250 ml) double cream
- Pinch of salt
- 1 vanilla pod
- 3 eggs
- ¾ cup (125 g) sugar
- 3 small bread rolls
- 1½ tablespoons (30 g) butter
- 1 tablespoon (10 g) sultanas, soaked in water
- 1½ tablespoons (20 g) apricot jam
- Pinch of confectioner's sugar

Bring the milk, cream, pinch of salt, and vanilla pod to a boil.

Mix the eggs and sugar together; add the simmering milk and cream. Pass mixture through a sieve.

Cut the rolls into thin slices and butter them. Arrange in a buttered ovenproof dish. Add the soaked raisins and milk mixture. Sprinkle the remaining butter on top and poach carefully for 35 to 40 minutes in a double-boiler. Sprinkle with apricot jam and dust with confectioner's sugar.

Bread and Butter Pudding may be served with double cream or canned fruit.

The *WESTWOOD MARQUIS*
HOTEL and GARDENS

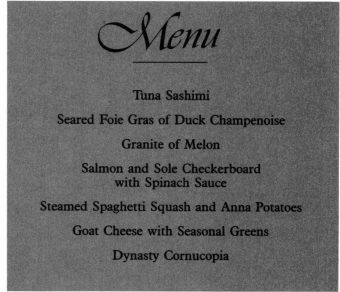

Menu

Tuna Sashimi

Seared Foie Gras of Duck Champenoise

Granite of Melon

Salmon and Sole Checkerboard
with Spinach Sauce

Steamed Spaghetti Squash and Anna Potatoes

Goat Cheese with Seasonal Greens

Dynasty Cornucopia

The Westwood Marquis Hotel and Gardens spared no expense in creating the decor, menu and ambiance of the "Dynasty Room." The results are as stellar as their world famous patrons. They come for the gracious service, elegant presentation and superb cuisine they know to be unique to the Westwood Marquis.

Seared Foie Gras of Duck Champenoise

Servings—6
Portion—1 slice

1-2½ pound (1¼ kg) fresh whole duck foie gras
2 tablespoons (30 g) butter
¼ cup (60 g) shallots
2 cups (½ L) Brut champagne
2 cups (½ L) chicken stock
1 cup (¼ L) heavy cream
2 tablespoons (30 g) cornstarch or arrowroot
1 teaspoon (5 ml) honey
2 tablespoons (30 ml) extra virgin olive oil

Garnish:
½ pound (225 g) champagne grapes
1 bunch chervil

Melt butter in 10-inch (25 cm) sauté pan and lightly brown shallots. Deglaze with champagne and reduce liquid to ½ the volume. Add chicken stock. Reduce again to ¼ the volume. Add cream and boil for 5 minutes. Thicken sauce with cornstarch or arrowroot. Add honey and stir well. Strain through fine china cap. Place champagne sauce over hot water bath.

Cut 6 5-ounce (140 g) slices of foie gras. In large skillet, quickly sear both sides of foie gras in hot oil. Remove from pan and place on paper towel to blot extra fat. Immediately set the foie gras on a warm salad plate and pour the champagne sauce over. Arrange the grapes and chervil leaves around the plate.

Salmon and Sole Checkerboard with Spinach Sauce

Servings—6
Portion—1 slice

3 bunches fresh spinach, stems removed
1½ pounds (675 g) fresh salmon
1½ pounds (675 g) fresh lemon sole
4 cups (1 L) white wine
2 cups (½ L) clam juice
4 shallots, chopped
2 pinches black pepper

Clean spinach.

Cut both salmon and sole into 24 1-inch (2.5 cm) strips, making 48 strips. Weave four strips each of sole and salmon (per serving) under and over each other to create checkerboard.

Mix white wine, clam juice, shallots and pepper in 2-inch (5 cm) deep sautéuse and simmer.

Using a wide spatula, slide checkerboards into simmering court bouillon and cook for 3-4 minutes. Gently remove and place on paper towel.

Strain bouillon through fine china cap. Add spinach to bouillon and cook for 1 minute. Remove from heat. Purée in a blender.

Place checkerboard in center of plate and pour sauce around. Garnish with julienne of tomato or garnish of your choice.

Dynasty Cornucopia

Servings—8
Portion—¾ cup (180 g)

Cornucopia Batter—
   1 cup (225 g) all-purpose flour
   1½ cups (340 g) powdered sugar
   ½ cup (120 ml) egg whites
   ½ cup (120 ml) heavy cream
   Wax paper
   4 ounces (115 g) dark chocolate

Mousse—
   8 egg yolks
   2 cups (450 g) sugar
   3 tablespoons (45 g) unflavored gelatin
   ½ cup (120 ml) water
   1 pint (½ L) fresh strawberries, puréed
   4 ounces (120 ml) Kirsch liqueur
   12 egg whites
   2 cups (½ L) heavy cream, whipped

Vanilla Sauce—
   2 egg yolks
   ½ cup (100 g) powdered sugar
   ¼ piece vanilla bean, slit
   1 cup (250 ml) heavy cream

Decoration—
   1 mango, puréed
   ½ pint (¼ L) fresh raspberries, puréed
   Fresh fruit in season

Sift together dry ingredients. In a medium bowl, mix egg whites and cream; add dry ingredients. Mix 3 minutes at high speed. Pre-heat oven to 350°F (180°C). Cut 8 pieces of wax paper into 5½″ × 5½″ (14 cm × 14 cm). Pour and spread a thin layer of the mixture covering each piece of wax paper. Place in oven for 8–10 minutes or until firm and light brown in color. Remove from oven. While still hot, remove wax paper. Hold the two opposite corners of the square and wrap each side towards the center, under and over to form the cornucopia. Let cool.

Melt chocolate. Dip the closed end of the cornucopia in the chocolate. Set aside.

In a medium bowl, beat yolks until pale yellow. Add 1 cup (225 g) sugar. Beat until sugar is dissolved.

In a small bowl, combine gelatin and ½ cup water. Place over hot water bath. Stir to dissolve gelatin. Combine gelatin with puréed strawberries and Kirsch liqueur.

In a separate bowl, beat egg whites to soft peaks. Add sugar, 1 tablespoon (15 g) at a time, beating well after each addition. After all the sugar has been added, beat until stiff peaks form. Fold egg whites into strawberry purée. Add cream. Refrigerate 20 minutes.

Place egg yolks, powdered sugar and slit vanilla bean into a bowl. Let stand over hot water bath. Add cream and whisk to a thick consistency. Remove from heat and whisk until cool.

Fill a pastry bag with strawberry mousse. Fill each cornucopia. Arrange fresh fruits as desired. Pour 1 tablespoon (15 ml) each of vanilla sauce, mango, and raspberry purée on plate to serve.

GRAND HOTEL NATIONAL

Menu

Creme of Yellow Mushrooms

Fillet of Baby Turbot
and Smoked Salmon

Medallions of Veal
and Goose Liver with Turnips

Island of Fresh Fruits

A unique dining experience awaits you at the "von Pfyffer Stube," which is named after the constructor of the Grand Hotel National, beautifully located on the lakeshore of Lucerne. We feature a creative market-fresh cuisine in a wood-panelled dining-room overlooking the lake. Our wine cellar matches the variety of our dishes.

Medallions of Veal and Goose Liver with Turnips

Servings—6
Portion—1 medallion

6 veal steaks
6 slices of fresh goose liver
2 tablespoons (30 ml) oil
2 tablespoons (30 g) butter
¾ cup (200 ml) beef stock
2½ cups (500 g) turnips, blanched
½ cup (120 ml) Port wine
1 teaspoon (5 g) fresh horseradish
2 teaspoons (20 g) chives
Salt and pepper

Pan-fry the seasoned veal steaks. Pour wine into hot skillet and reduce to ½. Add the beef stock and blanched turnips. Reduce again, blend in the butter, grated horseradish and chives. Season to taste with salt and pepper.

Pour sauce onto a hot plate and place veal medallion on top. Season and quickly pan fry the goose liver sepa-rately. Place it next to the veal on the plate. Serve at once as goose liver tends to cool very fast.

Creme of Yellow Mushrooms

Servings—6
Portion—¼ cup (60 ml)

¾ cup (180 g) fresh yellow mushrooms
3 tablespoons (50 g) butter
2 cups (425 ml) veal stock
1 cup (250 ml) double cream
1 teaspoon (5 g) shallots
Seasoning

Quickly sauté the shallots in 1 table-spoon (15 g) of butter. Add the mush-rooms and simmer for 5 minutes to-gether with veal stock. Add the double cream and rest of butter. Bring to boil. Blend in mixer and strain. Season to taste.

Fillet of Baby Turbot and Smoked Salmon

Servings—6
Portion—1 slice

2 tablespoons (30 ml) olive oil
6 slices of baby turbot
6 slices of smoked salmon
½ cup (120 ml) double cream
½ cup (120 ml) Béarnaise sauce
2 tablespoons (30 ml) white wine
Seasoning
6 leaves of fresh dill

Season the turbot fillets, dip them in olive oil, and grill them on a hot grid-dle. Reduce the white wine in the pan, add the double cream, and bring to boil.

Add Béarnaise sauce to taste. Place on a hot plate. Dress the grilled fish on top of the sauce and place the rolled smoked salmon opposite the sauce. Gar-nish with a dill leaf.

Island of Fresh Fruits

Servings—6
Portion—1 plate

5 egg yolks

⅓ cup (85 g) confectioner's sugar

⅔ cup (150ml) whipped cream

½ grated orange peel

1 kiwi

1 fig

1 orange in fillets

¼ cup (60 g) each of fresh raspberries, blueberries, strawberries, and boysenberries

½ mango

1 slice pineapple

Beat egg yolk with confectioner's sugar. Add whipped cream and grated orange peel. Place the cream in deep soup plates, and arrange cut fruit shapes on top. Glacé under broiler.

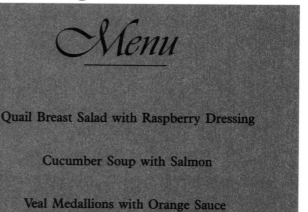

Park Hotel Vitznau

Menu

Quail Breast Salad with Raspberry Dressing

Cucumber Soup with Salmon

Veal Medallions with Orange Sauce

Chilled Sabayon of Champagne

The Park Hotel Vitznau sets like a pearl on the fair, verdant shores of Lake Lucerne in the romantic heart of Switzerland. Each guest is still king at the Park Hotel Vitznau, with a gourmet restaurant to pamper your palate at every meal.

Quail Breast Salad with Raspberry Dressing

Servings—6
Portion—2 breasts

- **12 quail breasts**
- **Leaves of green salad, red lettuce, lambs lettuce**
- **12 quail eggs, cooked**
- **12 tomato roses**
- **¼ pound (115 g) fresh mushrooms**
- **Chives to garnish**
- **Chervil to garnish**
- **1 cup (250 ml) raspberry vinegar**
- **1 cup (250 ml) walnut oil**
- **Salt, pepper, Worcestershire sauce to taste**

To make raspberry dressing, combine the vinegar, salt, and pepper. Add the oil in a thin stream, while stirring with a whisk until all of the oil is absorbed. Season to taste.

Season the quail breasts, sauté until cooked medium well, keep warm. In a bowl, mix the salad leaves and mushrooms with the raspberry dressing. Place leaves in the center of a plate. Cut the quail breasts and place on the lettuce. Sprinkle with dressing. Garnish with tomato roses, 2 halves quail eggs, chervil, and chopped chives.

Cucumber Soup with Salmon

Servings—6
Portion—1 cup

- **¾ cup (180 g) cucumber, peeled and freshly chopped**
- **1 tablespoon (15 g) shallots, chopped**
- **1 teaspoon (5 g) butter**
- **2 cups (425 ml) chicken broth**
- **2 cups (425 ml) 35% cream**
- **½ cup (120 ml) white wine**
- **Salt, pepper, Worcestershire sauce to taste**

Garnish—
- **Julienne of fresh salmon**

Heat butter, add the shallots and cucumber, and simmer for a few minutes. Add the white wine and chicken broth. Simmer for 15–20 minutes. Add the cream and let simmer for another 5 minutes. Strain through a cheesecloth, and season to taste.

Veal Medallions with Orange Sauce

Servings—6
Portion—3 ounces (85 g)

- **1¼ pounds (560 g) veal medallions**
- **⅓ cup (75 g) clarified butter**
- **3 tablespoons (45 g) shallots, chopped**
- **¼ cup (60 ml) white wine**
- **3½ cups (⅘ L) orange juice**
- **1 cup (250 ml) veal stock**
- **½ cup (120 g) unsalted butter**
- **Salt**
- **Freshly ground pepper**
- **Grand Marnier**
- **Orange segments**
- **Chervil**

Season the veal medallions with salt and pepper. Sauté in clarified butter carefully until golden brown and cooked medium well. Remove the meat and keep it warm. Sauté the chopped shallots in butter over moderate heat. Add white wine, orange juice, and veal broth, and reduce to ⅓ the original quantity and strain. Gradually work in the butter, and season with salt and Grand Marnier. Garnish with orange segments and a sprig of chevril.

Chilled Sabayon of Champagne

Servings—6
Portion—1 glass

8 egg yolks
1 cup (250 ml) champagne
½ cup (115 g) sugar
1 cup (250 ml) 35% cream
Pinch (1.5 g) natural gelatin, unflavored, dissolved in warm water

Combine the egg yolks, sugar, and champagne in a large bowl. Cook in a double boiler. Beat with a whisk until very fluffy and firm. Remove from the double boiler and continue beating until cold. Whip the cream until fluffy but not too stiff. Pour the melted gelatin into sabayon, while beating. Fold in the whipped cream and fill glasses. Garnish with chocolate cornet by piping a grape design on each sabayon. Serve with freshly baked lady fingers.

PALACE HOTEL

Menu

Salmon Terrine with Anchovy Butter

Small Herb Salad

Lobster in Cream Sauce

Partridge Toledana Style

San Marcos Cake

Through the stately wrought iron doors into the "Grill Neptuno," a tremendous sense of occasion and expectancy herald the delights of exceptional cuisine and service. This exclusive and distinguished restaurant—with its murals, ornate carved ceilings and authentic open Prussian grill—offers a local and international cuisine.

Salmon Terrine with Anchovy Butter

Servings—8
Portion—1 slice

1¾ pounds (800 g) smoked salmon
2½ tablespoons(45 g) anchovies
¼ cup (60 g) butter
Alfalfa sprouts
Modena vinegar
Mint
Chicory
Salt and pepper to taste

Cut salmon into long, fine strands. Press anchovies through a colander and blend with soft butter. Fill an earthenware dish with alternate layers of salmon and anchovy butter. Cool.

Remove and cut into ½ inch (1.28 cm) thick slices. Place on serving dish with herb salad.

Partridge Toledana Style

Servings—8
Portion—1 partridge

8 partridges
1 cup (¼ L) dry white wine
½ cup (250 ml) olive oil
3 tablespoons (40 g) garlic
3 tablespoons (50 g) onion
3 tablespoons (50 g) leeks
3 tablespoons (50 g) carrots
2 teaspoons (10 g) black pepper
2 bay leaves
Prepared poultry stock

Clean partridges and remove giblets. Sauté in oil until golden. Add vegetables, pepper, and bay leaves. Allow to simmer for a few minutes.

Add wine and stock. Boil until partridges are tender. Purée remaining liquid and allow to thicken. Garnish with vegetables.

Lobster in Cream Sauce

Servings—8
Portion—1 lobster

8 1-pound, 9 ounce (700 g) lobsters
7 tablespoons (100 g) carrots
7 tablespoons (100 g) leeks
7 tablespoons (100 g) green beans
7 tablespoons (100 g) white celery
⅞ cup (200 g) cream

Boil live lobsters with half of the vegetables for 10 minutes. Remove lobsters and allow liquid to cool.

Whip cream to a thick consistency. Slowly add the meat from the lobster heads, and the thickened stock for a delicate, light sauce.

Place the lobster meat in the center of a serving plate, with the head and tail completing the shape of a lobster. Cover the meat with the remaining vegetables in julienne strips and add sauce.

San Marcos Cake

Servings—8
Portion—1 slice

6 eggs
1 cup (200 g) sugar
½ cup (100 g) flour
1 cup (1 L) cream
¼ cup (60 ml) chocolate cream
1¼ cup (300 ml) syrup
⅔ cup (155 g) apple gelatin
1 cup (250 ml) brandy

1 slice of lemon rind
2 cups (½ L) water

Mix eggs with ½ cup (100 g) sugar, and blend well. Add flour. Bake in square sponge pan at 425°F (220°C) until done. Allow to cool.

Boil water, remaining sugar, lemon rind, and brandy for syrup.

Cut the cooled sponge into small squares. Spoon syrup over squares until well soaked. Add a layer of chocolate cream, then a layer of sponge. Top with another layer of whisked cream.

Blend 10 egg yolks with ¼ cup (50 g) sugar, to cover the cake. Use a hot metal branding iron on this yolk mixture to make it a golden color. With a piping bag, apply chocolate cream and apple gelatin to decorate.

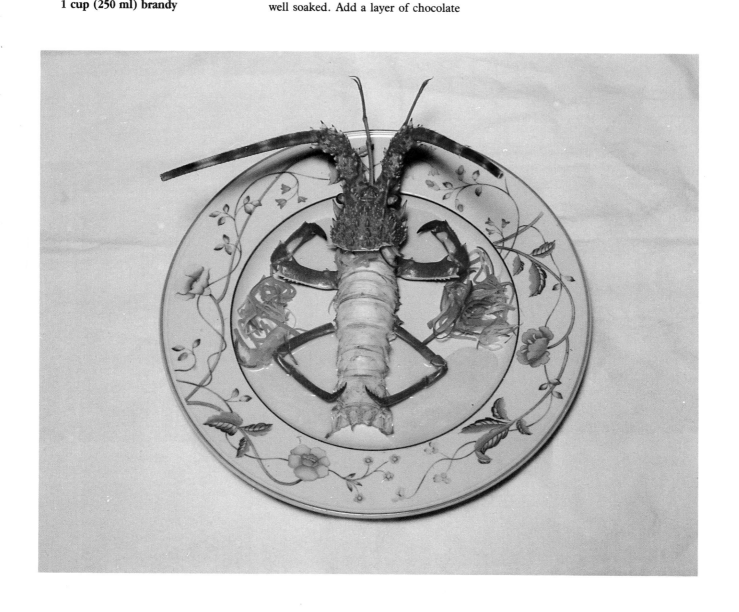

HOTEL BYBLOS ANDALUZ

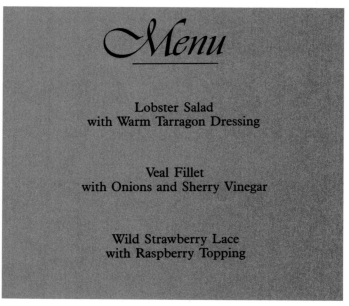

Menu

Lobster Salad
with Warm Tarragon Dressing

Veal Fillet
with Onions and Sherry Vinegar

Wild Strawberry Lace
with Raspberry Topping

The Hotel Byblos Andaluz offers you a wide range of sports facilities. Three restaurants and two bars are at your disposal. The French gastronomic cuisine restaurant, where a cosy atmosphere envelopes you in a typically Andalusian setting, is enhanced by the scent of flowers and the luxury of faultless service.

Lobster Salad with Warm Tarragon Dressing

Servings—4
Portion—¼ lobster tail

6 cups (1½ L) court bouillon
1 lobster
1 head lettuce
1 trevise
16 asparagus tips
1 tomato
1 teaspoon (5 g) finely chopped shallots
Pinch finely chopped fresh tarragon

Dressing—

1 cup (250 ml) Americaine
¼ cup (60 ml) virgin olive oil
¼ cup (60 ml) peanut oil
Juice of 1 lemon
¼ cup (60 ml) nage

Peel and clean all the vegetables. Cut coarsely and cook for 8 minutes in 5 cups (1¼ L) of boiling water. Add white wine and lobster; cook for another 15 minutes on high heat. Drain and cool. Remove the tail and cut into equal slices according to the rings on the underside.

For the dressing, combine Americiane, olive and peanut oils, and lemon juice. Thin dressing carefully with some court bouillon. Season with celery salt and pinch of cayenne.

Cover the bottom of serving plate with dressing. Place lettuce in the middle. Surround lettuce with lobster slices. Decorate with asparagus tips and tomato.

Veal Fillet with Onions and Sherry Vinegar

Servings—4
Portion—1 fillet

1 pound (450 g) veal fillet
2 medium-sized onions
2 cups (475 ml) beef stock
1 cup (250 ml) sherry vinegar
2 tablespoons (30 g) mushrooms
1 cup (250 g) spinach
¼ cup (60 ml) port wine
1 cup (250 g) potatoes
⅓ cup (75 ml) milk
½ cup (120 ml) fresh cream
2 eggs
Pinch of nutmeg

Quickly fry the veal fillet over high heat, keeping it underdone.

Peel, clean and cut the potatoes in thin slices. Put 3 layers in a tray to gratin.

In a separate container, blend the eggs, cream, milk and nutmeg. Whip well. Spread mixture over the potatoes, and bake for 90 minutes at 300°F (150°C).

Peel, clean and cook the spinach.

To make the sauce, steam veal. Add the chopped onions, and thin the sauce by adding vinegar, wine, and half of beef stock. Cook approximately 30 minutes. Strain the sauce. Allow to thicken. Season to taste and whip.

Place some spinach in the center of serving plate. Cut the meat into equal slices and cover with spinach. Place gratin on the plate. Pour the sauce in a circle around the meat.

Wild Strawberry Lace with Raspberry Topping

Servings—4
Portion—1 stack of 3 laces

Lace—
- **2 tablespoons (30 g) almonds**
- **¼ cup (60 g) sugar**
- **2 tablespoons (30 g) flour**
- **1 teaspoon (5 ml) corn syrup**
- **1 teaspoon (5 g) butter**
- **2 cups (½ L) water**
- **1⅛ cups (250 g) wild strawberries**
- **4 mint leaves**

Cream—
- **¾ cup (200 ml) milk**
- **2 egg yolks**
- **¼ cup (60 g) sugar**
- **2 tablespoons (30 g) flour**
- **¼ stick vanilla**
- **¼ cup (60 ml) fresh cream**
- **Dash wild strawberry liqueur**

Raspberry Topping—
- **⅔ cup (150 ml) raspberry syrup**
- **Juice of 1 lemon**

Mix almonds with sugar and flour. Add the corn syrup, melted butter and water. Mix until dough forms.

Divide the dough into 12 small balls and place on a baking sheet. Bake at 475°F (240°C) until lightly browned, approximately 6 to 8 minutes. Remove quickly from the sheet and cool.

Boil the milk with vanilla.

In separate bowl, mix egg yolks, sugar, and flour. Pour boiled milk into the mixture, and boil again for 7 to 8 minutes. Remove from heat and whip vigorously, then chill well. Whip the cream in a separate bowl.

Mix the very cold custard with the whipped cream, adding the wild strawberry liqueur. Blend the strawberries with the syrup and lemon juice. Strain through a fine sieve.

Decorate serving plates with raspberry topping. Lay 2 laces on a serving plate with a teaspoon of whipped cream on top of each. Add the wild strawberries. Finish with a single lace.

The Manila Peninsula

Menu

Quenelles of Dover Sole with Beluga and Malossol Caviars on Tomato and Cucumber Coulis

Essence of Venison with Truffled Ravioli

Fresh Gooseliver in Crunchy Puff Pastry on Fine Champagne Sauce

Veal and Prawns Wrapped with Tenderloin of Prime Beef

Fresh Berries of the New Season with Raspberry and Mango Pulp

The Manila Peninsula, located in Makati, the business center of Manila, is a strikingly elegant hotel where modern Manila congregates. "Old Manila" specializes in Filipino, grilled prime beef and seafood delicacies. Swiss and continental cuisine is served in "The Chesa," with its Swiss chalet setting.

Quenelles of Dover Sole with Beluga and Malossol Caviars on Tomato and Cucumber Coulis

Servings—6 to 8
Portion—4 ounces (115 g)

> 1¾ pounds (800 g) sole fillet, trimmed and cleaned
>
> 2 potatoes
>
> 2 leeks
>
> 2 onions
>
> 4 cloves garlic
>
> 1 cup (250 ml) cream
>
> 6 gelatin leaves
>
> 3½ cups (⅘ L) whipped cream
>
> 1¾ tablespoons (25 g) caviar

Sauce—

> 24 tomatoes
>
> 2 cucumbers
>
> ½ cup (125 ml) cream
>
> 2 tablespoons (30 g) butter, salt, pepper, dill leaves

Clean and wash sole fillets well. Cut potatoes, leeks, onions, and garlic into small cubes. Sauté with sole fillets; add the cream, and simmer until done.

Soak the gelatin in cold water and add to fish. Purée mixture in a blender until fine and allow to cool. Before the mixture sets, add the whipping cream and allow to cool completely. Form into quenelles.

Serve on the tomato coulis and add the cucumber sauce with cream. Garnish with dill leaves and caviars.

Fresh Gooseliver in Crunchy Puff Pastry on Fine Champagne Sauce

Servings—6 to 8
Portion—3 ounces (85 g)

> 1½ pounds (640 g) fresh gooseliver
>
> 1½ tablespoons (20 g) butter
>
> Salt and pepper to taste
>
> 1 pound, 5 ounces (600 g) puff pastry
>
> 1 egg wash or beaten egg
>
> 3½ cups (800 ml) champagne
>
> **Glacé de Viande**
>
> ½ cup (125 ml) cream

> 1 cup (250 g) grapes
>
> 2 tablespoons (30 ml) cognac

Sauté the gooseliver on both sides for a few seconds. Remove from pan and let cool. Roll out puff pastry and wrap individual gooselivers. Brush with eggwash, and bake for 8 to 10 minutes in a hot oven.

To make the sauce, reduce the champagne, add a little glacé de viande, add cream, and season with salt and pepper. Pour sauce on a plate, place the gooseliver pastry in the middle, and garnish with peeled and seedless grapes sautéed with cognac.

Veal and Prawns Wrapped with Tenderloin of Prime Beef

Servings—6 to 8
Portion—8 ounces (225 g)

> 1¾ pounds (800 g) beef tenderloin
>
> 1¼ pounds (560 g) veal tenderloin
>
> 4 large prawns

1 cup (225 g) veal farce

4 dried seaweed leaves

Sauce—

4 tablespoons (60 g) butter

4 tablespoons (60 g) fresh herbs (basil, marjoram, thyme, and rosemary)

3 cups (675 ml) fresh cream

½ cup (120 ml) white wine

Cut the veal and beef tenderloin in two flat square pieces. Skewer two large prawns to straighten. Boil them in fish stock and let cool. Remove from the shell and wrap in seaweed leaves, using only the center cut. Spread the veal farce very thinly on the veal and beef tenderloins. Roll the veal first around the prawns and then the beef around the veal. Press to create a leaf shape. Secure both ends with strings. Roast in a hot oven for about 15 to 20 minutes.

Allow to rest for a few minutes before slicing.

For the sauce, sauté the freshly chopped herbs in butter, deglaze them with white wine, and add cream. Reduce to preferred consistency. Season with salt and pepper.

Arrange the meat slices on the sauce and garnish with champignon potatoes and any vegetables in season.

Fresh Berries of the New Season with Raspberry and Mango Pulp

Servings—6 to 8
Portion—1 plate

¾ cup (150 g) fresh blueberries

¾ cup (150 g) fresh raspberries

¾ cup (150 g) blackberries

¾ cup (150 g) cowberries

¾ cup (150 g) white currant

¾ cup (150 g) wild strawberries

¾ cup (180 ml) raspberry sauce

¾ cup (180 ml) mango sauce

1 cup (120 g) chocolate

¾ cup (180 ml) fresh cream

Mint leaves

2 tablespoons (28 g) confectioner's sugar

Clean and wash the berries. To make the raspberry sauce, blend raspberries with confectioner's sugar. To make the mango sauce, purée fresh mango.

Cover the bottom of the serving plate with the raspberry sauce. Pour a little mango sauce in the middle. Use a toothpick to make a design with the two sauces. Mix all the berries together and pour them over half of the fruit mirror. Fold a small chocolate mold and place on the upper right side of the fruits. Pipe a cream rosette on the top of the chocolate and decorate with mint leaves.

MAUI PRINCE HOTEL

Menu

Spicy Hawaiian Shrimp
on Luau Leaf Pancakes
with Sweet Papaya Salsa

Maui Baby Corn and Lobster Chowder

Peppered Duck Salad
with Poached Pears and Walnuts

Steamed Salmon in Vermouth
with Fettucine and Fiddlehead Ferns

Chocolate Macadamia Nut Brittle Flan

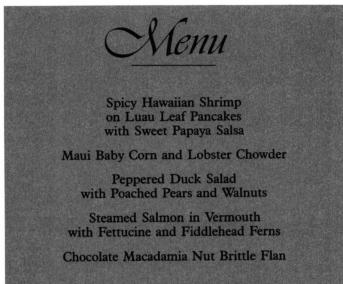

"The Prince Court" is a handsome candlelit room decorated in a simple but elegant style. Its fine rattan furnishings are highlighted by rich teak framed windows which fold back to afford each guest gorgeous ocean vistas. The chef's interpretations of American cookery are specially blended with fresh island resources of Hawaii.

Spicy Hawaiian Shrimp on Luau Leaf Pancakes with Sweet Papaya Salsa

Servings—6
Portion—2 pancakes

Spicy Grilled Shrimp—

- 1 pound (450 g) medium-sized shrimp
- 3 tablespoons (45 g) dry mustard
- ½ teaspoon (2.5 g) salt
- 1 teaspoon (5 g) sugar
- 1 teaspoon (5 g) wasabi powder
- ¾ cup (200 ml) stale beer
- 3 tablespoons (45 g) melted butter

Mix mustard, salt, sugar and wasabi together with enough beer to make a smooth paste. Gradually add rest of beer to make a thin mustard. Let stand 1 hour. Dip shrimp in mustard sauce and brush with melted butter. Grill over kiawe coals for 6 minutes. Do not overcook.

Luau Leaf Pancakes—

- 1 cup (225 g) fresh taro leaves, stemmed

- ½ cup (115 g) flour
- 1 egg
- 1 egg yolk
- ⅓ cup (75 ml) corn oil
- 1 cup (250 ml) milk
- ¼ cup (60 g) butter
- ¼ teaspoon (1.2 g) nutmeg
- ¼ teaspoon (1.2 g) each salt and white pepper

Cook taro leaves in water for 10 minutes. Drain and chop coarsely. Mix flour, eggs, and oil with whisk. Stir in milk and chopped taro. Add seasonings. Let stand for 1 hour. Sauté cakes in butter, 3 minutes per side.

Sweet Papaya Salsa—

- 1 papaya, peeled, seeded, and diced
- 1 small tomato, diced
- ¼ cup (60 g) chopped cilantro
- Juice of 1 large lime
- 1 tablespoon (15 g) sugar
- ¼ teaspoon (1.2 g) salt
- Chili or jalapeño pepper to taste

Mix all ingredients, adding chili peppers, lime, and sugar to taste.

Prepare sweet papaya salsa, pancake batter, and shrimp marinade 1 hour before serving. To serve, cook pancakes and keep warm. Grill shrimp and top with papaya salsa. Garnish with a lime and cilantro leaf.

Maui Baby Corn and Lobster Chowder

Servings—6
Portion—½ cup (115 g)

- 2 tablespoons (20 ml) virgin olive oil
- ½ cup (115 g) minced onion
- ½ cup (115 g) minced celery
- 3 tablespoons (45 g) minced shallots
- 2 tablespoons (30 g) minced garlic
- 2 tablespoons (30 g) diced smoked pork loin
- 1 cup (250 g) small new potatoes, diced
- 5 cups (1¼ L) chicken stock
- 3 cups (650 g) corn, freshly shucked

1 teaspoon (5 g) sugar

¼ teaspoon (1.2 g) fresh ground pepper

1 teaspoon (5 g) fresh thyme

2 cups (425 ml) heavy cream

1 teaspoon (5 g) salt

1 cup (250 g) sliced lobster medallions

3 tablespoons (45 g) chives

1 cup (250 g) sliced baby corn

Heat olive oil over medium high heat until hot. Add onion, celery, shallots, garlic, and smoked pork loin and sauté 2 minutes. Add fresh corn and sauté briefly. Add chicken stock, sugar, pepper, and thyme. Cook over medium heat, then purée in blender. Add heavy cream and season to taste. Add the potatoes.

Bring chowder to boil and garnish with lobster medallions, chopped chives, and sliced baby corn.

Steamed Salmon in Vermouth with Fettucine and Fiddlehead Ferns

Servings—6
Portion—1 fillet

6 6-ounce (180 g) fresh salmon fillets

¾ cup (200 ml) dry vermouth

¼ cup (60 g) each of diced leeks, celery, and onions

1½ cups (165 g) fettucine noodles

½ teaspoon (2.5 g) each salt and white pepper

½ cup (120 ml) fish stock

4 chopped shallots

½ cup (120 ml) heavy cream

2 teaspoons (10 g) salmon caviar

¾ cup (185 g) fresh fiddlehead ferns

Cook fettucine noodles. Lightly butter the bottom of a large sauté pan and sprinkle with chopped shallots, diced leeks, celery and onions. Lay the 6 salmon fillets on this mixture. Add ½ cup (120 ml) dry vermouth, fish stock, salt, and pepper. Cover the pan. Steam slowly, approximately 10 minutes, until cooked. Remove fish from pan and keep warm.

Reduce stock. Add remaining vermouth and heavy cream; season to taste. Toss warm fettucine in sauce and lay on plate. Place fish on top, ladle sauce over and garnish with salmon caviar. Sauté fiddlehead ferns to garnish.

Chocolate Macadamia Nut Brittle Flan

Servings—20
Portion—¹⁄₁₀ of a flan

1–2–3 Dough—

1 cup (225 g) sugar

2 cups (450 g) margarine

3⅓ tablespoons (60 ml) egg whites

3 cups (675 g) all-purpose flour

Cinnamon

Lemon extract

Vanilla extract

Mix sugar and margarine together lightly. Add egg whites. Sift together flour and cinnamon and add with the extracts to the rest of the mixture. Chill dough. Roll out dough and place in 2 9-inch (23 cm) pie shells. Bake at 400°F (200°C) until golden brown.

Filling—

⅔ cup (140 g) butter

1½ cups (340 g) sugar

½ cup (120 ml) cream

1 cup (150 g) macadamia nuts

1 tablespoon (15 g) cornstarch, dissolved in 1 cup (250 ml) cream

1 cup (250 ml) sour cream

2 eggs

4 egg yolks

¾ cup (180 g) semi-sweet chocolate

Melt butter and sugar and caramelize until golden brown. Add cream and macadamia nuts. Pour mixture into pie shells. Refrigerate.

Combine cornstarch-cream solution, sour cream, eggs, and egg yolks in saucepan over medium heat, whisking constantly. Let thicken, but do not boil. Remove from heat. Add chocolate and whisk until melted. Pour over brittle layer. Let set.

Garnish with whipped cream and chocolate shavings.

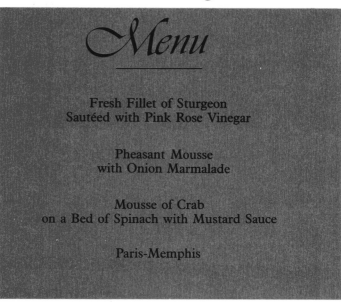

Menu

Fresh Fillet of Sturgeon
Sautéed with Pink Rose Vinegar

Pheasant Mousse
with Onion Marmalade

Mousse of Crab
on a Bed of Spinach with Mustard Sauce

Paris-Memphis

"Chez Philippe," The Peabody's signature restaurant, is regally situated on three marble tiers at the east end of the elegant lobby. Voted number one by Memphis *magazine for four years running, "Chez Philippe" is outstanding for its ambiance, service, and award-winning Nouvelle French cuisine.*

Fresh Fillet of Sturgeon Sautéed with Pink Rose Vinegar

Servings—2
Portion—2 fillets

- **4 3½-ounce (100 g) fillets of sturgeon**
- **2 ounces (60 g) butter**
- **2 ounces (60 g) snow peas, blanched, sliced in middle**
- **5 ears baby corn, blanched**
- **½ cob corn kernels, blanched**
- **2 shallots, thinly sliced**
- **1 cup (¼ L) rose vinegar**
- **¾ cup (180 g) butter**
- **Salt and pepper to taste**
- **6–8 pink rose petals**
- **½ red bell pepper, julienned**

Sauté fillets in butter, cooking slowly until done. Sauté vegetables in butter in a separate pan.

Place sautéed vegetables on plate. Place 2 fillets per plate on vegetables.

Reduce vinegar with shallots to ¾. Remove from heat. Whisk ¾ cup (55 g)

very cold butter into vinegar mixture. Season to taste. Pour over fillets.

Pheasant Mousse with Onion Marmalade

Servings—9
Portion—2 quenelles

- **1 large pheasant**
- **12 juniper berries, crushed**
- **1 tablespoon (15 ml) Dijon mustard**
- **4½ tablespoons (75 ml) butter, unsalted**
- **6 tablespoons (90 ml) whipped cream**
- **2 ounces (60 g) chicken or pheasant livers**
- **1 tablespoon (15 ml) brandy**
- **2 large onions**
- **1 teaspoon (5 ml) sugar**
- **4 cups (1 L) veal stock**
- **2 tablespoons (30 ml) currant jelly**
- **Salt and pepper to taste**

Season pheasant with salt and pepper, and roast pheasant in 2 teaspoons (10 ml) of oil with crushed juniper berries at 450°F (230°C) for 25 minutes. Remove meat from oven and set aside.

Quickly sauté chicken livers in butter, adding salt and pepper. In 3–4 minutes, deglaze with brandy. Put the following in a food processor: chicken livers, pheasant meat and juniper berries. Add mustard and 2 tablespoons (30 g) of butter. Purée until meat is very thin. Then add cream and process for a few more minutes. Season with more salt and pepper to taste. Refrigerate.

Peel and thinly slice onions. Sauté in butter with sugar and dash of salt until golden brown. Strain grease.

Remove grease from pan in which pheasant was cooked. Pour stock and currant jelly into pan. Reduce until ¾ of mixture remains. Strain and mix with onion marmalade.

When everything is cold, combine

pheasant sauce and pheasant mousse. Serve 2 quenelles with marmalade.

Mousse of Crab on a Bed of Spinach with Mustard Sauce

Servings—4
Portion—1 plate

    ¼ **pound (115 g) fresh crabmeat**
    1 **cup (250 ml) cream**
    1 **egg**
    2 **tablespoons (30 ml) Dijon mustard**
    1 **red bell pepper, puréed**
    ⅛ **pound (28 g) spinach, blanched**
    1 **tablespoon (15 ml) caviar**
    ¼ **cup (60 ml) white wine**
    2 **shallots**
    Salt and pepper to taste
    1 **teaspoon (5 ml) chives, sliced**

Butter 4 one-ounce (30 g) souffle cups. In each cup place 4 tablespoons (60 g) of crabmeat.

Mix ½ cup (125 ml) cream with salt and pepper, egg, and chives. Pour mixture into cups.

Bake in water bath for 20 minutes at 450°F (230°C).

Reduce sliced shallots and white wine to ¾. Add ½ cup cream. Reduce to ½ and add red pepper purée. Boil for 1 minute, then add mustard. Whip and continue cooking without boiling. Strain. Sauté spinach quickly in butter.

Place spinach in the center of the plate. Place crab mousse on top of spinach and cover with sauce. Place 1 teaspoon (5 ml) of caviar on each mousse. Decorate with a thin julienne of red pepper.

Paris-Memphis

Servings—6
Portion—⅙ layer

Chocolate Meringue—

    ½ **cup (125 g) egg whites**
    ¼ **cup (60 g) sugar**
    ¼ **cup (45 g) powdered sugar**
    1 **teaspoon (5 ml) cocoa**

Chocolate Ganache—

    4 **ounces (115 g) semi-sweet chocolate**
    ¼ **cup (60 g) heavy cream**

Vanilla Sauce—

    5 **egg yolks**
    ¼ **cup (45 g) sugar**
    2 **cups (½ L) milk**
    1 **teaspoon (5 ml) vanilla**

To make meringue, whip egg whites and sugar until they peak. Fold in *sifted* powdered sugar and cocoa. Pipe out in 1 inch (2.54 cm) circles (18 total) and pipe out ½ inch (1.2 cm) baby fingers. Bake at 175°F (97°C) for 2 hours or until completely done.

To make chocolate ganache, bring cream to a boil. Pour over chocolate pieces and stir. Stir occasionally until cold.

For vanilla sauce, mix egg yolks with sugar and vanilla. Add boiling milk. Mix over heat for 4 to 5 minutes.

Coat circles lightly with ganache. Then roll in crushed almonds. Stack circles and spread a light coat of ganache on top. Stack baby fingers on top. Sprinkle with sifted powdered sugar. Serve with vanilla sauce.

The Pfister Hotel

Menu

Smoked Nova Scotia Salmon "Gourmand"

Chilled Melon Soup

Veal Medallions "Salve"

Warm Goat Cheese

Ice Cream Pie "Pfister"

The Pfister Hotel has been a tradition in Milwaukee since 1893. On Milwaukee's fashionable East Side, the hotel is a historical landmark. Experience the Pfister of 1893 in the elegant, Victorian-styled "English Room." The restaurant has become an award-winning dining facility, obtaining national acclaim for its superb cuisine.

Smoked Nova Scotia Salmon "Gourmand"

Servings—6
Portion—3 ounces (85 g) salmon

- **1 pound (544 g) Nova Scotia smoked salmon, sliced**
- **1 cup (250 g) sliced chanterelles**
- **1 cup (250 g) sliced morels**
- **1 tablespoon (15 g) freshly chopped sorrel**
- **1 tablespoon (15 g) freshly chopped chervil**
- **1 tablespoon (15 g) freshly chopped parsley**
- **1 tablespoon (15 g) freshly chopped mint**
- **½ cup (126 ml) heavy cream**
- **2 tablespoons (30 g) chopped shallots**

Hollandaise Sauce—

- **3 egg yolks**
- **1 cup (250 g) clarified butter**
- **1 tablespoon (15 ml) lemon juice**
- **Pinch cayenne pepper to taste**
- **Salt and pepper to taste**

Sauce—

- **1 cup (250 ml) whipped cream, unsweetened**
- **1½ cup (350 ml) hollandaise**

To prepare the hollandaise, beat the egg yolks in a 1-quart (1 L) mixing bowl over simmering water until slightly cooked. Remove from heat and add the warm, clarified butter very slowly, while stirring with a wire whisk. Season with salt, pepper, and lemon juice.

Sauté the mushrooms with the shallots in butter. Add cream and reduce until the cream completely coats the mushrooms. Season with salt and pepper. Distribute the cooked mushrooms on six warm serving plates in compact piles. Cover the mushrooms with the sliced salmon. Place the chopped herbs in a wire strainer and blanch them in a hot water bath for just one second. Allow them to drain and sauté lightly. Coat the salmon with the herbs.

To make the sauce, gently fold the whipped cream into the hollandaise. Cover the salmon with the sauce, and broil until golden brown. Serve immediately.

Chilled Melon Soup

Servings—6
Portion—¾ cup (185 ml)

- **3 ripe cantaloupe**
- **3 ripe bananas**
- **Juice of 1 lemon**
- **¾ cup (185 ml) port wine**
- **6 small orchids**
- **Honey or orange juice, to taste**

Cut the melons crosswise into six melon halves of equal size. Scoop out the meat with a serving spoon. Take care not to pierce the rind of the melons.

Combine the meat of the melon with the remaining ingredients. Blend in an electric blender at medium speed until puréed. Pour the soup into the emptied melon rinds. Place these into soup bowls and garnish with an orchid.

Honey or orange juice can be added if more sweetness is desired.

Veal Medallions "Salve"

Servings—6
Portion—6 ounces (180 g)

12 3-ounce (90 g) veal medallions
1 cup (250 ml) white wine
**2 tablespoons (30 g) chopped
 shallots**
**1 tablespoon (15 g) freshly chopped
 basil**
12 slices prosciutto
3 cups (¾ L) heavy cream
12 fresh basil leaves for garnish
½ cup (120 ml) olive oil

Mix the white wine, shallots, and basil.
Wrap the veal with the prosciutto.
Place the medallions in a shallow pan
and cover with the wine mixture. Marinate for 4 hours.

Heat a large sauté pan over high heat.
Pour in oil and sauté the veal. Remove
the veal when browned, and place in a
slow oven to keep warm. Discard the
oil from the pan and pour in the marinade. Reduce this by ⅔, and add the
cream until thickened. Season with salt
and pepper to taste. Serve the veal over
the sauce and place 4 basil leaves on
each medallion for garnish.

Serve with sautéed brussel sprouts, zucchini, and yellow squash flavored with
tomatoes.

Ice Cream Pie "Pfister"

Servings—6
Portion—1 slice

1 pint (½ L) vanilla ice cream
**1 pint (½ L) chocolate almond ice
 cream**
**1 pint (½ L) pecan and praline ice
 cream**
1 cup (250 ml) honey
½ cup (20 ml) Grand Marnier
**1 cup (10 oz.) coarsely chopped
 walnuts**
**2 3-ounce (85 g) packages lady
 fingers**

Sprinkle the bottom of a 2-quart (2 L)
loaf pan with lady fingers. With a rubber spatula, spread the vanilla ice
cream evenly over the bottom. Drizzle
a generous layer of honey (⅓ cup —
75g) over the ice cream. Then sprinkle
Grand Marnier over this. Repeat these
steps using the chocolate almond ice
cream. Follow with the pecan praline
ice cream. Cover the top with lady fingers, and let this freeze overnight before slicing and serving.

Menu

Red Sea Shrimp

Roasted Red Pepper Soup

Warm Frog Leg Salad

Kiwi Sorbet

Roulade of Pheasant Breast
with Smoked Duck and Pistachios

White Chocolate Swan Paradise

Located on the Mississippi River in downtown Minneapolis, the new 97 room Whitney Hotel recreates the elegance of hotels of bygone days. In the mahogany-appointed "Whitney Grille," traditional American specialties are served by a staff that is as meticulously polished as the lobby's marble floors.

Red Sea Shrimp

Servings—6
Portion—4 shrimp

- 24 shrimp (about 15 to a pound)
- 3 cups (¾ L) French-style cocktail sauce
- ⅔ cup (150 ml) American-style cocktail sauce
- 2 lemons
- 6 sprigs fresh dill

French Cocktail Sauce—

- 2 cups (425 ml) mayonnaise
- ¼ cup (60 ml) tomato purée
- 1 teaspoon (5 g) horseradish
- Tabasco sauce to taste
- ½ teaspoon (2.5 g) cayenne pepper
- 2 tablespoons (30 ml) heavy cream

American Cocktail Sauce—

- 2 cups (425 ml) chili sauce
- ½ teaspoon (2.5 g) horseradish
- Tabasco sauce to taste
- ½ teaspoon (2.5 g) Worcestershire sauce
- 1 teaspoon (5 g) brown sugar
- ½ teaspoon (2.5 g) black pepper

Juice from 1 lemon
Pinch cayenne pepper

In a 4-quart (3¾ L) stockpot, poach fresh shrimp in a court-bouillon of carrots, celery, onions, leeks, lemons and 1 tablespoon (15 g) pickling spice. Chill shrimp, peel and devein.

For French Cocktail Sauce: combine all ingredients into 2-quart (2 L) mixing bowl.

Likewise, combine all ingredients for American Cocktail Sauce into a 2-quart (2 L) mixing bowl.

Place ½ cup (120 ml) of the French-style cocktail sauce on a 10-inch (25 cm) plate and spread until smooth. With a small pastry bag, lay lines of the American Cocktail Sauce across plate at approximately ½-inch (½ cm) intervals. Going in the opposite direction, pull a toothpick through the sauce from edge to edge at ½-inch (1.2 cm) intervals. Overlap shrimp at top of plate. Garnish with thinly sliced lemon wheels and a sprig of fresh dill.

Roulade of Pheasant Breast with Smoked Duck and Pistachios

Servings—6
Portion—6 to 8 slices

- 2 tablespoons (30 g) minced shallots
- 2 3-pound (1⅓ g) pheasants
- 10 ounces (285 g) smoked duck breast
- 2 cups (200 g) shelled pistachios
- ½ pound (225 g) pancetta (Italian style bacon in a loaf form)
- ¼ cup (40 g) lingonberries (fresh or jarred)
- 2 quarts (2 L) 40% heavy whipping cream
- 2 cloves garlic
- 10 leaves fresh sage
- 6 juniper berries
- 1 orange (zest from orange, poached for 2 minutes)
- 1 teaspoon (5 ml) cognac (optional)
- Salt and white pepper to taste
- 1 egg white

Debone breasts completely and skin. Cover breasts with plastic wrap and pound until thin and close to square.

With a meat grinder or food processor, grind the smoked duck, trimmings from pheasants, (everything other than the breasts), garlic, 3 ounces (85 g) pancetta, fresh sage, juniper berries, and orange zest. Gently fold the egg whites, cognac, salt, and pepper into mixture in a 4-quart (3¾ L) bowl.

In a food processor, grind whole pistachios. Lay out pheasant breast and thinly coat with the pistachios, then coat with the smoked duck mixture. Roll tightly and set aside.

Make sure the remaining pancetta is well chilled. Slice approximately 20 round paper-thin slices and lay them out on parchment paper. Cover each pheasant roulade with 5 slices (3 on bottom, 2 on top) and secure edges with toothpicks.

To make the sauce, use a 6-quart (5¾ L) sauce pan, and reduce heavy whipping cream to ½ original volume. Sauté shallots until translucent. Add cognac, lingonberries, the reduced cream, salt, and white pepper to taste.

Preheat oven to 400°F (200°C). Place roulades on a 13-inch × 18-inch (396 cm × 549 cm) pan and bake for 15 minutes.

Place ½ cup (120 ml) sauce on each plate. With an electric knife, gently slice roulades and place on top of sauce.

White Chocolate Swan Paradise

Servings—6
Portion—1 swan

White Chocolate Mousse—
   ½ pound (225 g) white chocolate
   ¼ cup (60 ml) milk
   1 tablespoon (15 ml) Grand Marnier
   1½ cups heavy (350 ml) cream

Dark Chocolate Sauce—
   ¼ pound (115 g) bittersweet chocolate
   3 tablespoons (45 ml) water
   4 tablespoons (60 ml) corn syrup
   2 tablespoons (30 g) unsalted butter
   4 teaspoons (20 ml) Grand Marnier

Royal Icing—
   1 cup (140 g) powdered sugar
   1 egg white
   ½ teaspoon (2.5 g) cream of tartar
   ½ cup (75 g) sliced almonds, toasted

To make white chocolate mousse: fill a 2-quart (2 L) pan ¼ full of water and bring to a simmer. Place 2-quart (2 L) mixing bowl over pan to melt white chocolate. In a separate pan, heat milk until warm. Whip heavy cream until stiff. Add the warm milk to the melted chocolate and gently fold in the whipped cream. Add Grand Marnier and set aside.

To make dark chocolate sauce: fill a 2-quart (2 L) sauce pan ¼ full of water and bring to a simmer. Place 1-quart (1 L) mixing bowl on top, and slowly melt the bittersweet chocolate. Remove from heat and stir in corn syrup and unsalted butter. Add Grand Marnier and remove from heat.

To make the royal icing: add first three ingredients in a small mixing bowl and mix until smooth. Using a pastry bag with a small tip, pipe on parchment paper in the shape of a swan's head.

Dip two large kitchen spoons in water. Then scoop ½ cup (115 g) of the white chocolate mousse with one spoon. Use the second spoon to shape the body of the swan.

Spread 1 tablespoon (15 ml) chocolate sauce on plate. Set body of swan onto chocolate sauce. Put head in place and garnish with 3 sliced toasted almonds and chocolate wings (which can be purchased at any specialty baking shop).

Menu

Fresh Salmon Tartare with Dill

Lobster Bisque

Florentine Salad with Lemon Dressing

Rack of Lamb Basted in Mustard

Chilled Fresh Fruit Topped with Sabayon

Le Grand Hotel, located at the crossroads of Montreal's cobblestone streets and bustling boulevards, offers visitors a memorable dining experience in the new "Chez Antoine Bistrot-Grill." Elaborately decorated in La Belle Epoque style, this bistro specializes in true French delicacies grilled over imported and Canadian wood.

Fresh Salmon Tartare with Dill

Servings—6
Portion—3 ounces (35 g)

- 1 pound (450 g) fresh salmon fillets
- 1 tablespoon (15 g) chopped dill
- 1 teaspoon (5 g) granular salt
- 1 teaspoon (5 g) sugar
- Juice of 2 lemons
- 1 teaspoon (5 g) fresh ground pepper
- 1 teaspoon (5 g) chopped capers
- 1 teaspoon (5 g) horseradish
- 1 tablespoon (15 ml) 15% cream
- ½ cup (120 ml) sunflower oil

Garnish:

- 4 pumpernickel slices
- 12 stalks of chives
- 6 cherry tomatoes
- 6 lettuce leaves
- 6 half lemons

Cover the salmon fillet with dill, salt, sugar, lemon juice, pepper, and sunflower oil. Marinate for 3 days, covered in refrigerator, turning the fillet every 12 hours.

Remove fillet from marinade and finely chop. Place chopped pieces in a bowl. Mix in chopped capers, cream, and horseradish.

Place a portion of the tartare on a bed of lettuce in the center of the plate. Garnish with chives, cherry tomatoes, pumpernickel, and lemon half.

Serve immediately.

Lobster Bisque

Servings—4
Portion—8 ounces (225 g)

- ¼ cup (60 ml) vegetable oil
- 1 chopped celery stalk
- 1 chopped onion
- 1 chopped small leek
- 1 garlic clove
- 1 2-pound (900 g) lobster cut into pieces, in shell
- 3 ounces (85 g) tomato paste
- 2 fresh tomatoes
- 1 teaspoon (5 g) chopped tarragon
- 2 bay leaves
- 3⅓ tablespoons (50 ml) white wine
- 3⅓ tablespoons (50 ml) brandy
- 1 pint (½ L) fish stock

Garnish:

- ½ cup (120 ml) 35% cream, (whipped)
- 1 tablespoon (15 g) chopped chives

Brown celery, onion, leek, and garlic. Add lobster pieces in shells and cook for 4 to 5 minutes, stirring constantly. Flambé with brandy, pour in white wine, tomato paste, and tomato pieces. Add chopped tarragon, bay leaves and fish stock. Stir and simmer for 20 minutes over medium heat.

Remove lobster pieces from mixture. Separate the meat from the shells. Slice meat to be used for garnish. Return lobster shells to soup mixture and simmer for 20 minutes.

Remove shells. Blend mixture in blender and put through a sieve. Season

to taste with salt and cayenne pepper.
Pour bisque in soup plate, add 1 tablespoon (15 ml) of whipped cream in the center of the plate. Sprinkle with pieces of lobster and chopped chives.

Florentine Salad with Lemon Dressing

Servings—4
Portion—1 salad

1 package fresh spinach
2 sliced hard boiled eggs
2 sliced ripe tomatoes
4 black olives
½ cup (60 g) fresh oyster mushrooms

Dressing:

½ cup (120 ml) almond oil
Juice of 1 lemon
1 teaspoon (15 g) chopped chives
1 teaspoon (15 g) chopped tarragon
Salt and freshly ground pepper to taste

Wash spinach leaves and place in center of plate. Slice tomatoes in wedges and arrange around spinach. Add egg slices with olives and mushroom pieces over spinach to decorate.

Mix lemon juice, tarragon, and chives together. Slowly stir in almond oil. Add salt and pepper to taste.

Rack of Lamb Basted in Mustard

Servings—6
Portion—1 rack

6 racks of lamb (cleaned, approximately 6 ribs)
3 tablespoons (45 g) Dijon mustard
1 teaspoon (15 g) chopped fine herbs
1 teaspoon (5 g) honey
2 tablespoons (30 g) breadcrumbs
1 tablespoon (15 ml) butter
1 tablespoon (15 ml) oil

Season rack of lamb with salt and pepper. Sauté in a frying pan with oil and butter.

Blend mustard, honey, and fine herbs. Baste the racks of lamb with this mixture in preheated oven at 400°F (200°C) for 15 to 20 minutes, until medium rare. Sprinkle breadcrumbs over the lamb and broil for 1 to 2 minutes.

Chilled Fresh Fruit Topped with Sabayon

Servings—4
Portion—1 plate

2 egg yolks
2 teaspoons (10 g) sugar
2 teaspoons (30 ml) white wine
4 kiwis
8 ripe strawberries
1 small cantaloupe, in Parisian balls
1 red apple
4 mint leaves

Mix egg yolks, sugar, and white wine together in a bowl in a double boiler. Whip the mixture until it thickens. (Be careful not to let the water get too hot so that the egg yolks become overcooked.)

Slice fruit and place creatively on a plate. Pour sabayon mixture over fruits and place plate under broiler until the sabayon becomes golden brown.

Decorate with mint leaves and serve immediately.

HOTEL BAYERISCHER HOF MÜNCHEN

Menu

Salad from Baby Rock Lobster
with Sherry Dressing

Cream of Cress Soup with Croûtons

Medallions from Saddle of Venison
with Elderberry Sauce, Broccoli, Chanterelles,
and Schupfnudeln

Bavarian Cheese Assortment

Thickened Cherries with Parfait

The Hotel Bayerischer Hof offers luxurious furnishings with precious antiques. The traditional "Grill Restaurant" features both international and regional cuisine, with zither music in the evenings. The "Palais Montgelas" highlights Bavarian dishes with an extensive range of wine and beer.

Salad from Baby Rock Lobster with Sherry Dressing

Servings—8
Portion—1 salad

  4 **live rock lobsters, 1 pound (450 g) each**

Sherry Dressing—

  ⅓ **cup (75 ml) sherry**
  ⅓ **cup (75 ml) sherry vinegar**
  ⅓ **cup (75 ml) walnut oil**
  ⅓ **cup (75 ml) hazelnut oil**
  Juice of ½ lime
  Salt to taste
  White pepper from mill to taste
  1 **teaspoon (5 g) chervil**
  1 **teaspoon (5 g) minced tarragon**
  8 **sorrel leaves**

Poach live rock lobsters in boiling vegetable stock for 10–12 minutes, leaving in stock for 10 minutes. Halve lengthwise, remove intestines. Cut the rock lobster tail into 5 equal medallions and marinate slightly with sherry vinegar. Place different salad greens such as watercress, oak leaf, Lollo Rosso, Batavia, fillets of tomatoes and basil leaves on serving plate. Arrange lobster on greens. Mix sherry dressing ingredients and serve with salad.

Cream of Cress Soup with Croûtons

Servings—8
Portion—1 cup (250 ml) soup

  8 **cups (2 L) water**
  1⅛ **pounds (500 g) giblets**
  2 **cups (450 g) vegetable bouquet (made with celery, onion, leek, parsley roots, shallot, 1 leaf white cabbage or savoy cabbage, 1 garlic clove, 1 twig thyme, 1 bay leaf, 2 tablespoons (30 g) sea salt, 10 white minced peppercorns)**
  6 **egg yolks**
  ½ **cup (115 g) cress, finely chopped**
  2½ **tablespoons (40 g) butter**
  1¾ **cups (400 ml) cream**
  4 **cups (1 L) poultry stock**

Place all ingredients into a large copper pot. Boil for 1 hour, skimming as needed. Reduce to 4 cups (1 L). Simmer until temperature reaches 203°F (95°C), then strain. Add egg yolks, finely chopped cress, butter, and cream. Whip to a froth over hot water. Add poultry stock, whip with a mixer, and pour into soup bowls. Serve with white bread croûtons.

Medallions from Saddle of Venison with Elderberry Sauce, Broccoli, Chanterelles, and Schupfnudeln

Servings—6
Portion—1 medallion with vegetables

  6 **venison medallions**
  1 **pound (450 g) crushed venison bones and trimmings**
  1¼ **cups (300 g) vegetables (onions, carrots, celery, shallots), diced**
  2 **juniper berries**
  4 **pimiento corns**
  1 **tablespoon (15 g) salt**

1 garlic clove

Black peppercorns

1½ tablespoons (20 g) tomato purée

1 teaspoon (10 g) redcurrant jelly

2 tablespoons (30 ml) wine

2 tablespoons (30 ml) red wine vinegar

4 cups (1 L) water

¼ cup (60 g) ripe elderberries

½ pound (225 g) broccoli

1¾ pounds (800 g) chanterelles

2¼ pounds (1 kg) jacket potatoes

6 tablespoons (100 g) potato flour

4 egg yolks

2 tablespoons (30 g) salt

1 teaspoon (10 g) nutmeg

1 teaspoon (10 g) pepper

Remove the skin of the venison and cut into proportional medallions. Marinate slightly with 1 tablespoon (15 ml) gin, fresh crushed pepper and 1 tablespoon (15 ml) of hazelnut oil. Cover the meat refrigerate.

In a 4-quart (4 L), pot heat olive oil and peanut oil and brown the bones. Heat the oven to 410°F (210°C) and bake until golden. Add the diced vegetables, then the remainder of the ingredients except the wine, vinegar, and jelly. Add wine and evaporate it completely. Add vinegar and 4 cups (1 L) of water, let evaporate completely, then add water and the jelly. Bake 2½ hours at 350°F (180°C). Strain the sauce, skim and season, reducing to ½ quart (½ L). Add the elderberries.

Clean the broccoli, and boil in salted water for a few minutes. Plunge immediately in ice water. Sauté in buttered pan and season lightly with salt.

Sauté chanterelles in buttered pot with finely minced shallots. Season lightly with salt.

Schupfnudeln (potato-noodles)—

Peel and press cooked dried jacket potatoes. Mix potato flour, 4 egg yolks, salt, nutmeg, and pepper. Form small rolls (4–5 per person), 0.4 inches (1 cm) thick × 2.4 inches (6 cm) long. Blanch in salted water and plunge into ice water. Sauté in buttered pan until golden.

Flour the medallions, sauté them in melted butter, for 2 minutes on each side. Set aside for 10 minutes. Strain sauce into the pan, skimming it. Pour the sauce on the medallions. Garnish with elderberries and serve with the side dishes.

Thickened Cherries with Parfait

Servings—8
Portion—1 parfait

1 cup (225 g) morello cherries

1 cup (225 g) heart cherries

½ cup (115 g) emperor cherries

Ice Parfait—

1 cup (250 ml) whipped cream

2 eggs

1 tablespoon (15 g) vanilla sugar

1 gelatin leaf

¼ cup (40 g) sugar

2 egg yolks

2 tablespoons (30 ml) kirsch

Remove pits and poach cherries in stock of sugar, cherry juice and kirsch. Thicken with cornstarch, add cinnamon and vanilla sugar.

Combine eggs, vanilla sugar, sugar and egg yolks. Whip to a cream over hot water. Place container in ice water and add gelatin, whipped cream, and kirsch. Pour into cups or forms and freeze for 3 hours at −10°F (−18°C). Hold the forms or cups under hot water to loosen the parfait. Unmold on a flat plate, garnish with cherries, cream, chocolate, and raspberries. Serve warm cherries separately.

Bavarian Cheese Assortment

Servings—6
Portion—½ cup (125 g)

½ cup (125 g) Mountain cheese

½ cup (125 g) Bavarian Blue

½ cup (125 g) Bavarian Brie

½ cup (125 g) Bavarian brown mold cheese

½ cup (125 g) Caraway cheese

½ cup (125 g) Bavarian fresh goat cheese with chives

Attractively arrange cheeses on a plate. Garnish with grapes and pears or radishes. Serve with salted butter and country bread.

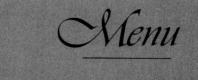

Menu

Ratatouille Dumplings with Crabmeat

Stuffed Zucchini Blossoms

Grilled Veal Chop
with Smoked Mushroom Ragoût
and Coriander Crème Fraîche

Roasted Santa Rosa Goat Cheese

Chilled Consommé of Berries
with Late Harvest Riesling
and Mexican Marigold Mint

Meadowood Resort is nestled in its own valley, within the Napa Valley. One can enjoy the elegant resort ambiance of "The Starmont Restaurant," with a formal interior and large deck that overlooks the golf course, the manicured croquet lawns and the wooded hills beyond.

Ratatouille Dumplings with Crabmeat

Servings—6
Portion—3 medallions

For the dumplings—

¼ cup (60 ml) olive oil

½ cup (125 g) finely diced zucchini

½ cup (125 g) finely diced eggplant

½ cup (125 g) finely diced yellow
bell pepper

½ cup (125 g) finely diced red bell
pepper

½ cup (125 g) finely diced green bell
pepper

½ cup (125 g) finely diced red onion

1 cup (250 g) peeled, seeded and
finely diced tomato

2 tablespoons (30 g) chopped garlic

1 pound (450 g) lump crabmeat

1 tablespoon (15 g) chopped fresh
basil

Salt and white pepper to taste

30 3-inch (7.6 cm) round dumpling
wrappers (or wonton wrappers cut
with a 3-inch (7.6 cm) round
cookie cutter)

For the saffron sauce—

2 pinches saffron

3 tablespoons (45 ml) boiling water

Juice of 2 lemons

Grated zest of 1 lime

1 cup (250 ml) olive oil

¼ cup (60 ml) sour cream

Pinch of cayenne pepper

Salt to taste

18 veal medallions

For the dumplings, heat the olive oil in a large sauté pan, and sauté the zucchini, eggplant, yellow, red and green pepper for 5 minutes. Drain, and mix the vegetables with the red onion, garlic, tomato, and crab. Cook slowly, uncovered, until the vegetables are soft. Then drain, adjust seasoning, stir in basil, and refrigerate. When cooling, place a heaping teaspoon (5 ml) of the filling in the center of each dumpling.

Dust the veal medallions lightly with flour. Heat the oil over medium high heat, and when hot, brown the veal. Remove from pan and deglaze the pan

with white wine. Place pan in oven and bake for 7 to 10 minutes, depending on the thickness of the medallions.

To serve, arrange 3 medallions and some of the dumplings on plates. Garnish with the hot vegetables, and spoon the sauce around the sides.

Stuffed Zucchini Blossoms

Servings—4
Portion—3 blossoms

For the zucchini—

12 zucchini blossoms

3 tablespoons (45 g) unsalted butter

12 medium shrimp, peeled, deveined
and diced

½ cup (30 g) fresh breadcrumbs

2 tablespoons (30 ml) sour cream

1 tablespoon (15 g) chopped dill

2 tablespoons (30 g) ground walnuts

Salt and pepper to taste

For the sauce—

¼ cup (115 g) unsalted butter,
softened

½ cup (125 g) finely chopped fennel

1 tablespoon (15 g) finely chopped shallots

2 tablespoons (30 ml) tarragon vinegar

⅓ cup (75 ml) dry vermouth

3 tablespoons (45 ml) heavy cream

1 tablespoon (15 ml) lemon juice

Salt and pepper to taste

Gently clean the squash blossoms, removing centers. Heat 1 tablespoon (15 ml) of the butter over medium heat. Sauté the shrimp until cooked, and then remove from heat and add the breadcrumbs, sour cream, dill, walnuts, salt and pepper to taste. Stuff the mixture into the squash blossoms. Set aside until ready to cook.

For the sauce, heat 1 tablespoon (15 g) of the butter in a small saucepan. Sauté the fennel and shallots gently for 3 minutes. Then add the vinegar and vermouth. Reduce by half over high heat. Add the cream and reduce slightly. Beat in the butter, bit by bit, then season with lemon juice, salt, and pepper.

To serve, preheat the oven to 300°F (150°C). Heat the remaining butter and saute the flowers on both sides for 1 minute. Place in the oven for 3 minutes to finish. Place 3 blossoms on each plate.

Grilled Veal Chop with Smoked Mushroom Ragoût and Coriander Crème Fraîche

Servings—8
Portion—1 chop

8 - 10 ounce (285 g) center cut veal chops

¾ cup (180 g) each mushrooms: shiitake, pleuriottes, oyster and white mushrooms

1 cup (250 ml) veal stock

½ cup (125 ml) port wine

½ cup (125 g) chopped shallot

3 tablespoons (85 g) fresh butter

Salt and pepper to taste

1 cup (250 g) cilantro leaves

Coriander Crème Fraîche—

1 cup (250 ml) crème fraîche
(Or, if not available):

1 teaspoon (5 g) cayenne

½ cup (120 ml) buttermilk

2 cups (425 ml) heavy whipped cream

1 tablespoon (15 g) fresh ground coriander

Beat together all ingredients for coriander crème fraîche. Place in glass jar in a hot spot for six hours. Then refrigerate for 24 hours before using.

In hot smoker, smoke mushrooms for two hours using grapevine wood chips. Place in covered container for one night.

To prepare veal, sauté shallots with butter and chopped mushrooms. Add port wine. Reduce to glaze and add veal stock. Reduce to half and add fresh butter. Keep seasoning on the side.

Season veal chops before grilling. Grill to preferred doneness.

Place sauce on plate with veal chops over the sauce and crème fraîche. Add chopped cilantro leaves to garnish.

Chilled Consommé of Berries with Late Harvest Riesling and Mexican Marigold Mint

Servings—4
Portion—1 bowl

1 cup (250 ml) Late Californian Harvest Riesling wine

1 cup (250 g) raspberries

1 cup (250 g) strawberries

1 cup (250 g) blackberries

4 bunches redcurrant

1 bunch Mexican marigold mint

Syrup—

1 quart (1 L) white wine

½ quart (½ L) water

10 black peppercorns

3 cups (675 g) sugar

Boil all ingredients together for 5 minutes over low heat. Refrigerate for 2 hours.

Add the following to mixture: mint stems, juice of 1 lemon, and wine. Put in refrigerate overnight. Strain after refrigerating and freeze for 3 hours.

Place berries and redcurrant in bowls. Blend frozen syrup for 15 seconds and add mint leaves. Serve with berries.

GRAND BAY HOTEL
AT EQUITABLE CENTER

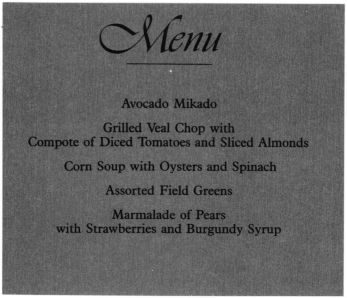

Menu

Avocado Mikado

Grilled Veal Chop with
Compote of Diced Tomatoes and Sliced Almonds

Corn Soup with Oysters and Spinach

Assorted Field Greens

Marmalade of Pears
with Strawberries and Burgundy Syrup

In keeping with the dramatic renaissance of Midtown Manhattan's West Side, the hotel's lavish dining room is highlighted by an eclectic menu of enticing international items. The chef's creations reflect a dedication to presenting the freshest of seasonal products with sumptuous yet understated elegance.

Avocado Mikado

Servings—6
Portion—½ avocado

3 avocados, peeled, seeded and sliced into a fan

18 smoked salmon roses

3 heads endive

fresh chives

3 tablespoons (45 ml) dressing

Dressing—

1¼ cups (275 ml) olive oil

2 shallots, (peeled and minced)

2 tablespoons (30 g) Dijon mustard

1 tablespoon (15 ml) Worcestershire sauce

½ cup (120 ml) red wine vinegar

Salt and pepper to taste

Place sliced avocado in a fan shape on plate. Place smoked salmon roses on three points around plate. Garnish with endive and chives. Top with the dressing.

To make the dressing, place shallots in bowl with mustard and Worcestershire. Whip in a small amount of oil at a time. Strain, and ladle over avocado.

Grilled Veal Chop with Compote of Diced Tomatoes and Sliced Almonds

Servings—6
Portion—1 chop

6 10-ounce (285 g) veal chops, French style

10 tomatoes, roughly chopped

1 Spanish onion, finely diced

2 cloves garlic, finely minced

2 cups (425 ml) veal stock

1½ cups (225 g) almonds, sliced and chopped

Grill veal chops and then place in 350°F (180°C) oven for 8–10 minutes to finish cooking. To prepare sauce, sauté onions, add garlic and sauté until onions are transparent. Add almonds and sauté until light brown. Add tomatoes and sauté well. Add veal stock and reduce until it reaches the consistency of a compote. Serve sauce as an accompaniment next to the veal chop. Serve with seasonal vegetables.

Corn Soup with Oysters and Spinach

Servings—6
Portion—½ cup (120 ml)

2 8-ounce (225 g) cans sweet corn kernels (not cream corn)

6 ounces (200 ml) fish fumet

⅔ cup (150 ml) heavy cream

18 oysters

1½ pounds (675 g) fresh spinach

Chopped chives

Salt and pepper to taste

Purée corn in blender. Add fumet and heat. Add cream and season with salt and pepper. Heat oysters in pan with their own juice until firm, then place in

bowl with cleaned cooked spinach.
Pour soup over oysters and spinach,
and garnish with chopped chives.

Marmalade of Pears with Strawberries and Burgundy Syrup

Servings—6
Portion—1 pear

   6 **pears**
   1 **vanilla bean**
   1 **cup (250 ml) white wine**
   2 **tablespoons (30 g) sugar**
   24 **strawberries**
   18 **mint leaves**

Peel and core pears. Cut in ⅛ inch
(.3 cm) strips. Sauté in butter with
white wine, sugar, and vanilla bean.
Cook until soft, yet "al dente". Allow
to cool and chop pears roughly. Place
on plate and top with sliced strawberries arranged to look like a flower. Use
3 mint leaves on top and surround with
syrup when ready to serve.

Syrup—

   4 **cups (1 L) burgundy**
   1 **cup (225 g) sugar**

Reduce burgundy and sugar until the
mixture reaches a syrup consistency.
(The syrup will get thicker as it cools,
so test it as it reduces.)

UNITED NATIONS PLAZA HOTEL

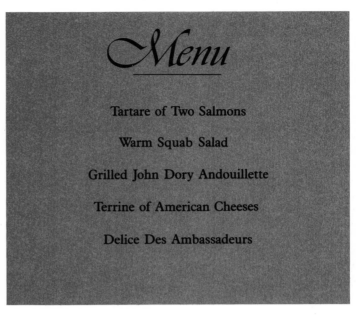

Menu

Tartare of Two Salmons

Warm Squab Salad

Grilled John Dory Andouillette

Terrine of American Cheeses

Delice Des Ambassadeurs

The dramatic interior of the "Ambassador Grill" is one of the most beautiful in the city. Soft lighting from a vaulted glass ceiling provides a warm, inviting atmosphere. Italian marble, smoked glass, fresh flowers, imported china and crystal set the tone for personal service and a memorable evening.

Tartare of Two Salmons

Servings—8
Portion—¼ pound (115 g)

- 1 pound (450 g) smoked salmon, cut into 24 slices
- 1 pound (450 g) fresh Norwegian salmon, skinned and boned
- 8 quail eggs
- Vinegar

Marinade—

- ½ stalk fresh fennel
- 4 teaspoons (20 g) sugar
- 4 teaspoons (20 g) salt
- ½ lime

Tartare Sauce—

- 1 hard-boiled egg, chopped
- 4 small cornichons
- 1 teaspoon (5 g) capers
- 2 sprigs fresh dill
- 2 sprigs fresh parsley
- 2 tablespoons (30 g) grated horseradish
- ½ cup (120 ml) mayonnaise
- Pepper for seasoning
- ½ lemon, for juice

Garnish:

- **Dill or seaweed (also called Pouce Pierre, if available)**

Combine marinade ingredients in a food processor. Blend until mixture reaches a paste consistency. Spread paste on fresh Norwegian salmon and wrap in plastic wrap. Chill for at least 24 hours.

To make the tartare sauce, chop hard-boiled egg, cornichons, capers, dill and parsley, and mix well with the horseradish, mayonnaise, lemon juice, and pepper.

Poach the quail eggs for 30 seconds in simmering water with a little vinegar. Cool in ice water.

Remove salmon from refrigerator. Scrape away and discard any excess marinade paste. Pat salmon dry with paper towels. Cut the salmon in small dices and mix with the tartare sauce. Mixture should hold together with a moist but firm consistency.

In the center of each plate, place a small patty of the marinated salmon and arrange 3 slices of smoked salmon around it. Top with one quail egg and garnish with dill or seaweed.

Warm Squab Salad

Servings—8
Portion—½ squab

- 4 squabs
- ¾ pound (340 g) duck foie gras (cut in 8 pieces)

Salad—

- ¾ cup (180 g) green beans (very thin)
- ¾ cup (180 g) frisee lettuce
- ¾ cup (180 g) mache lettuce
- ¾ cup (180 g) radicchio lettuce
- ¾ cup (180 g) Bibb lettuce hearts

Dressing—

- 2 teaspoons (10 ml) hazelnut oil
- 2 teaspoons (10 ml) olive oil
- 2 teaspoons (10 ml) sherry vinegar
- Salt and pepper for seasoning

½ tablespoon (10 g) fresh thyme
½ tablespoon (10 g) fresh basil
½ tablespoon (10 g) fresh chervil

Jus—
½ cup (115 g) tomato dices
¾ cup (180 g) carrot mirepoix
¾ cup (180 g) onion mirepoix
1 teaspoon (5 ml) raspberry vinegar
½ cup (115 g) butter

Garnish—
1 turnip
2 carrots
24 baby onions
1 teaspoon (5 ml) raspberry vinegar

Bone the squab and refrigerate the breasts and the legs. Sauté squab bones in a hot pan with some oil. When bones are brown, add carrots, onions, thyme, bay leaves and sauté until the onions begin to brown. Deglaze with sherry vinegar and add sufficient water to cover the bones. Boil until liquid is reduced by ½.

Cut the carrots and turnips into 1-inch (2.5 cm) length football-like shapes. Blanche in boiling water for 30 seconds. Cool in ice water. Marinade with raspberry vinegar.

Wash the frisee, mache, radicchio and Bibb lettuces. Cut into 1-inch (2.5 cm) wide strips.

To prepare the dressing, mix sherry vinegar with olive and hazelnuts oils. Add herbs and seasoning.

Season squab breast and legs with salt and pepper. Sauté in hot pan with oil until golden brown (medium inside). Rest in warm place. Slightly season duck foie gras, and sauté for 15 seconds on each side. Set aside in a warm place. Deglaze the pan with squab jus. Reduce by ¼ and add butter. Set aside.

Finally, mix salad greens with raspberry dressing. Place in center of plate. Arrange sliced squab breasts, legs, and foie gras on top of the salad. Surround with vegetable garnish and serve topped with squab jus.

Grilled John Dory Andouillette

Servings—8
Portion—½ John Dory

4 John Dory fish, 2 pounds (900 g) each
½ pound (250 g) sea scallops, chilled
½ pound (250 g) raw shrimp, chilled
1 cup (250 ml) heavy cream, chilled
¼ cup (60 g) anchovies, chilled

2 tablespoons (30 g) diced leek
2 egg whites
1½ cups (340 g) pork fat
1¼ cups (275 ml) hollandaise sauce
⅓ tablespoon (5 g) mustard powder
1¾ cups (400 g) cucumbers
1¾ cups (400 g) snow peas
1¾ cups (400 g) tomatoes
1¾ cups (400 g) potatoes
Salt and pepper to taste
1 tablespoon (15 g) butter

Fillet the John Dory and remove skin. Cut fillet open like a wallet. Season with salt and white pepper.

Blend shrimp and scallops into a paste. Add anchovies and egg whites. Blend. Add heavy cream slowly and blend again. Refrigerate.

Blanch the diced leek in boiling salted water for 30 seconds. Strain and cool in ice water. Dry. Mix with mousseline and season. Put into a pastry bag.

Fill opened fish fillets with mousseline. Fold around mousseline and wrap fish in pork fat. Form into sausage-like shape.

Cut potatoes and cucumbers into oval shape pieces. Cook potatoes and blanch cucumbers, snow peas, and whole tomatoes. Chill in ice water. Peel tomato and cut each into eighths and remove seeds.

Grill the John Dory rolls, 5 minutes on each side and place back in the oven at 380°F (190°C) for 15 minutes.

Add mustard powder to hollandaise sauce and season to taste.

Finally sauté vegetables and potatoes briefly in butter and a few drops of olive oil to re-heat them. Do not allow to brown.

Place John Dory on plate. Put hollandaise sauce in the center of the plate and arrange vegetables around the sauce. Garnish with thyme sprig.

Menu

Medallions of Lobster with Yellow Pepper Coulis

Tomato and Celeriac Cream with Fresh Basil and Sambuca

Salad Milan

Breast of Chicken with Saffron Risotto

Poached Pear and Sauce Anglaise and Gorgonzola Cheese

Key Lime Soufflé Glacé with White Chocolate Cup

Medallions of Lobster with Yellow Pepper Coulis

Servings—6
Portion—1 lobster

- 6 1¼-pound (560 g) live lobsters
- 8 cups (2 L) court bouillon
- 3 feet (7.6 cm) butcher twine

Pepper Coulis—

- 4 large yellow peppers
- 2 tablespoons (30 g) chopped shallots
- 1 cup (250 ml) dry white wine
- ¼ cup (60 ml) champagne vinegar
- 2 tablespoons (30 g) scallion whites, finely chopped

Remove tails and claws from live lobster. Tie two tails together with shells to the outside. Cook the three sets of tails and all claws in court bouillon for 12 minutes. Remove from water and cool in ice water. Remove lobster meat from shell without cutting or ripping meat. Starting from the tail of the lobster meat, slice medallions. Set aside with the shelled claw meat.

To make the yellow pepper coulis, char yellow peppers on all sides on a hot grill. Remove and place in a brown paper bag to steam. When cooled, remove skin and all seeds. Roughly dice yellow pepper. Sauté shallots, garlic, and yellow pepper for 3 minutes over medium heat. Add white wine, champagne vinegar, and thyme, and cook for 5 minutes. Place all ingredients in a blender and purée. Strain purée with a fine strainer. Chill coulis.

To serve, cover bottom of plate with yellow pepper coulis. Shingle lobster medallions in center of plate, placing a claw on each side with tomato diamonds above and below the medallions. Place sprig of opal basil at the top of the plate.

Tomato and Celeriac Cream with Fresh Basil and Sambuca

Servings—6
Portion—1 cup (250 ml)

- 4 pounds (1¾ kg) whole plum tomatoes, peeled and seeded
- 2 celeriac, cleaned and ground in a food processor
- 2 onions, roughly cut two 2-inch (5 cm) pieces
- 2 shallots, roughly cut two 2-inch (5 cm) pieces
- 1 tablespoon (15 g) chopped garlic
- 4 cups (1 L) chicken stock
- 4 cups (1 L) heavy cream
- Salt and pepper
- 3 tablespoons (50 g) Sambuca Romana
- ¼ cup (60 g) butter

Sachet Bag—

- 1 bunch fresh basil, chopped
- Basil stems
- 3 bay leaves
- 1 tablespoon (15 g) crushed fresh black pepper

Sauté onions and shallots in butter until translucent. Add the garlic and cook until light brown in color. Add the celeriac and cook for 2 minutes, stirring constantly. Add the tomatoes, stock and sachet bag. Cook for 40 minutes. Remove from heat and purée the mixture in a high-speed blender. Pass through a fine strainer and return to heat. Add the cream to adjust consistency; salt and pepper; cook 15 minutes. Finish with chopped basil and Sambuca. Garnish with small whole fresh basil leaf to serve.

Breast of Chicken with Saffron Risotto

Servings—6
Portion—1 breast

> 6 10-ounce (285 g) skinless chicken breasts
> 1 cup (200 g) risotto
> 3 cups (¾ L) chicken stock
> 1 pinch saffron
> 2 cups (120 g) breadcrumbs
> 1 cup (225 g) flour
> 4 eggs
> 1 bay leaf
> 2 teaspoons (10 g) minced garlic
> ½ cup (115 g) whole butter
> 1 cup (225 g) clarified butter

Sauté onion, celery, and garlic in whole butter for approximately 8 minutes. Add risotto and stir until all grains are wet. In a separate saucepan, simmer chicken stock with saffron. When hot, add to the risotto and stir until simmering. Simmer 15 minutes uncovered or until all the liquid is absorbed.

Remove skin and fat from chicken breasts. Cut a pocket lengthwise in the breasts and season the pocket with salt and pepper. Stuff pockets with cooled risotto, pressing risotto firmly into pockets, leaving room for pocket to close. Season outside of breast with salt and pepper, and dredge breast in flour, egg, and breadcrumbs. Set aside. (This can actually be prepared 24 hours in advance.)

Heat clarified butter. Place chicken in sauté pan and cook until golden brown on bottom side. Turn over and place pan in 350°F (180°C) oven for 20 minutes, making sure top is golden brown. Slice chicken crosswise into 6 slices and shingle slices onto serving plate. Garnish with tomato crown, olive, sprig of parsley, and lemon zest.

Key Lime Soufflé Glacé in White Chocolate Cup

Servings—6
Portion—1 chocolate cup

White Chocolate Cup—
> 1 pound (450 g) white chocolate
> 1 tablespoon (15 ml) vegetable oil

Key Lime Soufflé Glace—
> 4 eggs
> 2 yolks
> 1 cup (225 g) sugar
> 4 cups (1 L) heavy cream
> ¼ cup (60 ml) lime juice

Chocolate Ganache—
> ½ cup (115 g) semi-sweet chocolate
> 2 cups (425 ml) heavy cream

To make chocolate cup, wrap six 8-ounce (250 g) paper cups with plastic wrap. Tuck ends into top of paper cup. Melt white chocolate in a double boiler with oil. When smooth, dip each cup into the chocolate and place chocolate side down on waxed paper. Place in freezer until hard. If chocolate is too thin, cups may have to be dipped twice. When chocolate is solid, remove cup and peel away plastic.

To prepare cups for glacé mixture, cut six strips of wax paper 8 inches × 6 inches (20 cm × 15 cm). Wrap one strip around each cup and tape to secure. Paper should cover each cup, and there should be a large overhang.

To make ganache, melt chocolate in double boiler until smooth. Slightly warm the heavy cream and whisk into chocolate. Remove from double boiler and let cool.

To make soufflé glacé, heat egg yolks, eggs, and sugar until sugar dissolves. Remove from heat and whip mixture until it is double the volume and lemon-colored. In separate bowl, whip cream into soft peaks. Set aside. Add lime juice to egg mixture. By hand, fold whipped cream into eggs. Carefully spoon soufflé into prepared cups. Divide evenly. After soufflé is in cups, spoon ganache into the center, pushing the chocolate downward into the center. Freeze 4 hours or overnight.

To serve, peel away wax paper collar and sift cocoa powder over the top.

The Peabody Orlando has embraced a number of the grand traditions long associated with the original in Memphis, Tennessee, including elegant restaurants and renowned cuisine. "Dux," offers cuisine best described as New American, amidst a setting that, while new, evokes the serenity and style of a fine old home.

Sweetbread Salad with Radicchio and Spinach with Walnut Oil Vinaigrette

Servings—6–8
Portion—¼ cup (115 g)

2 2½-pounds (1¼ kg) sweetbreads
4 golden apples
½ pound (225 g) bacon
1 large head radicchio
2 bunches spinach
½ large carrot
1½ stalks celery
¼ medium-sized onion
2 leeks (white only)
2 bay leaves
6 sprigs thyme (fresh, if possible)
8 black peppercorns
1 cup (250 ml) white wine
1 cup (225 g) butter
All purpose flour, to dust
Walnut Oil Vinaigrette—
1 egg yolk
2 teaspoons (10 g) Dijon mustard
5 teaspoons (25 ml) red wine vinegar
2 cups (425 ml) walnut oil
Salt and pepper to taste

This recipe requires a "court-bouillon," which is a composition of vegetables, spices, herbs, and stock and/or water. The purpose of this method of cooking is to add flavor to the product being prepared. It will also be used as a tool to help clean the delicate sweetbreads. The first step of this recipe should be done the night before serving.

Soak sweetbreads in cold water, changing frequently, for 1 hour. Gently trim sweetbreads to remove bulk sinew. Do not break apart. With ½ cup (115 g) butter, sauté vegetables, spices, and herbs in 2–3 quart (2–3 L) saucepot. When this mixture begins to release its aromatic flavors, deglaze with white wine. Reduce to one-half the original volume.

Carefully mix the sweetbreads with the vegetables. Add 1–1½ quarts (1–1½ L) water. Be sure water volume is correct—enough to allow sweetbreads to cook freely, but not too much to lose flavor from the "court-bouillon."

Bring water to boil. Gently poach sweetbreads 5–7 minutes. When the surface of the sweetbreads appears "hardened," plunge in cold bath for 2 minutes. Place between two pieces of cloth and put under a light weight overnight.

Wash spinach and radicchio. Dry with salad spinner. Finely julienne and reserve. Peel apples and soak in cold water with a touch of lemon. Sauté bacon evenly and drain on paper towel. Reserve ¼ of fat and slowly brown apple pearls in it.

Slice sweetbreads in ½-inch (1.3 cm) medallions. Season them with salt and pepper and lightly dust them with flour. Sauté with remaining butter and minced shallots, turning once until golden brown, over medium heat. Remove medallions and drain on a paper towel. Toss spinach and radicchio together with walnut oil vinaigrette (directions follow). Salt and pepper to taste. Weave salad on center of plate. Place warm sweetbread medallions on top and garnish with apples and bacon.

To make walnut oil vinaigrette, whip egg yolk to blend smoothly. Blend in mustard, salt, white pepper, and red wine vinegar. Add oil in a slow stream, incorporating liquid as you proceed. Unused vinaigrette may be refrigerated in a closed container for 7–10 days. If it becomes too thick, add a little water or wine to thin.

Breast of Pheasant with Sautéed Spinach, Golden Raisins and Port Wine Sauce

Servings—4
Portion—½ breast

  2 pheasants 1½–2 pounds
     (450–675 g) each
  2 bunches spinach
  Baby vegetables
  1½ cups (350 ml) port wine
  6 tablespoons (85 g) golden raisins
  2 sliced shallots

Stock—

  4 cups (900 g) butter
  1 carrot
  ½ onion
  2 stalks celery
  2 leeks (white only)
  8 peppercorns
  1 bay leaf
  4 thyme leaves

Use boning knife to remove breast and legs of pheasant. Reserve breasts. Chop legs, carcass, and stock vegetables into 1-inch (2.5 cm) pieces. Place bones in 2½ quart (2½ L) stock pot with cold water just covering. Gently bring to a boil. Skim as required. Add stock vegetables, spices, and herbs. Let stock simmer slowly for 1–1½ hours. Strain and allow stock to cool before adding port wine sauce.

Sauté shallots in 1½ quart (1½ L) saucepot. Add port wine and reduce by ⅔ or when reduction looks glossy. Add 1 quart (1 L) of pheasant stock and reduce this by ½. Slowly whisk in 3 cups (675 g) of butter on medium heat. As sauce begins to thicken, lower heat. Strain with fine china cap. Add golden raisins and keep in warm water bath until served.

Blanch vegetables in boiling, salted water. Plunge in ice water and drain on towel. With ¼ cup (55 g) butter in sauté pan, brown pheasant breasts, skin side down.

Finish in 350°F (180°C) oven, if needed. Sauté spinach in brown butter, drain on towel. Arrange on plate under pheasant. Toss vegetables with 1 tablespoon (15 g) butter. Add salt and pepper to taste. Place decoratively at top of plate. Slice pheasant breast and fan on top of spinach sauté. Ladle sauce around pheasant and serve.

Raspberry Soufflé

Servings—4–6
Portion—1 mold

  6 egg whites
  4 egg yolks
  ½ cup (120 ml) raspberry purée
  3 cups (600 g) fresh raspberries
  ⅔ cups (140 g) granulated sugar
  Pinch of salt
  ½ teaspoon (5 ml) butter

Evenly butter and sugar inside of soufflé molds. Refrigerate. Preheat oven to 400°F (200°C). Place oven rack on lowest position to allow soufflé to rise.

Separate yolks from whites. In two bowls (preferably stainless steel), whip egg whites to a soft peak. Mix yolks with remaining sugar and raspberry purée. Fold ⅔ of whites into yolks. Make folds with rubber spatula from bottom center to outside of bowl. Do not swirl mixture, as the whites will lose their stiffness. Add remaining whites in the same manner.

Place 6–8 raspberries in bottom of each mold. Fill to the top with raspberry and egg mixture, being careful not to disturb butter and sugar inside mold. Place in 425°F (220°C) oven for 7–10 minutes or until soufflé is dark brown on top and 1½–2 inches (3.7–5.0 cm) above mold. Do not open oven while soufflé is cooking. Dust with confectioner's sugar. Serve immediately.

ROYAL HOTEL

Menu

Salad of Lobster, Papaya, Avocado and Tomato

Consommé with Caviar and Asparagus Cream Soup

Three-Spined Stickleback and Foie Gras Sauté
with Sour-Sweet Tomato

Roasted Lamb Flavored with Green Pepper

Grand Dessert "Chambord" Style

Fancy Biscuits

The Royal Hotel, conveniently located in the center of Osaka, offers easy access to the city's business, shopping, and sightseeing areas. Located on the 29th floor and decorated in the elegant French court style, the "Restaurant Chambord" serves the finest French cuisine in an atmosphere of relaxing music.

Salad of Lobster, Papaya, Avocado and Tomato

Servings—8
Portion—1 lobster

  8 11-ounce (300 g) lobsters
15 cups (3½ L) court bouillon
1¼ cups (285 g) mayonnaise dressing
  2 large tomatoes
  2 avocados
  1 papaya

Court Bouillon—

  ½ cup (115 g) carrots
  ½ cup (115 g) onions
  ¼ cup (60 g) celery
  ¼ teaspoon (1 g) anise
  1 bouquet garni
  1 tablespoon (15 g) whole
    peppercorns
Rind of 4 oranges
2½ tablespoons (45 g) salt
16 cups (3¾ L) water
  ½ cup (120 ml) wine vinegar
  2 cups (425 ml) white wine
  1 pinch fennel

Mayonnaise Dressing—

  ½ cup (115 g) mayonnaise
  3 tablespoons (45 ml) red wine
    vinegar
3⅓ tablespoons (50 ml) heavy cream
  ½ cup (120 ml) shrimp bouillon
Salt and pepper to taste
Truffles, chopped
Chervil

Skewer lobsters to straighten and boil in court bouillon 7–8 minutes. Let the lobsters cool in the bouillon. Remove shells and slice each lobster into 6–8 pieces, but retain the original shape.

Scoop papaya and avocado into half-inch (1.5 cm) diameter balls. Peel tomatoes and cut the flesh with a half-inch (1.5 cm) diameter round cutter to make tomato "coins."

Add red wine vinegar, heavy cream, salt and pepper to the mayonnaise. Pour in lobster-flavored bouillon a little at a time.

Pour sauce onto the plate and arrange avocado, papaya, and tomatoes in that order. Place the lobster in the center. Garnish with chopped truffles and chervil.

Consommé with Caviar and Asparagus Cream Soup

Servings—8
Portion—¼ cup (60 ml) consommé and ¼ cup (60 ml) asparagus cream soup each, layered

  ⅔ cup (140 g) caviar

Asparagus Cream Soup—

  4 cups (1 L) chicken bouillon
2¼ pounds (1 kg) asparagus
1¼ cups (275 ml) heavy cream
  1 or 2 egg yolks
  1 tablespoon (15 g) cornstarch
Sugar and salt to taste

Consommé Jelly—

  5 cups (1¼ L) consommé
  3 onions
  1 tablespoon (15 g) celery
  2 tablespoons (30 g) carrot
2½ tablespoons (50 g) shallot

1 bouquet garni

1 tablespoon (15 ml) tomato purée

1 pound (450 g) lean meat (for soup)

Clarification—

1 tablespoon (15 g) leek, chopped

1 tablespoon (15 g) carrot

1 tablespoon (15 g) celery

1 or 2 egg whites

Gelatin

To make asparagus cream soup, mix ingredients listed above. Make consommé with ingredients listed and pour the vegetables and egg white mixture over the consommé.

Pour consommé into sundae glass, filling ⅓ full and refrigerate. When set, spread caviar over the surface and pour remaining consommé over caviar. Refrigerate.

Pour the asparagus cream soup over the consommé jelly in the sundae glass and serve.

Three-Spined Stickleback and Foie Gras Sauté with Sour-Sweet Tomato

Servings—8

Portion—1 piece

8 2-3-ounce (60 g-70 g) pieces three-spined stickleback

1⅛ cup (250 g) fresh foie gras

Dark veal stock

Sauce Tomato Vinaigrette—

4 large tomatoes, peeled, seeded, and chopped

½ cup (200 ml) tomato juice (made from pressing tomato flesh in a juicer)

2 teaspoons (10 ml) sherry vinegar

3 tablespoons (45 ml) olive oil

2 tablespoons (30 g) chives, chopped

Salt and pepper

Cut each three-spined stickleback into 3 pieces and sauté in olive oil. Coat foie gras with flour and sauté. Add sherry vinegar, tomato juice, and dark veal stock to make sauce for foie gras.

Mix tomato flesh, tomato juice, sherry vinegar, olive oil, salt and pepper in a double boiler. Warm so that tomato flesh retains its shape. Add chopped chives to taste.

Roasted Lamb Flavored with Green Pepper

Servings—8

Portion—4 pieces

4 racks of lamb

1¼ cups (285 g) Girolle mushrooms

32 green asparagus

Chicken Mousse—

¾ pound (340 g) chicken breast

2 whole eggs

⅔ cup (140 g) butter

⅔ cup (150 ml) cream

Whole green peppers

Remove skin, fat, and bones from the racks of lamb and make into fillets. Brown at high heat.

Mix together ingredients for chicken mousse in a blender. Thinly spread chicken mousse on greased cheesecloth.

Wrap the fillets in the cheesecloth, roll, tie with string, and roast. Roast and then boil tendons and bones of lamb to make juice for sauce.

Place sautéed Girolle mushrooms in the center of serving plate. Place 4 stalks asparagus per serving on the plate. Cut each fillet of lamb into 8 pieces and place 4 pieces on each plate.

THE BREAKERS

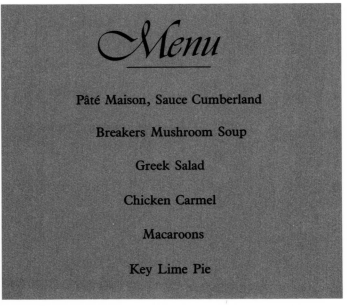

Menu

Pâté Maison, Sauce Cumberland

Breakers Mushroom Soup

Greek Salad

Chicken Carmel

Macaroons

Key Lime Pie

The Breakers, a Mobil Five-Star, AAA Five-Diamond resort in the heart of Palm Beach, offers a variety of exciting dining experiences. Soaring frescoed ceilings and 15th century Flemish tapestries are the setting for the classic cuisine and superlative service featured in the elegant "Florentine" and "Circle" dining rooms.

Breakers Mushroom Soup

Servings—8
Portion—1 cup (250 ml)

6 tablespoons (90 g) butter

3¾ pounds (1½ kg) fresh mushrooms, chopped (reserve ½ pound (225 g) and slice for garnish.)

1 cup (250 g) onions, chopped

½ cup (115 g) celery, chopped

3 cloves

6 tablespoons (90 g) all-purpose flour

8 cups (2 L) chicken stock

2 cups (425 ml) heavy cream

¼ cup (60 ml) dry Marsala wine

¼ cup (60 ml) dry sherry

Salt and pepper to taste

Dash of nutmeg

Fresh garlic, minced

Melt butter in a 4-quart (4 L) saucepan. Add chopped mushrooms, onion, celery and garlic. Sauté until mushrooms soften and lose their liquid. Dust flour over mixture and continue cooking for approximately 2 minutes. Stirring constantly, add chicken stock and bring to a full boil. Reduce heat and simmer for approximately 15 minutes (until flour cannot be tasted.) Blend and purée mixture in food processor or blender. Return to saucepan. Stir in cream and let set for 5 minutes on low heat. (Do not boil.)

To prepare garnish, heat dry Marsala and dry sherry. Add sliced mushrooms and blanch until softened and add to soup.

Season with salt, white pepper and nutmeg.

Chicken Carmel

Servings—8
Portion—1 breast

8 6-ounce (180 g) chicken breasts, boned

¾ cup (180 g) crabmeat

2 teaspoons (10 g) chopped shallots

2 cups (450 g) fresh mushrooms, sliced

2 tablespoons (30 g) chives, freshly chopped

2 tablespoons (30 g) pimiento, chopped

6 eggs (4 eggs reserved for egg wash)

¼ cup (60 ml) milk (reserved for egg wash)

2 cups (300 g) raw almonds, sliced and chopped

Flour for dredging

½ cup (115 g) butter, clarified

Sauce—

¼ cup (60 g) butter

¼ cup (60 g) flour (for roux)

3 cups (¾ L) chicken stock

1 cup (250 ml) white wine

Salt and white pepper to taste

Worcestershire sauce to taste

Brown shallots with mushrooms in 2 tablespoons (30 g) of clarified butter, until mushrooms exude juices and liquid is reduced. Add chives and pimientos. Fold in crabmeat and eggs.

Flatten chicken breasts, skin side down. Divide crabmeat mixture into 8 equal portions and place on chicken breasts. Roll. Freeze stuffed breasts for a few minutes to firm.

Lightly dust firm, stuffed breast with flour. Dip in egg wash (whipped egg and milk mixture), then in almonds. Lightly brown in skillet with seam side down, then cover with foil. Bake in a 325°F (170°C) oven for 15 minutes or until done.

To make the sauce, mix melted butter and flour (roux) over low heat. Stirring continuously, cook a few minutes until color changes slightly. Slowly add chicken stock, continuing to stir, and bring to a simmer. Add wine, bring to boiling point. Reduce heat, and let simmer until thickened.

To serve, cut in slices crosswise so that the stuffing shows. Place some sauce on each plate and place chicken roll over the sauce. Serve additional sauce on the side. Serve with saffron rice and a bouquet of fresh seasonal vegetables.

Macaroons

Servings—5 dozen
Portion—2 macaroons

> **1 cup (225 g) granulated sugar**
> **6 egg whites**
> **2 tablespoons (30 g) almond paste**
> **2 cups (160 g) flaked, fine coconut**
> **⅓ cup (75 g) all-purpose flour**
> **3 drops vanilla**
> **Pinch of salt**

In a double boiler, combine sugar, egg whites, almond paste, and salt. Heat until sugar is dissolved. Remove from direct heat. Add coconut and flour to mixture, mix thoroughly, add vanilla and place in piping bag. Pipe onto baking sheet lined with parchment paper (approximately 1 inch (2.5 cm) in diameter) or spoon onto sheet pan. Mixture will not spread.

Bake 375°F (190°C) for approximately 15 minutes, until tops of macaroons are light brown in color. (Watch carefully as ovens may vary browning time.)

Key Lime Pie

Servings—8
Portion—⅛″ (3mm) slice

Filling—

> **3 egg yolks**
> **⅔ cup (150 ml) lime juice**
> **3 cups (¾ L) condensed milk**

Crust—

> **5 tablespoons (75 g) shortening**
> **7 tablespoons (105 g) cake flour**
> **2 tablespoons (30 g) sugar**
> **¼ teaspoon (1.2 g) salt**
> **1 whole egg**
> **3 tablespoons (45 ml) milk**

Mix above crust ingredients, roll out and shape into pie shell. Bake at 375°F (190°C) until light brown.

For filling, mix egg yolks, lime juice, and condensed milk until smooth and creamy. Pour into pre-baked pie shell and bake for 15 minutes at 350°F (180°C).

Cool pie and then top with whipped cream and decorate with slices of fresh lime.

Hôtel Le Bristol

Menu

Crawfish Salad with Fresh Beans
and Tarragon Sauce

Escalope of Fresh Salmon "Floralie"

Marc de Bourgogne Liqueur Sorbet

Saddle of Lamb with Garlic Cream Sauce

Chavignol Goat Cheese Served on Toast

Delicate Mousses with Fresh Fruit Sauces

The Hotel Le Bristol, just a few steps away from the Champs Elysées, features a French style garden, banqueting facilities, swimming pool and sauna. The Chef de Cuisine has been elected Meilleur Ouvrier de France, and the restaurant nominated the best hotel restaurant in Paris.

Crawfish Salad with French Beans and Tarragon Sauce

Servings—4
Portion—1 salad

40 crawfish
2½ cups (525 g) French beans
1 bunch tarragon
1 chopped shallot
2 tablespoons (30 ml) raspberry vinegar
5½ tablespoons (80 ml) corn oil
1 cup (250 ml) cream
1 carrot
1 onion
Cayenne pepper
Twig of thyme
Laurel leaf
1 cup (250 ml) white wine
1 lemon

Wash the crawfish thoroughly, removing the intestines. Bring white wine, 8 cups (2 L) water, carrot, sliced onion, twig of thyme, laurel leaf, and a few slices of lemon to a boil. Add crawfish and boil for 4–5 minutes. Remove and shell.

Place crawfish on a serving of French beans seasoned with raspberry vinegar, corn oil, and chopped shallot. To prepare tarragon cream, lightly flavor cream with lemon. Pour one large spoonful of chopped tarragon and juice of half a lemon around salad. (This dish can also be prepared with shrimp.)

Escalope of Fresh Salmon "Floralie"

Servings—4
Portion—1 steak

1½ pounds (675 g) fresh salmon fillet
1¼ cups (285 g) tomatoes, peeled and sliced
1¼ cups (285 g) cucumber, sliced
½ cup (120 ml) white wine
½ cup (120 ml) fresh cream
Bunch chives
1 shallot
½ cup (120 ml) Noilly Prat vermouth
⅔ cup (140 g) butter
Salt and pepper to taste

Cut the salmon fillets into 4 steaks. Season with salt and pepper and cover with tomato and cucumber slices. Place in buttered dish, add chopped shallot, white wine, Noilly Prat, and cover. Bake in oven at moderate heat approximately 15 minutes. Place on platter and keep warm. Strain the sauce into a saucepan, reduce to one-half. Remove from heat and add cream. Mix in small bits of butter. Garnish serving dish with finely chopped chives and pour sauce around each steak.

Saddle of Lamb with Garlic Cream Sauce

Servings—4
Portion—1 fillet

3½ pounds (1½ kg) saddle of lamb
¾ cup (180 g) garlic
2 cups (425 ml) cream

1 teaspoon (5 g) thyme

2 cups (450 g) tomatoes

2 cups (450 g) zucchini

4 pieces toast

½ cup (115 g) butter

¼ cup (60 ml) olive oil

Cut fillets from the saddle and trim. Season with salt and pepper and sauté in butter and thyme. Fillets should retain pink color. Peel the garlic cloves and simmer in cream. Crush mixture with a mixer, adding a small bit of butter. Glaze the toast with butter, and place in the middle of each plate. Spread with garlic cream, then lay slices of lamb in cream. Surround lamb alternately with tomatoes and slices of zucchini cooked in olive oil.

Delicate Mousses with Fresh Fruit Sauces

Servings—4
Portion—1 mold

½ cup (115 g) fruit pulp (cherry, peach, or raspberry)

2 egg yolks

2 tablespoons (30 g) fine sugar

2 leaves gelatin

2 egg whites

1 tablespoon (15 g) granulated sugar

Mousse—

To prepare mousse, mix pulp, fine sugar, and egg yolks in a saucepan. Whisk until boiling. Dip the gelatin leaves in cold water and strain well. Add to pulp mixture and cool.

Firmly whip egg whites with granulated sugar and add to pulp mixture. Place in small ramekin molds. Refrigerate approximately 2 hours. Unmold.

Fruit Sauces—

To prepare fruit sauces, combine mint, 1 cup (250 ml) water, ½ cup (100 g) sugar, 2½ tablespoons (50 g) mint leaves, and leaf gelatin.

Combine 1 cup (250 g) raspberry pulp, ⅓ cup (75 g) sugar, juice of ½ lemon. Combine 1 cup (250 ml) orange juice, ⅓ cup (75 g) sugar, and leaf gelatin.

Arrange the three sauces with three mousses on a serving plate. Dress the mousses by laying a raspberry on the raspberry mousse, a mint leaf on the peach mousse and a caramelized cherry on the cherry mousse.

The Pointe

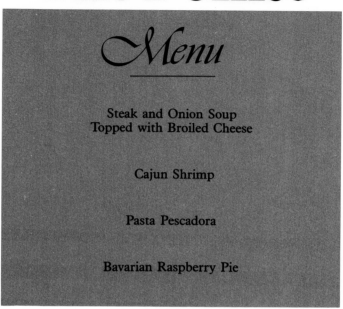

Menu

Steak and Onion Soup
Topped with Broiled Cheese

Cajun Shrimp

Pasta Pescadora

Bavarian Raspberry Pie

After sampling entrees from restaurants throughout the country, surveying opinions of food and entertainment editors nationwide, and tasting, testing and re-testing, The Pointe on South Mountain is proud to present to the Valley, "Pointe In Tyme," the first restaurant in America to feature culinary fame from around the nation.

Steak and Onion Soup Topped with Broiled Cheese

Servings—20
Portion—6 ounces (200 ml)

1–1½ large onions, julienned
1 pound (450 g) cooked beef, julienned
4 quarts (3¾ L) beef stock
1 cup (250 ml) sherry
1 teaspoon (5 g) chopped garlic
1 teaspoon (5 g) whole thyme
3 tablespoons (30 g) clarified butter
3 tablespoons (30 g) bacon grease
Kitchen bouquet
Roux

Sauté onions in butter and bacon grease until blanched. Add sherry, garlic, and thyme, cook 5 minutes. Add beef stock and bring to a boil. Add roux to thicken, kitchen bouquet to desired color, and add salt and pepper to taste.

Pour soup into 6-ounce (200 ml) serving bowls. Place large crouton on top. Place 1-ounce (30 g) slice of Swiss cheese on crouton. Melt under broiler. Serve immediately.

Cajun Shrimp

Servings—1
Portion—4 shrimp

4 jumbo shrimp (shelled and cleaned, tails intact)
2 tablespoons (30 g) Cajun spice
Lemon slices
2 tomato wedges
6 snowpeas

Dredge shrimp generously in Cajun seasoning. Sauté in about 1 ounce (30 g) of butter in a hot frying pan for approximately 2 minutes. Serve with ¼ cup (60 g) Cajun butter on side. Garnish with lemon slices, 2 tomato wedges, and 6 snowpeas. It can also be served with garlic toast.

To make Cajun butter, mix 2 cups (450 g) unsalted butter with 2 teaspoons (10 g) of Cajun spice. Blend well and serve as a dip at room temperature.

Pasta Pescadora

Servings—1
Portion—3 ounces (85 g)

Pescadora Sauce—

½ teaspoon (2.5 g) whole thyme
⅛ bulb shallot, chopped
⅛ bulb fresh garlic, chopped
1 teaspoon (5 g) ground sage
1 cup (250 ml) milk
2 cups (425 ml) chicken stock
½ cup (120 ml) half-and-half
½ cup (120 ml) heavy cream
¼ cup (60 ml) sherry
4 jumbo shrimp
¼ cup (60 g) whole baby clams
3⅓ tablespoons (50 ml) heavy cream
¼ cup (60 g) sliced mushrooms
1 tablespoon (15 g) chopped shallots
½ teaspoon (2.5 ml) garlic, freshly minced

3 ounces (85 g) linguini

2 tablespoons (30 g) lemon zest and chopped chives (combined weight)

2 tablespoons (30 g) grated Parmesan cheese

½ cup (120 ml) sherry

Sauté shallots, garlic, thyme, and sage in clarified butter. Deglaze with sherry. Add chicken stock and reduce by ⅓. Add milk, half-and-half and heavy cream. Bring to boil; thicken with roux and strain through cheesecloth.

Sauté shrimp in clarified butter until half-cooked, approximately 1 minute, until opaque.

Add mushrooms, shallots, and garlic and sauté. Remove shrimp from pan. Deglaze with sherry; reduce by ½. Add ¼ cup (60 ml) Pescadora sauce. Stir and simmer for 1–1½ minutes. Remove from heat, add baby clams.

Heat linguini in hot water and drain. Place linguini on plate, pour remaining sauce over generously. Place shrimp in row over top, add Parmesan cheese. Sprinkle with zest of lemon and chopped chives. Garnish plate with two lemon wheels and parsley.

Bavarian Raspberry Pie

Servings—8
Portion—1 1" (2.5 cm) slice

1 8-inch prepared pie shell

¾ cup (180 g) raspberry filling

¼ cup (60 ml) egg whites

¼ cup (60 g) granulated sugar

1½ tablespoons (15 ml) lemon juice

2 drops pure vanilla extract

2 drops pure almond extract

1½ cups (350 ml) heavy cream (whipped)

Use an egg wash to seal pie shell. Line shell with sliced almonds, and pre-bake until shell is golden brown.

Beat egg whites and sugar to stiff peaks. Blend together vanilla and almond extracts, raspberry filling, and lemon juice. Fold in meringue, fold in heavy cream (already whipped).

Spoon ingredients into pie shell (should be heaping). Line outer edge with sliced almonds. Freeze until served.

THE HEATHMAN HOTEL

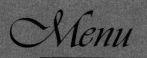

Menu

Terrine of Northwest Game Meats
with Horseradish Cream

Chicken Consommé with Garden Vegetables

Salad of Seasonal Greens

Quail with Wild Rice and Roasted Shallots

Chanterelle and Leek Sauté

White Ganache-Covered Poached Pears

The Heathman Hotel offers a varied menu of classic cuisine, distinguished by its selections of Pacific Northwest seafood and game. Take afternoon tea by the fire in the "Tea Court." After a concert next door at the Performing Arts Center, return for a nightcap and soft piano music in our graciously restored "Lobby Lounge."

Salad of Seasonal Greens

Servings—4–6
Portion—1 salad

   ¼ cup (60 g) smoked salmon or
      scallops

   Mixed seasonal greens

Dressing—

   **2 cups (450 g) frozen or fresh pearl
      onions**

   ½ cup (75 g) golden raisins

   2 tablespoons (30 g) curry powder

   4 cups (1 L) white wine vinegar

   1 cup (250 ml) olive oil

   Salt and pepper to taste

   **1 tablespoon (15 g) fresh garlic,
      chopped**

In a saucepan place ½ cup (120 ml) of the olive oil and bring to medium high heat. Sauté the pearl onions, garlic, raisins, and curry until the onions brown evenly. Reduce the heat to medium and add the vinegar. Simmer until the volume is reduced by ⅔ and remove from heat. Allow to cool. Gradually whisk in the remaining olive oil. Season to taste with salt and pepper. Toss the greens and smoked salmon or scallops with the dressing and garnish with lemons, limes, and tomatoes.

Quail with Wild Rice and Roasted Shallots

Servings—8
Portion—1 quail

   8 boneless whole quail

   4 cups (800 g) cooked wild rice

   8 shallots, peeled and left whole

   1 cup (250 ml) dry sherry

   ½ cup (120 ml) white wine vinegar

   Salt and pepper to taste

   **1 teaspoon (5 g) dried thyme or 1
      tablespoon (15 g) fresh thyme**

   1 cup (250 ml) heavy cream

Season the cavities of the quail with a pinch of salt, pepper, and thyme. Fill the cavities with wild rice so the quail plump slightly. Place in a shallow roasting pan with peeled shallots, taking care that none of the birds touch one another. Add the sherry, vinegar, and any remaining thyme to the pan. Roast at 425°F (220°C) until the birds and shallots are golden brown. Prick a quail at the joint and the juice should run pink to clear (20 minutes–½ hour). Remove the birds from the pan, and arrange them on a serving platter with the shallots. Pour the pan juices into a small saucepan, and reduce by simmering to ¼ the original volume. Add the heavy cream and continue to reduce by simmering until sauce thickens (about 5–10 minutes). Season to taste with salt and pepper. Serve the sauce around the birds and shallots on the platter with fresh herb garnish.

Chanterelle and Leek Sauté

Servings—4
Portion—½ cup (115 g)

1¾ cups (400 g) fresh chanterelle
  mushrooms, sliced

1 cup (225 g) leeks, julienned

1 teaspoon (5 g) minced garlic

2 teaspoons (10 g) minced shallots

1 cup (250 ml) chicken stock

1 cup (250 ml) white wine

1 cup (225 g) whole leaves of fresh
  basil

2 teaspoons (10 ml) lemon juice

1 teaspoon (5 ml) olive oil

Salt and pepper to taste

2 tablespoons (30 g) whole softened
  butter

Lemon wedges and basil to garnish

Sauté the oil in a large pan until it begins to turn blue. Place garlic and shallots in the hot pan, reduce heat to medium, and stir constantly. When the mixture becomes golden brown, add the wine, lemon juice, and chicken stock. Reduce the mixture by ½ at a steady simmer. Add the mushrooms and leeks. Continue to reduce until the mushrooms and leeks are cooked thoroughly (3–5 minutes). Remove and place on a warm serving dish. Whisk the softened butter into the pan, and season to taste with salt and pepper. Arrange the basil leaves on the mushrooms and leeks, and top with the sauce. Garnish with lemon and basil.

White Ganache-Covered Poached Pears

Servings—6
Portion—1 pear

Poaching Liqueur—

1 bottle Riesling wine

2 cups (500 g) sugar

4 whole cloves

2 bay leaves

1 vanilla bean

6 whole ripe Bartlett pears

Ganache—

1¼ cups (285 g) white Callebaute
  chocolate

1 cup (250 ml) heavy cream

Garnish:

6 mint sprigs

Combine Riesling, sugar, and spices in pan and bring to a simmer. Meanwhile, peel the pears as smoothly as possible, leaving the stems and removing the core from the bottom side of the pear. Place the pears in the simmering syrup and poach until they are tender, about 20 minutes. Remove from the liqueur and set aside to cool.

Strain the poaching liqueur and return it to the saucepan. Reduce to a medium syrup and remove from heat. Bring the heavy cream to a simmer and remove from heat. Stir in the white chocolate gradually, until dissolved and a smooth ganache is reached.

Pat the pears dry and cut a small portion of the bottom of each so they stand upright. Place in a shallow dish or pan and carefully ladle the ganache over each to achieve a smooth coating. Allow the pears to cool completely. Serve on dessert plates with the poaching syrup around each and a mint sprig for garnish.

Ambasciatori Palace Hotel

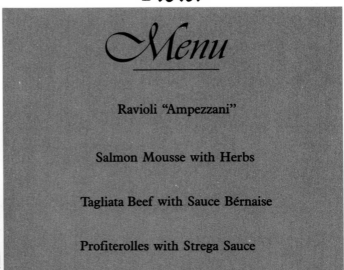

Menu

Ravioli "Ampezzani"

Salmon Mousse with Herbs

Tagliata Beef with Sauce Bérnaise

Profiterolles with Strega Sauce

The Ambasciatori Palace Hotel is situated in the heart of Rome, in the center of the famous Via Veneto, one of the most beautiful streets in the world, opposite the Embassy of the United States of America. The best Italian cuisine can be found at the famous "Grill-Bar ABC" and on "La Terrazza" from May to October.

Ravioli "Ampezzani"

Servings—6
Portion—1 plate

> 2¼ pounds (1 kg) beetroot
> ⅔ cup (150 g) butter
> ½ cup (15 g) cottage cheese
> Salt to taste
> 5 eggs
> Breadcrumbs
> 2½ cups (500 g) flour
> 2 cups (½ L) milk
> 5 level teaspoons (25 g) poppy seeds

Garnish—

> Hard cheese, mature and strong
> tasting

To make the filling for the ravioli, peel and slice the beetroot and mash with a fork. Melt butter in a pan, and sauté the mashed beetroot. Pour beetroot into a mixing bowl, add cottage cheese, salt, 2 eggs, and enough breadcrumbs to obtain a firm consistency.

To make the pasta, sift flour in a mound on the work surface. Make a well in the center and break 3 eggs into it. Salt to taste. Start to draw the flour into the center, working the eggs and flour together with the fingers. Add milk slowly. When dough is firm, knead it thoroughly until very smooth. Cover and let sit for about 30 minutes. The dough will lose some of its elasticity. Divide dough into 2-3 pieces and roll out as thinly as possible. Set aside. Roll each piece.

Cut into circles, add 1 teaspoon (5 g) of beetroot filling, and then fold over to a semicircular shape. Press the edges down.

Simmer in salted boiling water for 15 minutes. Drain and cover ravioli with remaining melted butter, poppy seeds, and grated cheese. Serve immediately.

Salmon Mousse with Herbs

Servings—6
Portion—1 mold

> 1¾ cups (400 g) cooked salmon,
> skinned and boned
> 1 spirit glass of cognac
> 1¾ cups (400 g) butter
> 1 bouquet of mixed cooking herbs
> 1 bowl of ice

Melt butter on low flame in a small pan. Set aside. Sieve salmon and put into a stainless steel bowl, place on top of the bowl of ice. Slowly add the melted butter, stirring gently with a whisk until the mixture begins to thicken. Remove from ice. Salt to taste and add thinly chopped herbs and cognac. Put into 6 molds and chill for 1 hour. Decorate and serve.

Tagliata Beef with Sauce Béarnaise

Servings—6
Portion—4 slices

> 1¾ pounds (800 g) beef rib roast
> Olive oil
> Salt and pepper
> Sauce Béarnaise

Sauce Béarnaise—

> **3 tablespoons (45 ml) wine vinegar**
> **6 peppercorns**
> **½ bay leaf**
> **1 blade mace**
> **1 slice onion**
> **2 egg yolks**
> **Salt and pepper to taste**
> **2½ cups (500 g) butter**
> **1 teaspoon (5 g) tarragon, chervil and parsley (chopped)**
> **Pinch of chives, or grated onion**

Bone the meat and marinate for 1 hour in olive oil, salt, and pepper. Slowly cook the meat on grill for about ½ hour, turning it to cook all parts. When cooked, scallop the meat. Then replace rib roast on bone with cooking string.

Put the vinegar, peppercorns, bay leaf, mace, and slice of onion into a small pan and reduce to 1 tablespoon (15 ml). Set aside.

Beat yolks in a small basin with a pinch of salt and a pat of butter. Strain vinegar mixture and set on a pan of boiling water. Turn off heat and stir until thickened. Add small pieces of softened butter, each about the size of a hazel nut, stirring constantly.

Season with pepper. Add the meat glaze, herbs, and chives or grated onion. Keep warm and use as required. The finished sauce should have the consistency of whipped cream.

Pour the Béarnaise sauce slowly on top of roast and grill until gratiné. Serve immediately.

Profiterolles with Strega Sauce

Servings—6
Portion—1 profiterolle

Basic Chou Pastry—

> **½ cup (120 ml) water**
> **½ cup (115 g) flour**
> **6 tablespoons (80 g) butter**
> **3 eggs**

Filling—

> **1 cup (250 ml) milk**
> **½ cup (120 ml) cream**
> **½ cup (115 g) sugar**
> **¼ cup (60 g) flour**
> **4 egg yolks**
> **¼ cup (60 ml) Strega liqueur**
> **Pinch salt**

Chou pastry—

Put water and fat into large pan. Sift flour onto a piece of paper. Bring contents of the pan to boil and when bubbling, remove pan, allowing bubbles to subside. Pour in all the flour at once. Stir vigorously until smooth (a few seconds).

Cool mixture for about 5 minutes, then beat in eggs, one at a time. Beat pastry until it looks glossy. It is then ready to be piped out, using a plain chou nozzle, or shaped with a spoon. Bake for 15 minutes at 425°F (220°C).

Filling—

Beat flour and sugar together, adding the 4 egg yolks, then the milk. Strain into a small saucepan, bring to a boil, stirring constantly with a wooden spoon. Simmer for 5 minutes. Allow to cool. Whip the cream and add cooled filling.

Place in a pastry bag and fill profiterolles. Add liqueur to remaining cream for a runny consistency, and pour over profiterolles.

Decorate with pistachios or glazed cherries. Refrigerate 30 minutes before serving.

LA MANSIÓN
DEL RIO HOTEL

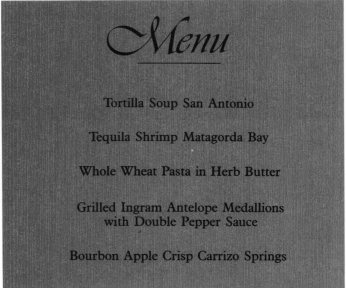

Menu

Tortilla Soup San Antonio

Tequila Shrimp Matagorda Bay

Whole Wheat Pasta in Herb Butter

Grilled Ingram Antelope Medallions
with Double Pepper Sauce

Bourbon Apple Crisp Carrizo Springs

"Las Canarias" is the specialty dining room of La Mansión del Rio. The hotel is rich in Texas history. The original structure was built in 1852 as the St. Mary's Law School. The restaurant specializes in Southwest cuisine, and combines fine food with the gracious hospitality of San Antonio and Texas.

Tortilla Soup San Antonio

Servings—6
Portion—1 cup (¼ L)

- **2 tablespoons (30 g) chopped garlic**
- **2 yellow onions, diced**
- **2 tablespoons (30 g) whole butter**
- **3⅓ tablespoons (55 ml) olive oil**
- **1 poblanos**
- **2 jalapeños**
- **6 ounces (180 g) canned Italian tomatoes**
- **¾ cup (200 ml) tomato sauce**
- **5½ cups (1⅔ L) chicken stock**
- **1½ teaspoons (8 g) ground chili powder**
- **1½ teaspoons (8 g) ground cumin**
- **1 teaspoon (5 g) leaf oregano**
- **¼ bunch cilantro**
- **Salt and pepper to taste**
- **1 teaspoon (5 g) Oaxacan cheese, shredded**
- **1 teaspoon (5 g) julienned tortillas**
- **½ teaspoon (3 g) green onion, chopped**

Roast and peel poblanos; remove seeds and stem.

In a 6 quart (6 L) pot, sauté onions in whole butter until translucent. Add peppers, garlic, and spices. When peppers are tender, add tomato sauce, crushed Italian tomatoes, and chicken stock.

Bring to a boil and simmer for ½ hour.

Serve in hot soup bowl and garnish each serving with shredded Oaxacan cheese and julienned tortillas. Top with chopped green onion.

Tequila Shrimp Matagorda Bay

Servings—6
Portion—3 shrimp

- **18 green shrimp**
- **¾ cup (200 ml) José Cuervo Tequila**
- **3¾ cups (8½ dl) heavy cream**
- **⅓ cup (75 g) melted butter**
- **3 tablespoons (45 g) chopped green onion**

Heat butter and sauté shrimp until half done. Deglaze shrimp with tequila. Add heavy cream and reduce to desired thickness.

To serve, pour sauce on plate and lay shrimp on the sauce.

Whole Wheat Pasta in Herb Butter

Servings—6
Portion—1 serving

- **¾ cup (180 g) fresh whole wheat pasta**

Herb Butter—

- **1 teaspoon (5 g) butter**
- **1 teaspoon (5 g) thyme**
- **1 teaspoon (5 g) oregano**
- **1 teaspoon (5 g) fresh dill**
- **1 teaspoon (5 g) tarragon**
- **1 teaspoon (5 g) rosemary**
- **1 teaspoon (5 g) garlic**

Bring butter to room temperature, fold in seasonings. Place whole wheat pasta in boiling water. Cook for 2–3 minutes.

In a sauté pan, heat herb butter. When butter is hot, toss in pasta and sauté until pasta is hot.

Place pasta on hot plate and top with tequila shrimp and sauce.

Grilled Ingram Antelope Medallions with Double Pepper Sauce

Servings—6
Portion—3 medallions

> **18 2-ounce (60 g) antelope medallions**

Pound the meat until about ⅛ inch (0.3 cm) thick. Place medallions in a stainless steel bowl and cover with dry red wine for about 2 hours at room temperature.

Take medallions out of wine and dry. Dust with seasoned flour and grill on hot grill until done. When medallions are cooked to taste, place ¼ cup (60 g) double pepper sauce on hot serving plate. Place 3 medallions on the sauce. Serve with wild rice or potato.

Double Pepper Sauce—

> **4 teaspoons (20 g) chopped shallots**
> **⅔ cup (150 ml) sherry**
> **1⅓ cups (300 ml) heavy cream**
> **1⅓ cups (300 ml) brown sauce**
> **1 tablespoon (15 g) green pepper, chopped**
> **1 tablespoon (15 g) pink pepper, chopped**

In a heavy 1-quart (1 L) pot, add sherry and shallots. Reduce by three-quarters. Add heavy cream and reduce by one-half. Add brown sauce, green and pink peppers, and reduce by one-quarter.

Finish sauce with ¼ cup (60 g) unsalted butter.

Bourbon Apple Crisp Carrizo Springs

Servings—5–6
Portion—1 slice

> **4 Granny Smith apples**
> **2 tablespoons (30 g) salted butter**
> **2½ tablespoons (45 g) sugar**
> **½ teaspoon (3 g) cinnamon**

> **¼ cup (60 g) raisins**
> **1½ tablespoons (20 ml) bourbon**

Topping—

> **2⅔ cups (625 g) oatmeal**
> **1 cup (225 g) salted butter**
> **1 cup (200 g) brown sugar**
> **¾ cup (75 g) pecan pieces**
> **3⅓ tablespoons (55 ml) molasses**

Sauté diced apples and raisins in butter. Add cinnamon, sugar, and toss. Deglaze with bourbon and allow to cool.

For topping, melt butter, add oatmeal, brown sugar, molasses, and pecans, and mix until crumbs are formed.

Fill 1-quart (1 L) ovenproof dish with apple mixture. Top with topping mixture. Bake in oven at 350°F (180°C) until the center is hot.

Serve with ice cream.

Menu

Vegetable Terrine
with Italian Parsley and Walnut Oil Dressing

The Grant Grill Mock Turtle Soup

Lemon Sorbet with Champagne and Mint Leaf

Broiled Fillet of King Salmon
with Red Bell Pepper Sauce

Tomato and Mozzarella Salad

Fresh Raspberries with Marsala Zabaglione

"The Grant Grill," in the heart of San Diego's downtown business district, is a popular and long-standing gathering spot. The leather booths, dark mahogany wood and white tablecloths are especially appealing to San Diego's sophisticated crowd. Here, one can enjoy Continental cuisine, with daily special entrees using fresh ingredients.

Vegetable Terrine with Italian Parsley and Walnut Oil Dressing

Servings—16
Portion—1 slice

3 pounds (1⅓ kg) red bell pepper
3 pounds (1⅓ kg) yellow bell pepper
4 pounds (1¾ kg) shiitake mushrooms
3 medium zucchini
1 cup (250 ml) walnut oil
2 cups (425 ml) olive oil
¼ cup (60 ml) white wine vinegar
2 bunches Italian parsley
½ medium onion, finely chopped
½ cup (120 ml) dry white wine
Salt and freshly ground pepper

Place the peppers directly into the flame on top of a gas range. Burn them until black and immediately place into plastic bag. Put bag into refrigerator to steam peppers. This can also be done in a 500°F (222°C) oven. Coat the peppers with olive oil and bake on a sheet pan. In approximately eight minutes remove

from oven and place peppers into plastic bag; then refrigerate.

While the peppers are cooling, remove stems from mushrooms. Sauté in olive oil with chopped onion and half of the chopped parsley. Season to taste with salt and pepper.

Add wine and simmer 1 minute. Place the mushrooms in another container and cool at room temperature. Peel the peppers underwater with a slow running faucet. Rub the peppers gently to remove all of the charred skin.

When peeled, cut the peppers in half. Remove the stem and all of the seeds. Place peppers into a colander to drain. Next, wash zucchini and slice lengthwise about ⅛ inch (0.3 cm) thick. Arrange the slices on a sheet pan and bake in a 350°F (180°C) oven until the zucchini softens. Remove from sheet pan and cool.

Line terrine mold with plastic wrap. Beginning with the red bell pepper, place a layer in the bottom of terrine mold. Next add a layer of mushroom,

then yellow pepper, zucchini, red pepper, and so on until the terrine is filled. Press down lightly after each layer is added to remove any air pockets. Cover with plastic wrap. Turn over, lift off terrine mold, and carefully remove plastic wrap. (The natural gelatin in the vegetables holds the terrine together and is very delicate.) Slice ½ inch (1.3 cm) thick with a sharp knife. Place on chilled salad plates.

Combine walnut oil, olive oil, vinegar and remaining parsley. Mix well, season to taste with salt and pepper. Pour dressing around the terrine just before serving.

Broiled Fillet of King Salmon with Red Bell Pepper Sauce

Servings—6
Portion—1 fillet

6 7-ounce (200 g) fillets of king salmon
2 cups (425 ml) white wine

2 bell peppers, chopped, stem and seeds removed

¼ medium onion, chopped

1 cup (250 ml) cream

Salt and white pepper to taste

6 tablespoons (90 g) butter

Place the salmon in a shallow pan, add wine, bell peppers, and onion. Dot with butter and season lightly with salt and white pepper. Place under broiler and cook until done (approximately 8 to 12 minutes, depending on thickness of salmon). Drain liquid into blender, blend until smooth. Bring the cream to a boil, and whisk in the blended pepper mixture. Do not boil again. Season to taste, strain and ladle the sauce around the salmon. Serve immediately.

Tomato and Mozzarella Salad

Servings—6
Portion—1 salad

18 slices tomato

18 slices mozzarella cheese ⅛ inch (0.3 cm) thick

18 fresh basil leaves

½ cups (120 ml) olive oil

Arrange ingredients in a circular fashion, beginning with a tomato slice, then a slice of cheese, and finishing with a leaf of basil. Place in center of the plate, using three pieces of each per salad. Before serving, sprinkle with lemon juice and olive oil.

Fresh Raspberries with Marsala Zabaglione

Servings—6
Portion—1 glass

6 cups (1¼ kg) fresh raspberries (or any berry or fruit in season)

9 egg yolks

½ cup (120 ml) dry white wine

½ cup (115 g) sugar

3 ounces (75 ml) Marsala wine

Juice of 1 lemon

Place berries in six large glasses. Reserve six berries for garnish. Place remaining ingredients into a metal bowl and place in a hot water bath. Using a fine wire whisk, whip vigorously until frothy and stiff. Be careful that eggs do not coagulate. Serve warm over chilled berries. Garnish with reserved berries.

La Valencia Hotel

Menu

Chilled Avocado Soup
with Red Bell Pepper Sauce & Beluga Caviar

Crabmeat in Puff Pastry with
Beurre Rouge Sauce with Pinot Noir and Chives

Sky Room Salad with Orange Dressing

Kiwi Intermezzo

Assorted Seafood Plate with
Lobster and Spinach Sauces

Apple Turnovers
Raspberry and Mango Coulis

The La Valencia Hotel is a Mediterranean resort built in 1926. Nestled in the cliffs of exclusive La Jolla and overlooking the blue Pacific, the hotel presents its premiere restaurant on the tenth floor, "The Sky Room." Rated the most romantic spot in San Diego, "The Sky Room" features award-winning French cuisine.

Crabmeat in Puff Pastry with Beurre Rouge Sauce with Pinot Noir and Chives

Servings—8
Portion—1 puff pastry with 3 ounces (85 g) crabmeat

- **2–12-inch × 18-inch (30 cm × 45 cm) sheets of puff pastry**
- **1 egg, beaten**

Crabmeat Filling—

- **24 ounces (675 g) crab leg meat, chopped into ½-inch (1.3 cm) pieces**
- **½ cup (120 ml) herb and tomato sauce (see recipe below)**
- **4 tablespoons (60 ml) heavy cream**

Beurre Rouge Sauce with Pinot Noir and Chives—

- **1 cup (250 ml) Pinot Noir**
- **2 tablespoons (30 g) shallots, chopped**
- **1½ tablespoons (15 ml) red wine vinegar**
- **1 lemon, squeezed**
- **1 cup (225 g) butter: ½ unsalted, ½ salted**

Garnish:

- **1 cup (225 g) crab leg meat in strips**
  Chives, chopped

Herb and Tomato Sauce—

- **2 tablespoons (30 g) dried tomatoes**
- **2 whole fresh tomatoes**
- **2 tablespoons (30 ml) white wine**
- **¼ onion, minced**
- **1 bunch fresh basil**
- **2 pinch dry oregano**
- **1 clove garlic, minced**
- **3 tablespoons (45 ml) chicken stock**
  Salt and pepper to taste

Roll out puff pastry to ⅛ inch (0.3 cm) thick, and cut out 8 seashells of dough from cardboard stencil. Brush beaten egg on pastry. Bake at 375°F (190°C) for 15 minutes or until golden brown. Cut out center to make a well for crabmeat in pastry seashell.

Sauté crabmeat with herb and tomato sauce and heavy cream. Stir and simmer 3 minutes until the crabmeat is heated throughout.

Combine all ingredients for herb and tomato sauce, and cook until soft. Put in blender and strain.

Combine all ingredients for Beurre Rouge Sauce, except butter, and reduce until about 2 tablespoons (30 ml) of liquid remains. Add butter over heat stirring continuously. Remove from heat and pour onto serving plate underneath pastry seashell. Fill seashell with crabmeat. Garnish with sauce, strips of crabmeat, and chopped chives.

Assorted Seafood Plate with Lobster and Spinach Sauces

Servings—8
Portion—2½ ounces (72 g) swordfish, 1 ounce (30 g) sole, 1 ounce (30 g) salmon, 4 mussels, 2 crayfish, 1 shrimp

- **1¼ pound (560 g) swordfish, cut into 2½ ounce (75 g) portions**
- **½ pound (225 g) sole, cut into 16 6-inch × ¼-inch (15 cm × 0.6 cm) strips for braid**

½ pound (225 g) salmon, cut into 16 6-inch × ¼-inch (15 cm × 0.6 cm) strips for braid

32 mussels

8 shrimp, peeled, deveined and butterflied

½ cup (120 ml) white wine

Fish stock

2 cloves garlic

2 tablespoons (30 g) shallots

Pinch of oregano

Pinch of fresh parsley

4 tomatoes, seeded, peeled and diced

Butter

1 splash of Pernod

To braid sole and salmon, lay down alternating strips from left to right, sole, salmon, sole, salmon. Take the left sole and cross it over the salmon and the other sole. Take the right salmon and cross it over the sole and salmon. Continue the braid until the plait is completed. Use a sauté pan, and fill the bottom with wine. Sauté fish, covered, for about 3–4 minutes on high heat. Place braid on top of spinach sauce. Boil the crayfish in white wine and fish stock. When cooked, peel shells and use for garnishing.

Bring white wine, fish stock, clove of garlic, shallots, oregano, basil and parsley to boil in large saucepan. Add mussels, cooking until they open. Take mussels out of shells. Simmer mussel stock, add diced tomatoes, and reduce. Fill mussel shells with mixture and place mussel on top. Top with lemon, butter, and chives.

Sauté the shrimp in butter, garlic, fresh herbs, and Pernod for 3–4 minutes. Broil the swordfish on grill and place on top of Lobster Sauce (recipe follows). This assorted seafood entree is accompanied by steamed carrots tied with a strip of chive.

Lobster Sauce for Assorted Seafood Plate—

1 2-pound (900g) live Maine lobster

2 tablespoons (30 ml) olive oil

¼ cup (60 g) shallots

1 carrot, diced

2 celery stalks, diced

½ cup (120 ml) dry vermouth

3 cups (¾ L) fish stock

2 tablespoons (30 g) tomato purée

Salt and pepper to taste

1 teaspoon (5 g) thyme

1½ cups (340 g) butter: 1 cup (225 g) unsalted and ½ cup (115 g) salted

Crack shell into pieces. Place pieces in large sauté pan, sauté in olive oil with shallots, carrot, and celery until mixture turns red. Then reduce with vermouth, fish stock and tomato purée. Season with salt, pepper and thyme. Reduce to ¾ cup (200 ml) of liquid and strain. Add butter to strained sauce, and continue to whip over medium heat. Remove from heat just before all butter is melted and finish whipping. Pour on one half of serving plate.

Beurre Blanc—

1 cup (250 ml) white sauce

¼ cup (60 g) shallots

1½ cups (340 g) butter: ½ salted, ½ unsalted

Reduce white wine and shallots to 2 tablespoons (30 ml) of liquid. Whip in butter and continue stirring the sauce. Remove from heat when butter is melted, and pour in container. Store in warm spot until ready to use.

Spinach Sauce—

1 pound (450 g) fresh spinach

4 tablespoons (60 ml) white wine

1 teaspoon (5 g) fresh basil

Salt and pepper

1¾ cups (400 ml) Beurre Blanc

Sauté fresh spinach with white wine, basil, salt and pepper, until spinach wilts but is still green. Remove from heat and purée in blender. Add puréed spinach to Beurre Blanc and stir. Pour on one half of serving plate.

The STANFORD COURT

Menu

Sweet Red Pepper and Tomato Soup
with Corn and Toasted Cumin

Smoked Salmon and Sour Cream
and Warm Potato Pancake

Grilled Rabbit Loin
with Savory Rabbit and Chicken Paté
and Whole Grain Mustard Sauce

Salad and Mixed Lettuce and Greens
with Grilled Young Artichokes
and Maytag Blue Cheese

Raspberry Crème Brulée

Terra-cotta-hued tiled floors lead to two small private dining rooms and the wine bins where engraved brass plaques carry the names of the individual owners. Specialties include game, Hawaiian fish, Maine lobster, national and international produce. Delectable dessert items complete the dinner menu.

Sweet Red Pepper Soup with Corn and Toasted Cumin

Servings—4–6
Portion—1 cup (¼ L)

1 tablespoon (15 g) butter
3 medium onions, chopped
4 sweet red peppers, chopped
2 cloves garlic, minced
3 tablespoons (45 g) chili powder
4 cups (1 L) vegetable stock
2 tablespoons (30 g) miso
8 tomatoes, peeled, seeded, and chopped
1½ teaspoons (5–10 g) cumin seed
½ cup (120 ml) white wine
Salt to taste
¾ cup (180 g) fresh or frozen corn kernels
Sour cream for garnish
Cilantro leaves for garnish
Vegetable Stock—
3 medium onions, sliced
1 carrot, sliced
1 stalk celery, sliced
1 bay leaf

½ teaspoon (3 g) fresh thyme, chopped
10 parsley stems
8 cups (2 L) water

Melt butter in a heavy-bottomed 4-quart (3¾ L) saucepan. Add onion, and sauté until transparent. Add peppers and continue to sauté over low heat; add garlic and chili powder and continue sautéing until no liquid remains.

To prepare the stock, combine all the ingredients in a large pot, bring to a boil, and simmer for 1½ hours. Strain, discarding the vegetables.

In a separate pan, warm vegetable stock and whisk in miso, dissolving any lumps. Add tomatoes and stock to vegetables and simmer for about 40 minutes.

While soup simmers, toast cumin seeds in a dry frying pan to bring out aroma and flavor. Grind the seeds in a spice grinder, a mortar and pestle, or chop with a knife. Add the seeds, wine, and salt to the soup and purée in a blender

or food processor. Add corn, reheat and serve. Garnish each serving with a dollop of sour cream and a cilantro leaf.

Grilled Rabbit Loin with Savory Rabbit and Chicken Paté and Whole Grain Mustard Sauce

Servings—6
Portion—½ rabbit

Purchase 3 young tender rabbits from your butcher. Have the butcher remove and set aside the legs and loins. The remainder of the carcasses should be chopped into small pieces for the sauce. Marinate the loins and the legs in the following marinade overnight:

½ cup (120 ml) olive oil
2 medium onions, chopped
1 carrot, chopped
1 stalk celery, chopped
1 bunch parsley, chopped
4 cloves garlic, chopped
1 bunch fresh thyme, chopped

Drain off the excess oil and reserve marinade.

Whole Grain Mustard Sauce—

Brown chopped rabbit carcasses in oil, then add onion and carrot from marinade. When brown, add remaining vegetables and herbs from marinade.

Add 4 cups (1 L) white wine to the sautéed carcass meat, vegetable and herbs. Reduce wine until 1 cup of liquid remains; add 6 quarts (6 L) water and slowly bring to a boil. Skim off fat that rises to the surface. Reduce this mixture slowly, skimming occasionally, to 1 cup (250 ml). Strain the liquid. Mix 1 tablespoon (15 g) coarse mustard and 1 tablespoon (15 g) butter into liquid. Season as desired with salt and pepper.

Rabbit and Chicken Paté—

¼ pound (115 g) onion, chopped
1 tablespoon (15 g) butter
1 tablespoon (15 g) garlic, chopped
1 cup (225 g) rabbit livers
1 cup (225 g) chicken livers
⅓ cup (75 g) bacon, chopped
¼ cup (55 g) fresh breadcrumbs, chopped
¾ cup (200 ml) cream
3 eggs
⅛ teaspoon (.5 g) nutmeg
¼ teaspoon (1 g) pepper
¼ teaspoon (1 g) salt
Rabbit foreleg, roasted and diced
¼ bunch parsley, chopped

Soak breadcrumbs in milk. Sauté onions in butter, cool and blend with remainder of ingredients, except rabbit and parsley. Fold in rabbit foreleg meat and parsley. Butter a 4-ounce (120 ml) ramekin per person; fill ⅓ full, and bake in a water bath at 350F (177C) for approximately 20 minutes.

Prepare sauce and rabbit paté. Season rabbit legs and loins with salt and pepper. Grill over hardwood coals or broil in oven. Broil legs about 8–10 minutes under high heat. Broil loins about 3–4 minutes extra. For moist and juicy meat, cook only to medium-rare to medium.

To serve, arrange meat on a platter with the warm paté and pour the sauce over the meat.

Raspberry Crème Brulée

Servings—10
Portion—1 custard

9 large egg yolks
¾ cup (180 g) plus 2 tablespoons (30 g) sugar
4 cups (1 L) whipping cream
2 cups (450 g) raspberries

Preheat oven to 325F (163C). Prepare 10 individual ramekins, ½ cup (120 ml) each.

Lightly beat egg yolks. Add sugar and mix at low speed until smooth. Scrape bowl and beaters. Add cream and mix until all ingredients are combined.

Place 10 raspberries in each ramekin. Pour custard into the ramekins through a fine sieve. Set ramekins in a large, shallow pan, and add ½ inch (13 mm) hot water. Bake until the custard is set but not browned, about 50 minutes. Remove the ramekins from the water bath and cool to room temperature, refrigerate until firm. Do not top with caramel until ready to serve.

To serve, spread 1 tablespoon (15 g) of sugar evenly over top of each custard. Caramelize the sugar by placing under the broiler, watching carefully. Serve at once.

THE CLAREMONT
RESORT AND TENNIS CLUB

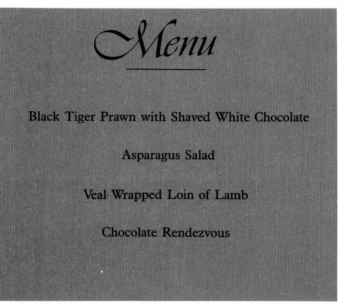

Menu

Black Tiger Prawn with Shaved White Chocolate

Asparagus Salad

Veal Wrapped Loin of Lamb

Chocolate Rendezvous

"The Pavilion Room" is the showcase for The Claremont Resort Hotel. Our breakfast and lunch menus, which rely heavily on traditional items, still provide interest and quality to our guests. The dinner menu has been designed to show our creativity without sacrificing the traditional standard menu items.

Black Tiger Prawn with Shaved White Chocolate

Servings—6
Portion—1 prawn

**6 black tiger prawns, 6–8 ounces
(180–225 g) each**
**¾ cup (180 g) white chocolate,
shaved**

Tangerine Sauce—

1 tablespoon (15 g) clarified butter
½ teaspoon (2.5 g) shallots, minced
1 cup (225 g) tangerine sherbet
½ cup (120 ml) champagne
1 sprig mint leaves

Sauté shallots in clarified butter until tender. Add sherbet, champagne, and mint leaves; reduce until syrupy over medium heat. Reserve.

Champagne Tarragon Sauce—

1 teaspoon (5 g) clarified butter
1 tablespoon (15 g) shallots, minced
½ cup (120 ml) fish stock

¼ cup (60 ml) champagne
**1 tablespoon (15 g) fresh tarragon,
finely chopped**
½ cup (120 ml) heavy cream

Sauté shallots in clarified butter. De-glaze pan with champagne; add tarragon and stock and reduce by ½ over medium heat. Add cream and reduce by ½. Reserve.

Grill tiger prawn over very hot fire, preferably mesquite, or broil. When done, peel and devein. Pool champagne tarragon sauce in center of a 7 inch (18 cm) plate. Form a narrow ring of tangerine sauce in the pool approximately 1 inch (2.5 cm) from the edge of the pool. With a knife, pull the tangerine sauce towards the edge of the pool, making a star pattern. Place the prawn in the center of the plate and sprinkle with white chocolate.

Veal Wrapped Loin of Lamb

Servings—6
Portion—4 slices

Veal Pâté—

**½ pound (225 g) veal striploin or top
round**
5 pistachio nuts, coarsely chopped
2 black truffles, coarsely chopped
1 tablespoon (15 ml) Madeira wine
1 egg white
1 tablespoon (15 ml) heavy cream
**½ teaspoon (2.5 g) fresh rosemary,
minced**
1 teaspoon (5 g) fresh thyme, minced

Run veal through food processor. Add salt, pepper, wine, egg whites and cream. Let run until smooth, *not* coarse. Remove from food processor and add truffles, pistachio nuts, and fresh herbs.

**4 large, fresh spinach leaves, cleaned,
stemmed, and steamed**
1 veal striploin or top round
1 lamb loin, completely trimmed

To wrap loin, slice veal lengthwise into approximately 4 one-ounce (30 g) pieces. Pound each piece into a rectangle approximately 5 inch × 7 inch (13 cm × 18 cm). Spread pâté over veal to ⅛ inch (.3 cm) thickness. Cut lamb loin into half lengthwise and wrap in spinach leaves. Place at one end of the veal and roll. Tie with butcher string and trim the ends. Cut roll into 2½ inch (6 cm) pieces, sear and roast 15 minutes in 350°F (177°C) oven. Serve with Truffle Madeira Sauce.

Chocolate Rendezvous

Servings—10–12
Portion—1 Rendezvous

Chocolate Pâté—
    3 tablespoons (45 g) butter
    6 tablespoons (85 g) chopped chocolate
    1 cup (250 ml) whipping cream
    4 egg whites
    3 tablespoons (45 g) sugar
    12 egg yolks
    ⅓ cup (75 g) sugar

Melt the butter and chopped chocolate together. Whip the whipping cream. Beat egg whites and 3 tablespoons (45 g) sugar to a soft peak. Beat the egg yolks and ⅓ cup (75 g) sugar until thick. Add melted chocolate and butter mixture. Fold in egg whites, then whipping cream.

Filling—
    2 cups (450 g) fresh raspberries
    3 egg whites
    1 tablespoon (15 g) sugar

Whip egg whites and sugar together until stiff peaks form. Wash and dry raspberries, then fold them into meringue.

Glaze—
    1 cup (225 g) chopped chocolate
    ¾ cup (200 ml) whipping cream
    3 tablespoons (45 g) butter

Heat whipping cream and butter together until they boil, then add chocolate. Keep warm.

Pour half the pâté mixture into a loaf

pan with straight sides 8 inches long × 3 inches wide × 3 inches deep or (20 cm × 8 cm × 8 cm). Freeze until mixture is set. When pâté is frozen, prepare filling. Pour a layer of filling over the first layer of pâté in the loaf pan. Freeze until filling is solid. Pour the remaining pâté mixture in and freeze overnight. When solidly frozen, remove loaf from pan and cover with chocolate glaze. Freeze until ready to serve.

Crème Anglaise—
    2 cups (425 ml) half-and-half
    ½ cup (40 g) shredded coconut
    2 tablespoons (30 ml) vanilla extract
    ¼ cup (60 g) sugar
    ⅓ cup (75 ml) Grand Marnier
    3 egg yolks

Heat half-and-half, coconut, and vanilla in a heavy saucepan over medium heat until very hot. *Do not let boil.* Whip egg yolks with sugar. Add hot milk mixture to yolks and heat in a double boiler for 15 minutes until thickened. Add Grand Marnier and strain through a chinoise or very fine strainer. Chill.

Raspberry Sauce—
    2 cups (450 g) fresh raspberries
    1 tablespoon (15 ml) Chambord liqueur

Purée berries and liqueur in blender. Strain to remove the seeds.

When ready to serve, remove chocolate pâté log from freezer. Pool slightly more than 2 tablespoons of crème anglaise on a 7 inch (18 cm) plate. Form 3 concentric rings of raspberry sauce 1 inch (2.5 cm) apart on the crème. With a knife, pull the raspberry sauce towards the edge of the pool, making a star pattern. Place a 1 inch (2.5 cm) slice of pâté in the center of the pool.

Garnish with fresh raspberries.

EL SAN JUAN HOTEL & CASINO

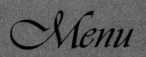

Menu

Salad of Tree Tomatoes
with Papaya and Pepper Chutney

Caribbean Lobster Bisque and Black Beans

Veal Mechada Wrapped in Banana Leaves
with Tamarind Sauce

Broccoli, Apio, Malanga, Yautia

Wild Raspberries with Almond Mousse

El San Juan Hotel & Casino offers elegant surroundings in an atmosphere of warm, efficient, impeccable service. Guests can choose "Le Pavillion" for elegant dining, "Dar Tiffany's" for spectacular beef and seafood, or "La Veranda" for casual 24-hour dining. For authentic Chinese cuisine, it's "Back Street Hong Kong."

Salad of Tree Tomatoes with Papaya and Pepper Chutney

Servings—8
Portion—1 salad

24 tree tomatoes
3 ripe papayas
3 yellow peppers
Jalapenó peppers to taste
1 pinch saffron
Nasturtium flowers
Maché lettuce

Make a small incision in one end of each tree tomato. Place in boiling water for approximately 1 minute. Remove tomatoes and place in cold water, remove skin, but leave stem in place.

Peel and deseed papayas. Chop in small chunks. Deseed and finely slice peppers. Place papayas, peppers, and saffron in one-quart pot and sauté until almost dry. Cool.

Slice tomatoes in thin slices. Place on dinner plate. Garnish with nasturtium and maché. Serve with chutney on a nasturtium leaf on the dinner plate.

Caribbean Lobster Bisque and Black Beans

Servings—8
Portion—½ cup (120 ml)

½ cup (120 ml) white wine
3 cups (¾ L) milk
4-¼ pound (115 g) lobster tails
6 tablespoons (85 g) butter
1 small carrot
1 stalk celery
1 small onion
Pinch paprika
Salt and pepper to taste
3 tablespoons (45 ml) sherry
3 tablespoons (45 ml) cognac
Worcestershire sauce or Tabasco sauce
½ cup (115 g) black beans

Melt the butter in a one-gallon pot. Cut lobster tails into large chunks and sauté in butter. Add the cleaned and cut vegetables and sauté until golden. Add salt, pepper, paprika, sherry cognac, white wine, Worcestershire sauce or Tabasco, then add the milk. Simmer for 10 minutes. Be careful not to boil the bisque after blending. Remove lobster, then simmer for another 20 minutes. Meanwhile, clean the lobster and discard the shells. Cut one half of the meat into chunks, returning the other half to the stock. Boil the black beans in salt water to cover until tender. Remove stock from heat and blend, including vegetables, very fine. Add the lobster meat and boiled black beans.

Garnish with chives and chervil

Veal Mechada Wrapped in Banana Leaves

Servings—8
Portion—1 loin
Mechada—

1 cup (225 g) goose liver
¼ cup (60 g) truffles peelings
½ cup (115 g) chorizos
2 whole carrots
½ stalk celery
1 big yellow onion

Chop all these items in the food processor.

4 pounds (¾ kg) veal loin
4 green banana leaves

Clean the veal loin and make 8 portions of 8 ounces (225 g) each. With a boning knife, make a hole through each portion and stuff with the mechada using a pastry bag.

Blanch the banana leaves over an open flame, then cut them into 6 inch (15 cm) long pieces. Wrap each stuffed loin in a blanched banana leaf. Poach in a pan with white wine. Place in oven at 275°F (140°C). Turn after 20 minutes and bake for another 20 minutes. Slice and serve on dinner plate with carrots, and julienne of potatoes. Serve with Tamarind Sauce.

Tamarind Sauce

Glacé de veau—

Veal bones
5 onions
5 carrots
7 stalks of celery
6 sweet chili peppers
Fresh herbs (chives, basil, chervil)
Red wine
Champignons mushrooms

Brown the bones in the oven in a roasting pan. Place pan on the stove over medium heat. Add ice to cover. Add the rest of the ingredients. Let the ice melt slowly without stirring. Skim scum until it subsides. Let the glacé boil slowly until it clears. Strain through a chinese cap colander with cheesecloth. Put the glacé in a stock pot and let boil until it reduces ¾ of the original amount.

Sauce—

⅔ cup (150 ml) tamarind pulp
⅔ cup (150 ml) glacé de veau
1 cup (250 ml) white wine
1 cup (250 ml) heavy cream

Soften the pulp in the wine and let boil at medium heat. Blend with the glacé and let boil and reduce to a syrupy consistence. Stir in the warm cream.

Wild Raspberries with Almond Mousse

Servings—8
Portion—1 mold

2 cups (425 ml) heavy cream
4 egg whites
1 cup (150 g) blanched almonds
2 tablespoons (30 ml) Amaretto
½ cup (115 g) sugar
1 tablespoon (15 g) gelatin

Grease 8 small dessert molds and sprinkle with sliced almonds. Blend blanched almonds and Amaretto into a paste. Whip heavy cream until stiff. Whip egg whites and sugar until soft peaks form. Fold almond paste and cream together. Fold in the egg whites, then the gelatin. Pour mousse in molds and refrigerate for at least 4 hours. To serve dip molds in warm water and turn onto a dinner plate.

Amaretto Sauce—

4 egg yolks
¼ cup (60 g) sugar
1 cup (250 ml) milk
1 teaspoon (5 g) flour
2 tablespoons (30 ml) Amaretto

Bring milk to a boil. Mix yolks, sugar, and flour. Temper yolk mixture, then add remaining milk. Over medium heat, whisk constantly until thickened. Let cool for 4 hours, then stir in Amaretto.

Garnish mousse with Amaretto sauce and raspberry jam. Garnish with raspberries and raspberry leaves or mint leaves.

SORRENTO HOTEL

Menu

Spinach Soup with Oysters, Pernod
and Crème Fraîche

Sorrento Salad

Sautéed Alaskan Spot Shrimp
in Scallop-Lime Butter with Sweet Cicely

Curried Rice Pilaf and Buttered Steamed Vegetables

Brownie-Meringue Torte
with White Chocolate Buttercream

The Sorrento Hotel, located in downtown Seattle, is renowned for its warmth and elegance in the traditional European style. The cuisine of the bountiful Pacific Northwest is featured in the intimate ambiance of the Sorrento's "Hunt Club Restaurant."

Spinach Soup with Oysters, Pernod, and Crème Fraîche

Servings—6
Portion—¾ cup (180 g)

- **2 tablespoons (30 g) shallots, peeled and chopped**
- **2½ tablespoons (45 g) chopped mushrooms**
- **¼ cup (60 g) butter**
- **1⅓ cups (300 ml) chicken stock**
- **2⅔ cups (¾ L) heavy cream**
- **1 large bunch spinach, cleaned (leaves only)**
- **2 tablespoons (30 ml) Pernod, to taste**
- **18 fresh oysters, shucked and cut into large pieces**

Melt butter, add shallots and mushrooms. Sauté and stir until softened. Add chicken stock. Reduce to about 1 cup (250 ml). Add cream. Reduce for several minutes more until mixture appears slightly thickened.

Purée spinach and soup in food processor or blender. Return to saucepan.

Add Pernod and bring to boil. Add oysters and simmer for 2–3 minutes, or until oysters are lightly cooked. Add salt and pepper to taste and more Pernod, if desired. Before Pernod is added, it should be warmed first in small pan, lit with a match, and the flames allowed to die.

Garnish each serving with a heaping tablespoon (30 g) of fresh crème fraîche.

Sautéed Alaskan Spot Shrimp with Scallop-Lime Butter and Sweet Cicely

Servings—6
Portion—10–12 shrimp

- **¾ pound (340 g) fresh scallops**
- **1 clove garlic, chopped**
- **2 tablespoons (30 ml) peanut oil**
- **2 tablespoons (30 g) plus 1 cup (225 g) softened unsalted butter**
- **1 tablespoon (15 ml) Worcestershire sauce**
- **¼ cup (60 g) sweet cicely, chopped**
- **2 tablespoons (30 g) chives, chopped**

- **60–72 Alaskan spot shrimp, unpeeled, preferably with roe**
- **¼ cup (60 g) butter**
- **¼ cup (60 ml) peanut oil**
- **Juice of 2 limes**
- **½ cup (120 ml) heavy cream**

Clean scallops and toss with chopped garlic.

Heat the peanut oil and 2 tablespoons (30 g) of butter. When almost smoking, add the scallops and sear quickly. Remove from pan immediately when lightly browned but still not cooked through. Drain in colander over a bowl. Allow to cool.

In a food processor, combine scallops with remaining butter, Worcestershire sauce, sweet cicely, and chives. Process until smooth. Reserve mixture.

Sauté half the spot prawns in half the butter and half the peanut oil. Repeat with the remaining prawns. Remove prawns from skillet and keep warm.

Add lime juice to skillet over low heat and stir to deglaze. Transfer liquid to a small saucepan, along with any juices which may have collected from the scallops. Bring to a boil. Add heavy cream and reduce until thickened. Over low heat, gradually whisk in scallop-butter mixture until smooth.

To serve, pour sauce over half of plate. Arrange shrimp over sauced portion, garnish with additional sprigs of sweet cicely. Accompany with curried rice pilaf and vegetables.

Brownie-Meringue Torte with White Chocolate Buttercream

Servings—12
Portion—¹⁄₁₂ of one 9 inch (23 cm) cake

Brownie Layers—

> **5 eggs**
> **2 cups (450 g) sugar**
> **½ cup (115 g) unsalted butter**
> **½ cup (115 g) semi-sweet chocolate**
> **1 cup (225 g) all-purpose flour, sifted**
> **1 cup (150 g) almonds, blanched and chopped**

Combine eggs and sugar in small saucepan. Stir constantly over low heat until warm to the touch. Transfer mixture to bowl of electric mixer. Beat on high speed for 10 minutes or until thick and light.

In a double boiler, melt chocolate and butter, stirring occasionally until smooth. Allow to cool slightly. Fold chocolate, flour, and almonds into egg and sugar mixture. Pour batter into a greased and floured 9 inch (23 cm) springform pan. Bake at 350°F (180°C) for 30 minutes. Allow to cool in the pan.

Cocoa Meringue Layer—

> **4 egg whites, room temperature**
> **1¼ cups (225 g) powdered sugar, sifted**
> **3 tablespoons (45 g) unsweetened cocoa, sifted**

In an electric mixer, beat egg whites until light and foamy (soft peaks that fall over at the tip when the beater is lifted). Gradually add the powdered sugar and beat until stiff but not dry (peaks form when beater is lifted). Fold in cocoa powder.

Transfer meringue to a pastry bag fitted with a star tip. Line a sheet pan with parchment paper. Pipe an 8 inch (20 cm) round of meringue onto the paper (about ¼ inch (7 cm) thick). Any remaining meringue can be used to make decorations. Bake at 225°F (110°C) for 2½ hours, or until dry and crisp.

White Chocolate Buttercream—

> **1½ cups (340 g) sugar**
> **½ cup (120 ml) water**
> **2 tablespoons (30 g) fresh mint**
> **Pinch of cream of tartar**
> **8 egg yolks**
> **3 cups (675 g) softened, unsalted butter**
> **1 cup (225 g) white chocolate, melted and cooled**

Combine sugar, water, and mint in a small saucepan. Bring to a boil, stirring to dissolve. Cover pan for one minute. Uncover pan and continue to boil without stirring until temperature reaches 246°F (119°C).

Beat egg yolks in bowl with an electric mixer until thick and light. Gradually pour sugar-water syrup into yolks, beating constantly. Continue to beat until cooled. Add butter, a pinch at a time, beating until smooth between additions. Beat in melted chocolate.

Unmold brownie cake from pan and cut horizontally into two layers. Spread buttercream over cut surface of each. Sandwich meringue layer between the two brownie layers, buttercream side in. Spread the top and sides of the cake with the remaining buttercream. Garnish with meringue decorations.

HOTEL LOTTE

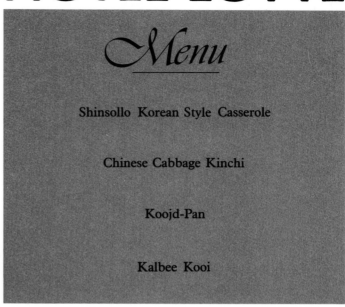

Menu

Shinsollo Korean Style Casserole

Chinese Cabbage Kinchi

Koojd-Pan

Kalbee Kooi

Hotel Lotte is a living, moving, striking collage of Western and Eastern cultures that join together to provide a unique atmosphere of warmth and hospitality. Dining in royal opulence on an assortment of traditionally prepared Korean delicacies, you can sit back and enjoy an authentic performance of Korean traditional dance.

Shinsollo Korean Style Casserole

Servings—2
Portion—½ casserole

Pan-Fried Fillet of Halibut Patties—
- ¼ **pound (115 g) halibut fillet**
- ½ **teaspoon (2½ g) salt**
- 1 **tablespoon (15 ml) salad oil**
- 2 **tablespoons (30 g) flour**
- 2 **eggs**
- **Dash of pepper**

Slice the halibut fillet and season with pepper and salt. Roll the slices in egg and sauté set aside.

Pan-Fried Parsley Patties—
- 1 **bunch parsley**
- ⅓ **teaspoon (1½ g) salt**
- 1 **tablespoon (15 ml) salad oil**
- 2 **tablespoons (30 g) flour**
- 2 **eggs**

Clean the parsley and cut into 6 inch (15 cm) slices. Roll parsley in egg, flour, and salt. Sauté the slices in a pan. Set aside.

Pan-Fried Beef Patties—
- ¼ **pound (115 g) ground beef**
- ⅓ **teaspoon (1½ g) salt**
- 2 **teaspoons (10 g) grated garlic**
- 1 **tablespoon (15 ml) salad oil**
- 2 **tablespoons (30 g) flour**
- 2 **eggs**
- ½ **teaspoon (2½ g) minced onion**
- **Dash of pepper**

Mix the ground beef with other ingredients. Form into patties ⅛ inch (3 mm) thin. Sauté and set aside.

Pan-Fried Tripe Patties—
- ¼ **cup (60 g) tripe**
- 1 **tablespoon (15 g) salt**
- **Dash of pepper**
- 2 **tablespoons (30 g) flour**
- 5 **eggs**

Clean the tripe with salt. Mix other ingredients with the tripe and press mixture into patties. Sauté, and set aside.

Pan-Fried Shrimp Patties—
- ¼ **pound (115 g) shrimp**
- ½ **teaspoon (2½ g) salt**
- ½ **teaspoon (2½ g) grated garlic**
- ½ **teaspoon (2½ ml) salad oil**
- 1 **tablespoon (15 g) flour**
- 5 **eggs**
- ½ **teaspoon (2½ g) minced onion**
- **Dash of pepper**

Shell and devein the shrimp. Mince shrimp and season with the condiments. Form into patties ⅛ inch (3 mm) thin. Sauté and set aside.

Pan-Fried Egg Patties—
- 10 **eggs, separated**
- ½ **teaspoon (2½ g) cornstarch**
- 1 **teaspoon (5 g) salt**

Season separated eggs with salt and cornstarch, adding cornstarch to yolk only. Sauté yolks and whites separately, pressing to ⅛ inch (3 mm) thin. Set aside.

Pan-Fried Mushrooms, Carrots and Red Peppers—
- 10 **mushrooms**
- ½ **pound (225 g) carrots**
- 1 **red pepper**

1 green pepper
Salt
Pepper

Soak and clean the mushrooms in fresh water. Season with pepper and salt. Sauté and set aside.

Clean and slice the carrot into ⅛ inch × 1½ inch × 2 inch (3 mm × 4 cm × 5 cm) pieces. Boil the slices in salted water. Set aside.

Seed the peppers and boil briefly in salted water. Set aside.

Sautéed Meat Ball—

¼ cup (60 g) ground beef
½ teaspoon (2½ g) salt
½ teaspoon (2½ g) grated garlic
1 tablespoon (15 ml) salad oil
1 tablespoon (15 g) flour
2 eggs
½ teaspoon (2½ g) minced onion

Combine all ingredients, form into one seasoned meatball. Roll in egg, and sauté. Set aside.

Chestnuts, Jujube, Ginko Nuts and Pine Nuts—

5 chestnuts
5 jujubes
25 ginko nuts
2 tablespoons (30 g) pine nuts
Salt

Cut the chestnuts in half and boil in water. Set aside.

Peel jujubes, cut into halves, and seed. Set aside.

Fry the ginko nut with salt in a pan and peel. Set aside.

Peel and clean the pine nuts. Set aside.

Beef and Beetroot—

1 pound (450 g) beef
2 tablespoons (30 g) salt
Dash of pepper
¾ pound (340 g) beetroot
1 teaspoon (5 g) grated garlic

Season the beef, boil and slice into ¹⁄₁₆ inch × ⅜ inch × 1⅛ inch (2 mm × 9 mm × 3 cm) cuts.

Season the beetroot, boil and slice into ¼ inch × 2 inch × 1⅛ inch (6 mm × 5 cm × 3 cm) cuts. Set aside.

The boiling water can be used for the gravy sauce below.

Gravy Sauce—

10 cups (2½ L) prepared gravy
1 teaspoon (5 g) salt
Dash of pepper
3 tablespoons (45 ml) soy sauce
2 tablespoons (30 g) garlic

Season the gravy with other ingredients.

Final Assembly—

In the bottom of a large casserole dish, place beef and beetroot. Slice all pan-fried patties, mushrooms, carrots, and peppers into 1½ inch × 1 inch (4 cm × 2½ cm) pieces and place in the casserole. Place sautéed meatball and all nuts into casserole on top of the patties. Pour gravy sauce over the casserole. Bring the dish to a boil.

Kalbee Kooi

Servings—5
Portion—2 ribs

10 beef ribs
½ cup (120 ml) soy sauce
1 teaspoon (5 g) pepper
1 pear
3 tablespoons (45 g) grated garlic
3 tablespoons (45 ml) refined rice liquor
¼ cup (60 g) sugar
2 tablespoons (30 ml) millet jelly
2 cups (½ L) water
2 tablespoons (30 g) minced onion
3 tablespoons (45 ml) sesame oil
2 tablespoons each (30 g) salt and sesame seed

Slice the ribs into 2 inch (5 cm) long cuts and wash. Move the feather-like beef portion to the edges of ribs. Mix soy sauce, sugar, millet jelly, and water and boil for 10 minutes. Grate pear and mix all condiments. Soak beef in the seasoned mixture. Charcoal-broil the marinated beef ribs.

Goodwood Park Hotel

Menu

Hot & Sour Sichuan Soup

Chicken with Dried Red Chili

Sautéed Shrimp with Hot Sauce

Crabmeat with Taiwanese Greens

Sichuan Pancake

The timeless elegance and charm of the nostalgic yesteryear are beautifully preserved in one of Singapore's truly grand old hotels, the Goodwood Park. Enjoy superb Sichuan dishes at the "Min Jiang Sichuan Restaurant" in a setting of regal splendor reminiscent of Imperial China, complemented by attentive service.

Hot and Sour Sichuan Soup

Servings—6–8
Portion—1 Chinese soup bowl

- 1 4 inch × 4 inch (10 cm × 10 cm) cake of white bean curd, cut into long strips
- ⅓ cup (75 g) shredded pork, mixed with:
    - ½ teaspoon (2.5 ml) soy sauce, cornstarch and ½ teaspoon (2.5 g) sugar
- ½ cup (115 g) canned bamboo shoots
- ¼ cup (60 g) fresh shrimp
- 2 tablespoons (30 g) chopped spring onion
- 1 tablespoon (15 g) cornstarch, mixed with ¼ cup (60 ml) cold water
- ⅔ tablespoon (10 g) shredded black mushrooms (soaked in water until it softens and opens up)
- 1 egg, beaten
- 5 cups (1¼ L) meat stock (beef, chicken or pork)
- 1 tablespoon (15 ml) soy sauce
- 1 teaspoon (5 g) salt
- 2 tablespoons (30 ml) black vinegar
- ½ teaspoon (2.5 g) white pepper
- ¼ teaspoon (1 g) sugar

Heat oil in frying pan. Fry shredded bamboo shoot and pork. Pour in meat stock. Bring to boil. Add bean curd, black mushrooms, shrimp, soy sauce and salt. Cover and boil for 2–3 minutes. Sprinkle with vinegar and pepper. Stir in cornstarch solution to thicken. Add 1 tablespoon (15 ml) oil. Slowly pour in beaten egg and stir well. Serve in casserole and garnish with chopped spring onions.

Chicken with Dried Red Chili

Servings—6–8
Portion—3–4 pieces

- 1 2 pound (900 g) chicken or 1 pound (450 g) chicken breast
- 8 pieces dried red chili, (each piece about 3 inches (8 cm) long)
- 1 teaspoon (5 g) chopped ginger
- 1½ tablespoons (20 g) cornstarch
- 1½ tablespoons (20 ml) cold water
- 1 tablespoon (15 ml) soy sauce
- 5 cups (1¼ L) oil

Sauce—

- 2 tablespoons (30 ml) soy sauce
- 1 tablespoon (15 ml) wine
- 1 tablespoon (15 g) sugar
- 1 teaspoon (5 g) cornstarch
- ½ teaspoon (2.5 g) salt
- 1 teaspoon (5 ml) sesame oil

Remove all bones from chicken, cut into 1 inch (2.5 cm) cubes, add soy sauce and cornstarch, stir evenly in one direction, and marinate for one-half hour. Wipe dried red chili clean, remove tips and seeds, and cut into 1 inch (2.5 cm) lengths. Fry chicken in boiling oil for half a minute. Remove chicken and drain off oil from frying pan. Heat 2 tablespoons (30 ml) oil and fry red chili until it turns black. Add ginger and chicken, stirring quickly. Add the seasoning sauce, stirring in cornstarch thoroughly until mixture thickens. Serve on oval platter.

Sautéed Shrimp with Hot Sauce

Servings—6–8
Portion—2–3 shrimp

1 pound (450 g) fresh shrimp, shelled and deveined

2 tablespoons (30 g) chopped spring onion

1 tablespoon (15 g) chopped ginger

4 cups (1 L) vegetable oil

2 tablespoons (30 ml) tomato sauce

1 tablespoon (15 g) minced fresh red chili

½ teaspoon (2.5 g) salt

½ teaspoon (2.5 g) sugar

3 tablespoons (45 ml) soup stock

2 tablespoons (30 g) cornstarch, diluted in 1½ tablespoons (20 ml) cold water)

1 teaspoon (5 ml) sesame oil

Marinade—

1 egg white

1 teaspoon (5 g) salt

1 teaspoon (5 ml) Chinese rice wine

1½ tablespoons (20 g) cornstarch

Marinate shrimp. Drain and deep-fry in oil. When the shrimp turn white, remove and drain oil from pan. Return 2 tablespoons (30 ml) oil to pan and stir-fry chopped spring onion and ginger. Add tomato sauce and chili, stirring quickly. Add soup stock, salt, and sugar. Cook for a few seconds and add cornstarch solution, stirring thoroughly. Add sesame oil and serve.

Sichuan Pancake

Servings—6–8
Portion—1–2 pieces

2 eggs

2¼ cups (300 g) wheat flour

1¾ cups (400 ml) cold water

⅓ cup (75 g) red bean paste or ground dates

6 cups (1½ L) oil

Beat eggs in a bowl, add flour and cold water. Mix well to form a batter. Heat a flat frying pan, rub with a little oil, and pour in two thirds of batter. Tilt the frying pan quickly to let the batter spread evenly to form a 12 inch (30 cm) diameter pancake. Cook over low heat for a few seconds and remove from pan. *Do not flip over.* Place the pancake on a board or large round platter, uncooked side up and add red bean paste or ground dates in the center. Spread paste out to measure approximately 10 inches (25 cm) long and 5 inches (13 cm) wide. Fold bottom edge up first, then fold the left and right sides toward the center to form an envelope. Brush top flap of pancake with remaining batter and fold down to seal. Heat oil until very hot. Deep-fry pancake for about 2 minutes until golden and crispy. Remove from oil and cut in half lengthwise. Cut each length into 6 equal pieces, resulting in a total of 12 pieces. Serve hot. .

SONOMA MISSION INN & SPA

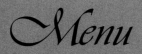

Menu

Grilled Eggplant and Goat Cheese Ravioli

Grilled Jumbo Sea Scallops

Mesquite Grilled Veal Chop

Sonoma Raspberry Tart

The Sonoma Mission Inn & Spa is a wine country landmark 40 miles north of San Francisco, offering 170 luxury guest rooms and a world-class European-style spa. It enjoys a reputation as the quintessential resort, renowned for superb dining at "The Grille," serving fresh, seasonal Wine Country cuisine.

Mesquite Grilled Veal Chop

Servings—6
Portion—1 chop

6 one-inch-thick ¾ pound (340 g) veal chops
6 slices yellow tomato
6 slices smoked veal breast
6 thin slices fontina cheese
12 basil leaves

Lay the veal chops on sides and cut parallel to the bones to create pockets. To make the stuffing: place the cheese slices in a row next to one another on the work surface. On top of each slice of cheese, layer one slice of smoked veal breast, one slice of tomato and two basil leaves. Fold the cheese over the tomato. Insert each cheese-stack stuffing into the veal chop pocket. Close the outside of each pocket with two toothpicks.

Place the chops in the center of a hot grill and sear them (using oak wood). When chops are seared, move them to the side of the grill and cook at me-

dium temperature to finish the cooking process (eight to ten minutes). The stuffing will become warm and melt the cheese. Be careful not to overcook the stuffed chops as the meat will dry out.

Grilled Eggplant and Goat Cheese Ravioli

Servings—6
Portion—1 plate

1 medium-sized eggplant
6 tablespoons (85 g) goat cheese
⅛ teaspoon (1 g) garlic
Oregano, salt and pepper to taste
2 pounds (900 g) pasta sheets
Sauce—
1 pound (450 g) zucchini
½ cup (120 ml) white wine
1 tablespoon (15 g) shallots
¾ cup (200 ml) cream
¼ cup (60 ml) chicken stock
Salt and pepper, to taste
2 tablespoons (30 g) peppers, roasted and finely diced

Roast and peel the eggplant. Allow to cool, then combine with goat cheese. Add garlic, oregano, salt, and pepper. Lay out pasta sheets, spread with mixture. Cut into round or square ravioli shapes.

Cook sauce ingredients until tender. Purée in blender until smooth, season to taste, and add peppers.

Cook raviolis in boiling salted water until done. Spread sauce on serving plates and place ravioli on top.

Grilled Jumbo Sea Scallops

Servings—6
Portion—3 scallops

1⅛ pounds (500 g) jumbo sea scallops
6 tablespoons (85 g) American sturgeon caviar
Assorted Sonoma greens (Baby red oak, frisée, basil)
Salt and pepper to taste
Vinaigrette—
½ cup (120 ml) California extra virgin olive oil

2 tablespoons (30 ml) lime juice,
   freshly squeezed

¼ cup (60 ml) champagne

1 teaspoon (5 g) shallots, finely diced

Salt and pepper to taste

Slice scallops into three pieces, place on grill and cook until tender. Season to taste. Wash and clean salad greens, arrange on serving plate. Place grilled scallops on top, put caviar in the center and spoon vinaigrette on scallops.

Sonoma Raspberry Tart

Servings—6
Portion—1 slice

Crust—

4 cups (900 g) flour

4 teaspoons (20 g) sugar

1 teaspoon (5 g) salt

1 teaspoon (5 g) grated lemon peel

2 cups (450 g) sweet butter, room
   temperature

4 teaspoons (20 ml) water, room
   temperature

2 teaspoons (10 ml) vanilla extract

Combine all ingredients. Chill dough at least one-half hour and roll it out to fit a shallow 10-inch (25 cm) spring form pan. Pre-bake at 325°F (160°C) eight-ten minutes. Remove from oven. Set aside.

Filling—

3 eggs

½ cup (115 g) granulated sugar

½ teaspoon (2.5 ml) vanilla extract

1 teaspoon (5 ml) raspberry
   schnapps

⅔ cup (140 g) sifted all-purpose flour

4 teaspoons (20 g) unsalted butter,
   melted and cooled

¾ cup (180 g) raspberry or strawberry jam

1¼ cups (285 g) marzipan

Confectioner's sugar

1½ cups (340 g) fresh raspberries

Prepare tart filling while crust is baking. Beat eggs with sugar, vanilla and raspberry schnapps until pale and yellow. Gently fold egg mixture, flour and butter together, adding one-third of each in turn. Set batter aside.

Roll the marzipan into a thin 10 inch (25 cm) round. Dust with confectioner's sugar to keep the marzipan from sticking.

Spread raspberry jam on the partially baked crust. Crust may be warm, but do not remove from pan. Place thinly-rolled marzipan over jam. Add fresh raspberries on top of the marzipan. Dust with confectioner's sugar. Pour tart filling over the berries and bake 15–18 minutes at 350°F (177°C). Remove from oven.

Topping—

1 cup (225 g) fresh raspberries or
   strawberries

½ cup (115 g) apricot jam

1 tablespoon (15 ml) water

While tart bakes, heat the apricot jam and water until the jam is melted. Remove the tart from the oven and dust with confectioner's sugar. Arrange two circular rows of raspberries around the edge. While the tart is still warm, carefully brush the raspberries with the melted jam to give them a special shine. If sauce runs onto the sugar, sprinkle a little extra sugar on the spots to restore the dusted look. Purée the remaining raspberries. Pour the purée on dessert plate and place slice of tart on the purée.

While the tart is still warm, add topping or dust the tart with confectioner's sugar and serve topped with fresh berries.

IMPERIAL HOTEL

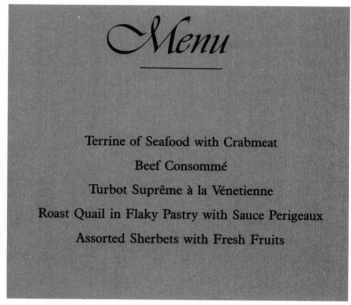

Menu

Terrine of Seafood with Crabmeat

Beef Consommé

Turbot Suprême à la Vénetienne

Roast Quail in Flaky Pastry with Sauce Perigeaux

Assorted Sherbets with Fresh Fruits

Inspired by the magnificent palace of Fontainebleau and the unsurpassed excellence of classical French haute cuisine, the Imperial's restaurant evokes a more gracious era of fine dining. We invite you to experience one of Tokyo's truly great epicurean delights.

Terrine of Seafood with Crabmeat

Servings—15
Portion—1 slice

½ pound (225 g) turbot
¾ cup (180 g) lobster tail
2 egg whites, divided into thirds
2 cups (½ L) heavy cream
3 tablespoons (45 g) pastry dough
Dash Pérnod
⅔ cup (140 g) scallops
Saffron, dissolved in water
Canned red pimiento
½ pound (225 g) crabmeat (from legs)

Blend turbot and lobster in blender, straining excess liquid. Place mixture in a pan on a bowl of ice cubes to chill. Add dash of salt and stir vigorously until well blended. Mixture should become opaque. Add egg whites in three separate blendings. Blend in the pastry dough. Add cream slowly while mixing. Add a dash of Pérnod. Divide mixture into three portions.

Shred scallops. Place half the portion into the three lobster and turbot mixtures equally. Add saffron to each portion. Put remainder of scallops into the pimiento and mix. Shred the crabmeat.

Prepare a terrine casserole pan 4 inch × 10½ inch, 3 inches deep (11 cm × 27 cm, 8 cm deep) buttering sides and bottom. Place scallop/pimiento mixture, shredded crabmeat, and saffron/scallop mixture into a piping bag. Squeeze into the casserole. Put casserole into a baking pan containing hot water to cover bottom of the pan. A towel should be put into the pan with the water. Bake in preheated oven at 320°F (160°C) for 40–45 minutes. Terrine is done when a skewer inserted into the casserole comes out hot. Remove terrine and slice in 15 slices.

Prepare two sauces for the terrine. Mix together 4 parts whipped cream and 6 parts mayonnaise; add a dash of lemon juice for the first sauce. Prepare a firm chilled, jellied consommé for the second sauce.

To serve, place terrine slice on center of serving plate. Place one sauce on one side of the plate, and place the second sauce on the other side.

Turbot Supreme à la Vénetienne

Servings—5
Portion—2½ ounces (70 g) turbot

6 tablespoons (85 g) chopped onions
6 tablespoons (85 g) chopped shallots
6 tablespoons (85 g) butter
4 tablespoons (60 ml) wine vinegar
2½ cups (550 ml) heavy cream
Several spinach leaves
Pinch of tarragon, chives, and parsley
Salt and pepper
5 2½ ounce (70 g) portions turbot
1½ cups (350 ml) white cooking wine

Sauté onions and shallots lightly in butter, then add wine vinegar. Stew until almost all liquid is evaporated. Add cream. After a few seconds, remove from heat and strain.

Blend spinach in blender and strain. Pour into a bowl set over simmering hot water. When liquid separates, discard liquid, leaving spinach paste. Mix 6 tablespoons (85 g) of butter with ¼ cup (60 g) of the spinach paste. Slowly blend spinach mixture into cream mixture over low heat. Add tarragon, chives, and chopped parsley.

Salt and pepper turbot and sprinkle a bit of white cooking wine on the fish. Wrap in plastic wrap and steam in steamer for 5 minutes. To serve, cover the turbot with spinach sauce. Garnish with boiled turnip cut into the shape of a flower, a bit of caviar and a fried basil sprout.

Roast Quail in Flaky Pastry with Sauce Perigeaux

Servings—2
Portion—1 quail

2 full-size quails, approximately 3½ ounces (100 g) each
2 tablespoons (30 g) fresh foie gras
Salt and pepper

Clean quail, cut open from back side, remove all bones except leg bones. Stuff breasts with fresh foie gras, then truss closed. Season with salt and pepper and bake at 480°F (250°C) until lightly browned. Remove from oven and cool, cover with pastry. Baste with egg yolk, then return to oven and bake at 450°F (200°C) for 15 minutes.

Pastry—

2½ cups (500 g) butter
5 cups (1 kg) flour
4 cups (1 L) ice water
2 tablespoons (30 g) salt
1⅛ cups (250 g) butter
¼ cup (60 g) flour

Mix together butter, flour, water, and salt. Roll out dough and fold into layers several times, re-rolling each time. Add the additional butter and flour, then roll out again until smooth.

Sauce Perigeaux—

12 cups (2¾ L) fond de veau
16½ cups (4 L) fond de veau lié

2¼ pounds (1¼ kg) sliced mushrooms
1¼ cups (285 g) truffles
1¼ cups (285 g) sliced scallions
2½ cups (550 ml) Madeira
1 tablespoon (15 ml) truffle juice
Salt and spices to taste

Make demiglaze sauce from the fond de veau and fond de veau lié. Add the mushrooms, scallions, truffles, Madeira, and truffle juice. Add salt and spices to taste and heat.

Serve quail with Sauce Perigeaux on the side, accompanied with sautéed string beans, sautéed mushrooms with scallions, or mousse of mushrooms.

PARK PLAZA HOTEL

Menu

Iced Scampi Soup with Mango Mousse

Carousel of Salmon with Red and Black Caviar Sauce

Calf's Liver with Sherry Vinegar and Cassis

Fresh Peaches Marinated with Grand Marnier Topped with Raspberry Coulis

The Park Plaza is a Toronto landmark, sitting on the doorstep of the fashionable Yorkville district, melding tradition with a feeling of contemporary European elegance. The "Prince Arthur Dining Room" has the charm of a Louis XV salon and classic cuisine enhanced by Cuisine Courante.

Iced Scampi Soup with Mango Mousse

Servings—6
Portion—½ cup (120 ml)

Soup—
  3 tomatoes
  2 red peppers
  1 clove of garlic
  ½ cucumber
  ½ cup (120 ml) white wine
  ½ cup (120 ml) white vinegar
  1 cup (250 ml) olive oil
  Pinch of salt and pepper
  2 slices white bread

Sauté vegetables, and simmer with remainder of ingredients until bread dissolves into mixture.

Mango Mousse—
  1 mango
  1 tablespoon (15 g) gelatin
  ½ cup (125 ml) whipped cream

Purée mango and fold into whipped cream stiffened with gelatin.

Garnish—
  6 scampi
  1 zucchini
  ½ red pepper

Garnish each serving with one scampi, slices of zucchini and red pepper.

Carousel of Salmon with Red and Black Caviar Sauce

Servings—6
Portion—3 ounces (85 g)

  1¼ pounds (560 g) salmon fillets, cut into strips
  1 pound (450 g) spinach
  1 cup (¼ L) white wine sauce
  ¼ cup (60 g) salmon caviar
  2 tablespoons (30 g) sturgeon (black) caviar

Clean and wash spinach, then sauté until leaves wilt. Cool. Place some spinach against one side of a salmon strip. Start from one end of the strip and roll salmon into a tight circle. Wrap a piece of foil around the carousel rolled strip to keep tight and in place. After rolling all the salmon strips wrap the whole carousel in plastic wrap. (This can be done in advance). Steam the salmon, using either a double boiler or vegetable basket. Remove when cooked and season. Heat white wine sauce, check seasoning, remembering that caviar is salty. Mix caviars into sauce then spread over salmon carousel, serve immediately.

White Wine Sauce—
  1⅓ cups (300 ml) fish stock
  ½ cup (120 ml) white wine
  2 cups (½ L) 35% cream
  4 mushrooms, sliced
  1 shallot, sliced
  Parsley and thyme to taste

Sauté diced shallot, deglaze with white wine. Reduce by one-half. Add fish stock, sliced mushrooms, parsley and thyme. Reduce to glaze. Add cream. Simmer until the consistency desired. Strain and keep warm.

Fresh Peaches Marinated with Grand Marnier—Topped with Raspberry Coulis

Servings—6
Portion—1 glass

> 6 ripe peaches, quartered
> ½ cup (120 ml) Grand Marnier
> ½ cup (115 g) raspberries
> ¼ cup (60 ml) Sauternes
> 6 tablespoons (85 g) sugar
> ½ bunch mint sprigs

Blanch whole peaches in boiling water until skin peels easily. Immerse in ice water to stop further cooking. Quarter peaches. Marinate peaches for two hours in Grand Marnier. Blend raspberries, Sauternes and sugar in a mixer until smooth.

Place peaches in a chilled glass and top with raspberry coulis. Garnish with mint sprig.

Calf's Liver with Sherry Vinegar and Cassis

Servings—6
Portion—1 ounce (30 g)

> ¾ cup (180 g) Provimi calf's liver, sliced
> 1 shallot
> ⅓ cup (75 ml) Cassis
> ⅓ cup (75 ml) sherry vinegar
> ½ cup (12 ml) veal stock
> ⅓ cup (75 g) butter
> 1 cup (225 g) flour

Finely dice the shallot. Sweat the shallot in 2 tablespoons (30 g) butter. When transparent, add Cassis and sherry vinegar and reduce by half. Add veal stock and reduce by one third. Remove sauce from heat and mount with 3 tablespoons (45 g) butter. Add another drop of Cassis for flavor. Season and keep warm.

Salt and pepper liver, then coat with flour, shaking off all excess. Sauté liver over medium high heat, about one minute on each side. Place on plate and then place sauce on top of liver.

Toronto
PRINCE HOTEL

Menu

Marinated Salmon with Mustard Sauce

Fiddlehead Soup

MacIntosh Apple Refreshment

Mignons of Veal on Spinach with Crayfish

Oka Cheese with Seasonal Leaves

Gratinated Peaches with Grand Marnier

The Toronto Prince Hotel offers you the best of both worlds: the luxury and convenience of a city, the parkland setting and recreational facilities of a true holiday resort. Dining is an adventure in choice, offering international cuisine, entertainment and dinner dancing in "Le Continental."

Marinated Salmon with Mustard Sauce

Servings—10
Portion—4 slices (100 g)

> **1 fillet from a 6–7 pound (2¾ kg–3¼ kg) fresh salmon, with skin**
>
> **1 bunch fresh dill**
>
> **¼ cup (60 g) coarse salt**
>
> **¼ cup (60 g) brown sugar**
>
> **2 tablespoons (30 g) white and black peppercorns, crushed**
>
> **4 cups (1 L) 35% cream**
>
> **2 tablespoons (30 g) English mustard**
>
> **2 tablespoons (30 g) Dijon mustard**
>
> **Salt and pepper to taste**
>
> **1 tablespoon (15 g) mustard seeds**

Place the salmon fillet, skin side down, in a long dish. Sprinkle with the salt, sugar, and crushed peppercorns. Cover with the dill and cover with plastic wrap. Refrigerate for 2–3 days. Clean the fillet with the back of a knife and slice very thinly at an angle.

Heat and reduce the cream to one-third and allow to cool. Mix the two mustards, and add some salt and ground black pepper to cream. Add mustard seeds.

Place salad leaves on plate, lay the salmon slices over the leaves. Serve mustard sauce on fillets or separately.

Garnish with Boston lettuce leaves, radicchio salad leaves, and lemon wedges.

Fiddlehead Soup

Servings—10
Portion—¾ cup (200 ml)

> **6 tablespoons (85 g) butter**
>
> **¾ cup (180 g) chopped onions**
>
> **1 pound (450 g) frozen fiddleheads**
>
> **1 cup (225 g) sliced raw potato**
>
> **6 cups (1½ L) chicken stock**
>
> **1 pinch thyme**
>
> **1 pinch white pepper**
>
> **Salt**
>
> **2 cups (425 ml) 35% cream**

Sauté onions in butter, add fiddleheads (keeping some for garnish) and spices and simmer over low heat for a few minutes. Add potato and chicken stock and simmer for approximately ½ hour. Blend to a smooth mixture. Heat again and add cream.

Garnish with additional fiddleheads and bread croutons.

MacIntosh Apple Refreshment

Servings—10
Portion—1 apple

> **10 MacIntosh apples**
>
> **½ cup (125 g) sugar (or to taste)**
>
> **Juice of 2 lemons**
>
> **2 cups (425 ml) 35% cream**

Grate the unpeeled apples with a medium grater. Mix in sugar to taste, lemon juice, and cream. Keep mixture in freezer for 1–2 hours.

Garnish with red cherry or strawberry.

Mignons of Veal on Spinach with Crayfish

Servings—4
Portion—3 mignons

- ¾ **pound (340 g) veal tenderloin, cut into 12 slices**
- **32 crayfish**
- **2 cups (425 ml) fish stock**
- **¼ cup (60 ml) white wine**
- **2 cups (425 ml) 35% cream**
- **¼ cup (60 g) butter**
- **½ cup (115 g) potatoes**
- **1 teaspoon (5 g) wild rice**
- **1 egg yolk**
- **2 tomatoes**
- **1 cup (225 g) fresh spinach leaves**
- **Black trumpet mushrooms**
- **Shallots**
- **Chervil**
- **Saffron**
- **Black pepper**
- **Salt**

Boil the crayfish, remove tails and peel. Reduce fish stock to half, add ¾ of the cream, and simmer slowly for about ½ hour. Reduce sauce a little, add white wine, saffron, salt and pepper to taste. Add remainder of cream.

Boil the potatoes and blend them. Cook the wild rice about 45 minutes. Add rice to potatoes along with egg yolk and salt. Mix together well. With two spoons form quenelles and poach them in either salt water or chicken stock.

Blanch the spinach and allow to cool. Sauté in butter with some shallots. Fillet the 2 tomatoes and quickly sauté them with a little chopped chervil and the black trumpet mushrooms.

Season veal mignons, with salt and pepper and sauté.

Put a ladle of sauce on serving plate and put some spinach in the center. Place 3 veal mignons on top and garnish with the sautéed tomatoes, chervil, and mushrooms. Place 4 wild rice quenelles on the plate and arrange the preheated crayfish tails, each garnished with a chervil leaf.

Gratinated Peaches with Grand Marnier

Servings—10
Portion—2 peach halves

- **Zest of 2 oranges**
- **Zest of 2 lemons**
- **Juice of 2 oranges**
- **Juice of 2 lemons**
- **2⅓ cups (475 g) sugar**
- **2½ cups (500 g) butter**
- **6 eggs**
- **3 cups (¾ L) 35% cream, whipped**
- **10 peaches, peeled and cut in half**
- **⅔ cup (150 ml) Grand Marnier**

Mix first seven ingredients well and bring to boil. Remove from heat and allow to cool. Fold the whipped cream into the mixture to make a gratin mousse.

Place two peach halves in 10 oven-proof ramekins. Sprinkle each with Grand Marnier and heat in the oven for 10–15 minutes until peaches are hot. Cover with gratin mousse and cook under broiler until slightly brown. Sprinkle a little Grand Marnier on top and serve.

Hotel im Palais Schwarzenberg

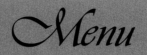

Menu

**Breasts of Quail Stuffed
with Goose Liver and Salad of Chanterelles**

Cream of Parsley Soup with Salmon Trout

Jack Salmon in Lemon Butter

**Calf Sweetbreads in Puff Pastry
with Fine Vegetables**

Chocolate Pudding with Whipped Cream

In the heart of the city, hidden within fifteen acres of beautiful gardens, the Hotel Im Palais Schwarzenberg is the preferred retreat of those who cherish a noble and elegant atmosphere. The food is superb: traditional Viennese cooking and international cuisine at its best.

Cream of Parsley Soup with Salmon Trout

Servings—4
Portion—½ cup

- 2 tablespoons (30 g) shallots, cut and washed
- 6 tablespoons (90 g) butter
- 6 tablespoons (90 g) crinkly parsley, cleaned
- 10 leaves uncrinkly parsley
- 2 cups (½ L) strong chicken stock
- 4 tablespoons (60 ml) white wine
- 1 dash lemon juice
- 1 cup (250 ml) double cream
- 2 tablespoons whipped cream
- Salt
- Pepper fresh from mill
- ¾ pound (340 g) salmon-trout
- 1 tablespoon (10 g) butter

Croutons—
- White bread without crust
- 2 tablespoons (30 g) butter

Put the washed parsley into boiling, lightly salted water. Bring to boil again and strain immediately. Sauté the shallots with ¼ cup (50 g) butter. Add parsley and deglaze with white wine; add chicken stock and remaining butter. Mix with double cream and boil exactly 3 minutes. Purée in mixer, then strain through a fine sieve. Heat once again and season with salt, pepper, and lemon juice. If necessary, whisk once more. Fold in whipped cream.

Fillet salmon trout. Skin, then cut each fillet into 4–6 equal parts. Roast on both sides in butter without browning.

Croutons—

Cut white bread into small cubes and roast in butter until golden brown in color. Drain on paper towels to absorb excess fat.

Ladle the soup into prewarmed plates, add the salmon trout, and sprinkle with croutons.

Jack Salmon in Lemon Butter

Servings—4
Portion—1 fillet

- 2 jack salmon, 1¾ pounds (800 g) each
- Salt
- Pepper
- Flour
- ⅔ cup (150 g) butter
- 2 tablespoons (30 ml) Noilly Prat
- 1 lemon, peeled and cut into quarters
- Salt
- 4 slices toast (2 days old)
- 3 tablespoons (45 ml) brown calf's stock
- Watercress

Fillet and skin jack salmon and remove bones. Season the fillets and dust lightly in flour. Set aside.

Reduce the Noilly Prat in a frying pan to half; add one-third of the butter and lemon slices. Salt and bring to a boil. Remove from heat and set aside.

Remove the crust of the toast and cut into small cubes. Roast slowly in 3 tablespoons (45 g) butter until golden brown.

Roast jack salmon fillets in last third of the butter until golden brown. Season once more and pour the butter over fillets. Serve the fish on prewarmed plates with lemon butter on top. Sprinkle drops of calf's stock on the lemon butter. Garnish with croutons and with watercress. Serve promptly.

Calf Sweetbreads in Puff Pastry with Fine Vegetables

Servings—2
Portion—¼ pound (115 g)

- ½ pound (225 g) sweetbreads
- ½ cup (115 g) meat farce
- 2 tablespoons (30 g) blanched, squeezed, and chopped herbs
- ¼ cup (60 g) blanched mengel
- ½ cup (115 g) puff pastry, rolled thin
- 3 blanched onions
- 5 blanched florets of broccoli
- 3 blanched, cut kohlrabi
- 1 truffle, cut in strips
- 4 cups (1 L) calf's glacé
- 3 tablespoons (45 ml) cognac
- 4 tablespoons (60 ml) white mushroom stock

Blanch sweetbreads. Remove veins and blood clots. Cover puff pastry with mengel and spread with farce. Sprinkle with the herbs. Put the sweetbreads on top and wrap with the pastry. Coat the pastry with egg yolk and bake for 20 minutes at 350°F (180°C).

Reduce the cognac. Add calf's glacé and white mushroom stock. Reduce and mix with butter.

Sauté all vegetables (except truffle) and serve with the sweetbreads. Garnish with truffle strips.

Chocolate Pudding with Whipped Cream

Servings—2
Portion—½ cup (120 ml)

Pudding—

- ½ cup (125 g) butter
- ½ cup (115 g) chocolate
- ½ cup (115 g) sugar
- ½ cup (115 g) hazelnuts, grated
- 6 egg yolks
- 6 egg whites
- 2 tablespoons (30 g) crumbs

Stir butter, chocolate, egg yolks, and half of the sugar until frothy. Add remaining sugar and egg whites. Whisk until stiff. Combine both mixtures and fold in hazelnuts and crumbs. Poach in a double boiler approximately 15–20 minutes.

Sauce—

- ½ cup (115 g) sugar
- 1¾ cups (400 ml) water
- 2 cups (½ L) cream
- ⅔ cup (150 ml) cacao
- 1¼ cups (275 ml) whipping cream

Bring all ingredients to a boil, stirring constantly.

Pour pudding into serving bowls and top with whipped cream sauce.

Menu

Marinated Smoked Salmon

Lobster Ravioli

Tournedo with Foie Gras and Black Grapes

Crème Bavaroise aux Pistaches

The Hay-Adams Hotel holds a long-standing tradition of hospitality and civility. This hotel has been restored to its original grandeur, a restoration recently hailed in Architectural Digest. *Our professional staff provides gracious, attentive, yet unobtrusive service.*

Marinated Smoked Salmon

Servings—6
Portion—3 ounces (85 g)

- **6 3-ounce (85 g) portions of smoked salmon**
- **3 large ripe tomatoes, seeded, peeled, and diced**
- **1 cup (250 ml) dry white wine**
- **½ cup (125 ml) red wine vinegar**
- **2 tablespoons (30 g) fresh thyme**
- **1 tablespoon (15 g) chives, finely chopped**
- **2 tablespoons (30 g) fresh basil, finely chopped**
- **2 tablespoons (30 g) fresh dill, coarsely chopped**
- **2½ cups (550 ml) hazelnut oil**
- **6 heaping teaspoons (35 ml) sour cream**
- **6 level teaspoons (30 g) Ostera caviar**
- **Salt and pepper to taste**

Mix white wine, red wine vinegar, all fresh herbs, hazelnut oil, diced tomatoes, salt and pepper to taste, remembering the salt already in the salmon. Let stand for 20 minutes.

Place a small amount of the marinade on a dinner plate; place smoked salmon on plate. Pour more marinade on salmon. Repeat for each serving. Place a heaping teaspoon of sour cream in the center of each serving. Garnish with a small teaspoon of the caviar, and a sprig of dill.

Lobster Ravioli

Servings—6
Portion—5 ravioli

- **2 pound (900 g) lobsters (with eggs if possible)**
- **60 wonton**
- **⅓ cup (75 g) tomato, peeled, seeded and diced**
- **⅓ cup (80 ml) fresh cream plus 1 cup (240 ml) fresh cream, warmed**
- **Salt and cayenne pepper to taste**
- **1 large egg yolk**
- **24 medium-sized morels, stalked and washed**
- **6 slices truffle**

Steam lobsters in convection steamer for 5 minutes. Separate tails and claws from lobsters and remove flesh of claws in one piece. Cut flesh from claws into scallops. Reserve coral and shells. Slice tails thin.

Spread 30 wontons out on work surface. Mix tomato and fresh cream. Season with salt, pepper, and cayenne to taste. Mix with lobster. Spoon about 1½ teaspoons (7.5 g) of the lobster mixture onto each of the 30 wontons. Brush remaining wontons with egg yolk and cover the prepared ravioli, pressing around filled portions to seal. With a 2½ inch (6 cm) cookie cutter, cut out ravioli.

Lobster Bisque—

- **Shells and carcasses from 2 lobsters**
- **2 tablespoons (30 ml) olive oil**
- **1 carrot, peeled and chopped**
- **1 onion, peeled and chopped**
- **1 celery stalk, peeled and chopped**
- **1¼ cups (275 ml) white wine**
- **1¼ cups (275 ml) water**
- **½ cup (120 ml) cognac**

2 tablespoons (30 g) tomato paste
½ teaspoon (2.5 g) tandoori spice
⅓ cup (75 ml) fresh cream
2 tablespoons (30 g) unsalted butter

Crush reserved lobster shells. Heat olive oil, add crushed lobster and sauté briefly. Add carrot, onion, celery and cook over medium heat, adding wine and cognac. Burn off spirits, add water and tomato paste and bring to a boil. Simmer for 25-30 minutes, then strain through a fine sieve set over a sauce pan. Return bisque to heat and reduce to about 1¼ cups (275 ml). Reduce heat to low and whisk in fresh cream. Set aside.

Poach ravioli in lightly salted, boiling-water for about 3 minutes. Remove from heat and drain. Reserve poaching liquid to use for heating the claws and morels. Combine the ravioli and warm fresh cream in a bowl. Toss to coat evenly. Heat bisque and season with tandoori and salt to taste.

Whisk in 2 tablespoons (30 g) butter and lobster coral into bisque over low heat. Do not boil. Place 5 raviolis in each of 6 heated dishes and spoon over the lobster bisque. Garnish with chervil, lobster claw, and morels.

Tournedo with Foie Gras and Black Grapes

Servings—6
Portion—1 tournedo

6 8-ounce (225 g) fillet mignons
3 tablespoons (45 g) clarified butter
4 tablespoons (60 g) unsalted butter
12 slices of fresh, raw foie gras
32 black grapes, seeded and peeled
3 tablespoons (45 g) chopped truffles
2 cups (425 ml) red wine
1 cup (250 ml) white wine
1 cup (250 ml) demi-glaze
Salt and pepper to taste

Season the fillets with salt and pepper. Heat clarified butter over high heat and sauté the fillets until medium rare, about 7–8 minutes, turning once. Re-

move from pan and keep warm.

Pour fat from pan and add 2 tablespoons (30 g) of unsalted butter. Heat over high heat and sear the slices of foie gras for about 10 seconds on each side. Remove with a slotted spoon and keep warm. Pour off all fat except 1 tablespoon (15 ml).

Sauté grapes over medium heat for one minute. Add red and white wine. Reduce by two-thirds, add demi-glaze, and reduce by one-half. Whisk in remaining butter and chopped truffle.

Place a slice of foie gras on top of each fillet with one to garnish the plate. Place 3 black grapes on each slice of foie gras.

Crème Bavaroise aux Pistaches

Servings—6
Portion—1 mold

1½ ounces (45 g) shelled pistachios
1 pinch salt
2 tablespoons (20 g) powdered sugar
3 egg yolks
¼ cup (60 g) granulated sugar
1⅛ cups (265 ml) milk
1½ packets unflavored gelatin, dissolved
1⅛ cups (265 ml) whipping cream, lightly whipped
¼ cup (60 ml) melted chocolate
Dash dark rum

Caramelize powdered sugar. Add pistachios and salt; cool. When cooled, chop into fine pieces.

Bring milk and 2 tablespoons (30 g) granulated sugar to boil. Mix egg yolks with the other half of the sugar until the mixture becomes lemon colored. With the mixer at low speed, add the boiled milk, then dissolved gelatin. Cool mixture until it begins to set. Fold in lightly whipped cream.

Divide this mixture in half. Fold the melted chocolate and rum into one half. Fold the caramelized pistachios in the other half. Pipe the chocolate mixture into the forms first, then the pistachio mixture. Refrigerate until set. Dip forms in hot water for a few seconds and unmold on plates. Sprinkle chopped pistachios on top and serve with strawberry sauce.

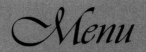

The Watergate Hotel

Menu

Tenderloin of Baby Boston Turkey
with Fresh Virginia Herbs and Cepes

Fresh Seafood Salad

Foie Gras with Fresh Asparagus
Fried Belon Oysters
Potato Ravioli
with Mirepoix of Coquilles St. Jacques

Cornet of Fresh Fruit with Lemon Ice Cream

Puff Pastry with Fresh Cream and Wild Strawberries

The landmark Watergate Hotel, in the nation's capital, is home to the award winning "Jean-Louis at the Watergate" restaurant." Culinary masterpieces are creative and unique, and served in an atmosphere of relaxed serenity.

Tenderloin of Baby Boston Turkey with Fresh Virginia Herbs and Cepes

Servings—6
Portion—½ turkey breast

2 baby Boston turkeys
Fresh sage leaves
Fresh dill sprigs
Fresh purple basil leaves
Fresh green basil leaves
Mesclum leaves
Fresh dandelion leaves
18 cepes
Shallots
2 tablespoons (30 ml) olive oil
Freshly ground pepper and salt
½ cup (120 ml) lime juice, freshly squeezed
½ cup (120 ml) lemon juice, freshly squeezed
¼ cup (60 ml) Jerez vinegar
2 cups (½ L) olive oil
¼ cup (60 ml) truffle oil

Reduce lemon and lime juice in saucepan to about ¼ cup (60 ml). Add vinegar, salt, and pepper, allow to cool. Whisk in olive and truffle oils in a slow stream until mixture is thoroughly emulsified.

Wash all herbs and salad greens thoroughly in cold water. Dry well. Brush off cepes and cut into julienne strips. Sauté finely chopped shallots and cepes in hot olive oil. Season with salt and pepper. Remove from flame and keep warm. Remove skin and any fat from turkey breast. Cut each breast in half, or to the size of the tenderloin. Salt and pepper all pieces and brush with dressing. Broil for 2 minutes without browning. Remove and keep warm in oven on low heat. Toss cleaned herbs and salad greens with 3 tablespoons (45 ml) of dressing to lightly coat. Arrange the salad attractively on center of plate. Reheat cepes for 1 minute and place on top of salad. Slice each halved turkey breast into five pieces. Arrange meat on top of cepes. Brush lightly with dressing and serve immediately.

Fresh Seafood Salad

Servings—6
Portion—1 salad

24 Venus clams
24 barnacles
12 crayfish
6 tomatoes, skinned
4 carrots, peeled and cut into 1½ inch (4 cm) julienne strips
6 stalks of celery, peeled and cut into 1½ inch (4 cm) julienne strips
4 leeks, washed thoroughly and cut into 1½ inch (4 cm) julienne strips
6 turnips, peeled and cut into 1½ inch (4 cm) julienne strips
5 tablespoons (75 ml) olive oil
3 tablespoons (45 ml) vinegar
4 cups (1 L) crayfish fumet
2 bunches fresh basil
½ pound (225 g) unsalted butter
Salt and freshly ground pepper

In a large pot, bring 1½ cups (350 ml) crayfish fumet to a boil. Add clams, cover and poach for 3 minutes or until clams open. Remove clams from shells, debeard and set aside. Reheat the same fumet, add barnacles and poach for 4 minutes. Remove and cut meat around the "foot" of the barnacle, set aside and discard fumet. To prepare the crayfish, remove the intestines by twisting and pulling out the middle tail fin while crayfish are still alive. Bring 2 cups (480 ml) crayfish fumet to a boil and poach the crayfish for 3 minutes. Remove meat from shells and set aside.

Slice sides of peeled tomatoes and cut into round shapes with a cookie cutter. Blanch julienne of carrots in hot water for 3 minutes. Add turnips and continue blanching for 2 minutes. Add celery and leeks and blanch an additional 2 minutes. Drain and plunge all vegetables in cold water.

Poach 2 bunches of basil in boiling salted water. Drain and purée, adding pieces of butter to the purée with the machine running. Continue whipping until creamy. Place basil butter in a saucepan with ½ cup (120 ml) of crayfish fumet. Whisk vigorously over high heat until emulsified. Remove from heat and place in blender. Add olive oil, vinegar, salt, and pepper. Blend for 1 minute.

Reheat clams, barnacles, and crayfish in warm crayfish fumet for 1 minute. Place sauce on bottom of serving plate. Arrange vegetables and fish on top and serve immediately.

Fried Belon Oysters

Servings—6
Portion—2 oysters

1 cup (225 g) unsalted butter, softened

1 cup (225 g) pressed caviar

12 Belon oysters, shucked

3 eggs

2 cups (450 g) flour

2 cups (240 g) brioche crumbs

Combine caviar and butter. Place squares of plastic wrap in the cups of a mini-muffin pan. Place 1 tablespoon (15 g) of caviar butter in each cup; top with a Belon oyster and another tablespoon of caviar butter. Holding corners of the plastic wrap, form the oysters into little balls. Freeze for one hour. Prepare egg wash by mixing whole eggs with salt and pepper. Prepare a tray of flour and another tray of brioche crumbs. Remove butter balls from the plastic wrap, coat with flour, egg wash, and then brioche crumbs. Freeze for one hour. Repeat flour, egg wash, and brioche procedure and freeze again. When ready to serve, deep-fry in 350°F (180°C) oil until golden brown, then place in oven at 300°F (150°C) for 3–4 minutes. Serve immediately.

Puff Pastry with Fresh Cream and Wild Strawberries

Servings—6
Portion—1 pastry

¼ pound (115 g) puff pastry (plus enough flour and sugar to roll out dough)

4 cups (1 L) whipping cream

4 tablespoons (60 g) sugar

4 tablespoons (60 ml) Grand Marnier

2 cups (450 g) fresh wild strawberries

Roll puff pastry to ⅛ inch (3 mm) thickness and refrigerate for 1 hour. Cut circles with a cookie cutter and refrigerate. Make one pile of flour and one pile of sugar. Dip one side of each circle into the flour and the other side into the sugar. With flour side down, roll out each circle to form an oblong shape. Prick center with fork and place on ungreased baking sheet. Bake at 375°F (190°C) for 10 minutes or until golden brown. Remove from oven, allow to cool, and cut in half lengthwise. Using a piping bag, fill halves with cream whipped with sugar and Grand Marnier. Arrange wild strawberries on top and serve immediately.

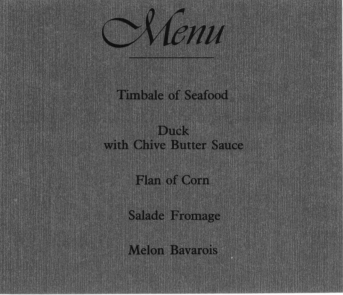

Menu

Timbale of Seafood

Duck
with Chive Butter Sauce

Flan of Corn

Salade Fromage

Melon Bavarois

Elegant and intimate, this 18th century-style mansion with genteel service and lavish period decor, hosts an excellent French restaurant. "Le Chardon d'Or" features two small dining rooms and French cuisine, rated the best in Northern Virginia, and among the best in the Washington, D.C. area.

Timbale of Seafood

Servings—2
Portion—1 timbale

- **1 teaspoon (5 g) unsalted butter**
- **3 tablespoons (45 ml) white wine**
- **1 shallot, peeled and finely diced**
- **3 sea scallops, cleaned and medium-diced**
- **1 shrimp, deveined and medium-diced**
- **½ cup (120 ml) heavy whipping cream**
- **½ lobster tail, cooked and medium-diced**
- **1 tablespoon (15 g) chives, finely diced**
- **⅔ cup (155 g) noodles (store-bought or fresh)**
- **2 egg yolks whipped with a little water**
- **¼ ounce (7.5 ml) golden caviar**
- **Fine sea salt and butcher's black pepper to taste**

Slightly sauté scallops and shrimp with shallot and white wine. In a separate pan, bring cream to a boil, then remove from heat. Add lobster to scallops and shrimp and cook just until reheated.

Add the lobster, scallops, and shrimp to the boiled cream, in addition to chives, cooked noodles, salt, pepper, and egg yolks. Place back on heat and stir continuously until mixture starts to thicken. Remove from heat, place in hot bowl, and whisk to an even consistency. Dab caviar in the center.

Duck with Chive Butter Sauce

Servings—2
Portion—½ duck

- **1 duck**

To prepare the duck: cut along the side of the breastbone, peeling back the meat as you go. Leave no meat on the bone. When the breast is totally off the bone, cut the surrounding fat, removing the fillet. Trim away the sinew, taking care to remove as little meat as possible.

Over medium heat, add 1 tablespoon (15 g) of clarified butter or oil. The pan should be hot, but not smoking. Place the duck breast flat-side down. Maintain a constant medium heat until the fat is rendered and the skin is crisp, about 10 minutes. If the fillet cooks too fast, the skin will brown or blacken before the fat is rendered. If it cooks too slowly, the meat steams or is boiled. Pour off excess fat. When the skin is crisp, turn the duck over and cook briefly on the other side until it feels springy, approximately 1 minute. Set fillet aside for 1 or 2 minutes.

Starting at the narrow end of the fillet, make ¼ inch (6 mm) slices on an angle. Place each slice at an angle, starting with the largest and going from left to right; on an oval plate. When finished, slices should be layered across, just above the middle of the plate, allowing space for the cooked flan just under the arranged duck slices.

Chive Butter Sauce

Servings—2
Portion—½ recipe

- **2 tablespoons (30 g) butter**
- **1 tablespoon (15 g) chopped chives**
- **1 tablespoon (15 g) tomato, blanched and diced**
- **1 clove garlic, cut in half**

Heat butter. Add chives and tomato. Add garlic halves and heat for 1 minute, then remove. Season with salt and pepper, and spoon lightly over the duck, flan, and exposed areas of the plate.

Flan of Corn

Servings—4
Portion—½ ounce (15 g) terrines

- **5 ears of fresh corn**
- **½ cup (120 ml) crème fraîche**
- **1 tablespoon (15 ml) chopped shallots**
- **3 tablespoons (50 g) butter**
- **1 cup (250 ml) chicken stock or consommé**
- **3 eggs, whole**
- **3 egg yolks**
- **1 tablespoon (15 g) chopped chives**
- **1 tablespoon (15 g) tomato, blanched and diced**
- **1 clove garlic**

Sauté three ears of corn in 2 tablespoons (30 g) butter with shallots for about 2 minutes; then add chicken stock and a pinch of salt and pepper. Cover and simmer for approximately 10 minutes or until the stock is reduced. Add the crème fraîche and remove from the heat. Purée in a food processor and strain. Cook the remaining two ears of corn in salt water until tender.

In a separate bowl, whip the eggs and egg yolks. Slowly add the puréed corn-crème fraîche mixture. Add the whole corn.

Bake in individual custard cups in a water bath at 350°F (180°C) for approximately 15–20 minutes.

Salade Fromage

Servings—2
Portion—½ of salad

- **2 heads Boston lettuce**
- **2 leaves radicchio**
- **3 leaves Belgian endive, sliced crosswise**
- **½ ounce (15 g) small diced tomatoes (from the meat of a blanched, peeled tomato)**
- **2 tablespoons (30 g) plain goat cheese**
- **3⅓ tablespoons (50 ml) hazelnut oil (marinated with peeled, smashed garlic and peeled, sliced shallots)**
- **Sherry wine vinegar to taste**
- **Fine sea salt to taste**
- **Black pepper to taste**

Clean Boston lettuce. Break lettuce and radicchio up into small pieces and add the endive. Mix together with a small amount of the vinegar and the hazelnut oil marinade. Season with salt and pepper to taste. Combine dressing and salad, toss lightly. Place on a plate in a light and airy way, paying special attention to the overall color contrast. Sprinkle with diced tomato and goat cheese.

HOTEL du PONT

Menu

Terrine from Pheasant with Foie Gras

Golden Pepper Soup

Rack of Lamb
with Meaux Mustard and Thyme en Croûte

Puff Potatoes and Steamed Vegetables

Salad

Cheese and Fruit

Peach Mousse with Amaretto Sabayon

The Hotel du Pont, central to Wilmington's business district and cultural attractions, offers a distinctive dining experience. The elegant "Green Room" features contemporary French cuisine. Classic American specialties are served amidst original Wyeth paintings in the intimate "Brandywine Room."

Terrine from Pheasant with Foie Gras

Servings—20
Portion—1 slice

1¼ pounds (560 g) pheasant meat from legs and thighs, cleaned of all sinew

1¼ cups (285 g) fatback

⅔ cup (140 g) bacon

1¼ cups (285 g) pheasant and chicken livers

6 tablespoons (85 g) fresh foie gras

1 teaspoon (5 g) ground coriander

6 each juniper berries, crushed

1 sprig rosemary, chopped

2 stems of thyme, chopped

1 clove garlic

Zest of ½ orange

Nutmeg, grated

Salt and pepper mill

½ cup (120 ml) dry vermouth

¼ cup (60 ml) Madeira wine

2 tablespoons (30 ml) armagnac

⅓ cup (75 ml) pheasant glaze

Garnish:

4 pheasant breasts

½ cup (115 g) foie gras

½ cup (115 g) pistachios, fresh with skin

The pheasant legs and thighs, fatback and bacon should be cut into cubes. Clean all nerves from the livers.

Quickly sauté the fatback and bacon in a hot skillet. Remove and strain. Return the strained fat to the skillet. When very hot, add the clove of garlic and quickly sauté the pheasant and liver to sear the meat. The meat should still be raw.

Place all in a shallow pan to cool. Keep the fatback and bacon separate. Cube the foie gras and mix with the pheasant and livers.

Marinate the meats with all the seasonings and alcohol. Cover tightly and let stand overnight in the refrigerator. Clean the foie gras for the garnish and marinate separately in cognac and Madeira; salt and pepper with the mill.

The next day, chill the grinder and its components. This prevents the fat from separating out of the fatback. Line the terrine mold with fatback. Quickly sear the breasts that will be used for the garnish and allow to cool.

Grind the fatback and bacon one time through the meat grinder using the fine plate.

Next, grind the livers and meat twice. Mix the meat farce and fat together and place in food processor. Blend quickly but thoroughly.

Remove from processor and place farce in mixing bowl. Add pistachios and season to taste.

Put a layer of the blended farce in the terrine mold. Place the foie gras that marinated overnight and place in the middle of the terrine, the length of the terrine. Add another layer of the farce and lay pheasant breasts on top. Place the remaining farce on top of the breasts. Cover with fatback.

Place mold in a water bath and poach

at 300°F for approximately 1 hour 10 minutes or until internal temperature reaches 120°F.

Golden Pepper Soup

Servings—8
Portion—¾ cup (200 ml)

1 medium onion, finely chopped
1 clove garlic, minced
4 yellow bell peppers, chopped
2 tablespoons (30 ml) olive oil
½ cup (120 ml) dry white wine
8 cups (2 L) chicken stock
2 cups (½ L) heavy cream

Sauté onions in olive oil until translucent.

Add peppers and garlic and sauté until soft.

Deglaze with white wine and reduce until almost all liquid is evaporated.

Add chicken stock. Reduce the volume by ¼. Add the heavy cream.

Reduce the volume again by ¼.

Remove from heat and purée in mixer. Strain through a fine china cap.

Return to heat and season to taste. Garnish with garlic croutons before serving.

Rack of Lamb with Meaux Mustard and Thyme en Croûte

Servings—8
Portion—4 half racks

2 whole trimmed racks of lamb
4 tablespoons (60 g) meaux mustard
8 sprigs fresh thyme
Salt and pepper
2 pounds (900 g) puff pastry
1¼ cups (275 ml) lamb jus

Season the racks of lamb and sear in hot oil. Let cool thoroughly.

Coat the racks with meaux mustard and place thyme leaves on top of racks.

Roll out puff pastry to approximately ⅛ inch (3 mm). Encase rack of lamb in puff pastry, sealing open ends with egg wash.

Place egg wash on outside of puff pastry. Place in 400°F oven for about 30 minutes or until puff pastry is golden brown. Let rest several minutes before serving. Place on top of lamb jus.

Peach Mousse with Amaretto Sabayon

Servings—8
Portion—½ cup (120 ml)

Mousse—

3 ripe medium peaches
½ cup (120 ml) white wine
½ cup (120 ml) water
Juice from ½ lemon
½ cup (120 ml) peach schnapps
2 tablespoons (30 g) gelatin
2 cups (½ L) heavy cream, whipped

Sabayon—

1 egg yolk
¼ cup (60 ml) white wine
¼ cup (60 ml) Amaretto
1 tablespoon (15 g) sugar

Raspberry Coulis—

½ (¼ L) raspberries
Sugar to taste

Skin and seed peaches and boil with water, white wine and lemon juice. Sugar may be added, if needed.

Dissolve gelatin in schnapps. When the peach mixture is approximately ¼ of its original volume, add the gelatin and mix well. Remove from heat and purée in blender until smooth.

Place in an ice bath and whisk. When mixture begins to thicken, fold in whipped cream. Place mixture in a shallow pan, about 1½ inches (45 cm). Cover and refrigerate until mixture is firm.

Place ingredients for the sabayon in a bowl and beat over a hot water bath until mixture is firm. Remove from heat and continue to whip until mixture cools.

Purée raspberries and sugar and strain to remove seeds.

Place 2–3 quenelles of the mousse onto chilled plates. Spoon some sabayon and coulis onto the plate.

BAUR AU LAC

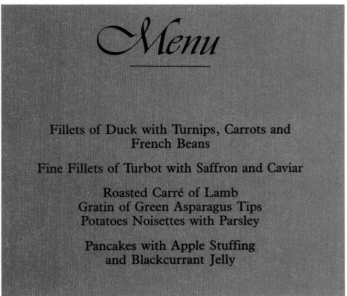

Menu

Fillets of Duck with Turnips, Carrots and
French Beans

Fine Fillets of Turbot with Saffron and Caviar

Roasted Carré of Lamb
Gratin of Green Asparagus Tips
Potatoes Noisettes with Parsley

Pancakes with Apple Stuffing
and Blackcurrant Jelly

The Baur au Lac, has a unique location on the shore of the lake, a few steps off the fashionable Bahnhofstrasse, the famous shopping and business center of Zurich. The elegantly appointed "Restaurant Francais" offers classic French cuisine and a famous selection of wines to which the treasures of our own cellerage contribute.

Fillets of Duck with Turnips, Carrots, and French Beans

Servings—4
Portion—¼ duck breast

1¾ pounds (800 g) duck breast
¼ cup (60 ml) peanut oil
1¼ cups (275 ml) red wine
1¼ cups (285 g) butter
Seasoning
Brown duck stock from bones and trimmings

Roast the duck breast in heated peanut oil in a 250°F (120°C) oven for 12–13 minutes until pink, basting constantly. Remove from pan and keep warm. Add the red wine to meat juice; deglaze. Add the slightly thickened brown duck stock, and reduce to desired consistency. Strain through a fine sieve. Stir in ½ cup butter. Carefully cut the meat lengthwise into thin even strips. Pour the well-seasoned sauce on a suitable plate. Place the duck strips on top. Garnish with turnips, glazed carrots, and French beans sautéed in butter.

Fine Fillets of Turbot with Saffron and Caviar

Servings—6
Portion—1 fillet

1 tablespoon (15 g) shallots, finely chopped
½ cup (120 ml) dry white wine
1 cup (250 ml) fish stock
1 pound (450 g) turbot fillets
½ cup (120 ml) cream
½ cup (120 ml) double cream
½ cup (120 ml) sauce velouté (velvet) of fish
Pinch of saffron
Seasoning
¼ cup (60 g) butter
6 tablespoons (85 g) Beluga caviar
1 tablespoon (15 g) dill
3 small lobster tails

Sauté shallots with 1 tablespoon (15 g) butter; add white wine and fish stock. Cut the fillets into fine slices; add to fish stock. Poach the fish and lobster tails approximately 1½ minutes. Re-

move and keep warm. Strain the stock through a fine sieve. Reduce stock, add the strained liquid, double cream and ¾ of the saffron. Reduce again, thicken with velvet sauce, and reduce to the desired consistency. Add remainder of butter, sprinkle with remainder of saffron. Pour the sauce into a suitable warm dish and arrange the fillets on top. Garnish each fillet with a tablespoon (15 g) of caviar, a tail of pared lobster, and sprigs of dill.

Roasted Carré of Lamb

Servings—12
Portion—½ pound (225 g)

½ cup (15 g) peanut oil
6 pounds (3 kg) carre of lamb
Seasoning
½ cup (15 g) butter

Skin and trim the lamb, carefully remove the nerves, and season with salt and pepper. Roast in hot oil for 12 minutes, basting constantly. Remove and allow to rest for 5–6 minutes in a fairly warm place. This will prevent the meat juices from running out when lamb is cut. Cut in slices and arrange on serving dish. Garnish with the gratin of green asparagus tips and the potatoes "noisettes." (See recipes below). Sprinkle with chopped parsley. Form a cordon around the meat with the slightly thickened meat juice and dot it with some brown butter.

Gratin of Green Asparagus Tips

Servings—12
Portion—¾ cup (180 g)

4½ **pounds (2 kg) green asparagus**
¼ **cup (60 g) salt**
2 **tablespoons (30 g) flour**
2 **tablespoons (30 g) butter**
1 **cup (250 ml) milk**
½ **cup (120 ml) cream**
⅔ **cup (140 g) Gruyère cheese, freshly grated**

Clean and tie the asparagus. Cook for 2 minutes in boiling salt water. Remove pan from the heat and let rest, covered, for about 20 minutes.

Prepare a white sauce (roux) with butter, flour, and milk. Simmer over low heat. Gradually whisk in ½ cup (120 ml) asparagus stock, stirring continuously. Season to taste and press through a towel. Add whipped cream.

Drain asparagus, cut to 4¾ inch (12 cm) lengths, place in serving dish. Coat the less attractive part of asparagus with sauce, sprinkle with grated Gruyère cheese, and broil.

Potatoes "Noisettes" with Parsley

Servings—12
Portion—¾ cup (180 g)

4½ **pounds (2 kg) potatoes**
¼ **cup (60 g) salt**
½ **cup (115 g) butter**
1 **tablespoon (15 g) finely chopped parsley**

Peel potatoes and wash thoroughly. Using spoon designed for potatoes noisettes, form equally small hazelnut-shaped balls. Cook in boiling salt water *à point* (only just cooked so that they remain crisp). Let drain. In small sauté pan, melt the butter, add the finely chopped parsley, and the cooked potatoes. Mix carefully and serve immediately.

Pancakes with Apple Stuffing and Blackcurrant Jelly

Servings—12
Portion—2 pancakes

2 **egg yolks**
2 **eggs**
½ **cup (115 g) flour**
½ **cup (120 ml) milk**
½ **cup (115 g) butter**
2 **cups (450 g) apples, sliced**
¼ **cup (60 g) sugar**
2 **tablespoons (30 g) sultanas, soaked in water**
1 **cup (225 g) blackcurrant jelly**
2 **tablespoons (30 ml) Calvados**
2 **tablespoons (30 g) icing sugar**
1 **cup (225 g) blue figs**
2 **teaspoons (10 ml) lemon balm**

Prepare a pancake batter with egg yolks, eggs, milk, flour, and ¼ cup (60 g) brown butter. Pass the mixture through a China cap. Fry 4 inch (10 cm) diameter pancakes.

Sauté apples and the sultanas in remainder of butter. Add sugar and deglaze with Calvados. Remove and let rest briefly. Fill lukewarm pancakes with apples and sultanas. Place 2 pancakes on each serving plate, cover with warm blackcurrant jelly. Garnish with thin slices of blue figs and lemon balm. Sprinkle with icing sugar and serve immediately.

INDEX

Anchorage—Hotel Captain Cook * Atlanta—Colony Square Hotel * Atlanta—The Ritz-Carlton Atlanta * Baden-Baden—Brenner's Park-Hotel * Baltimore—Harbor Court Hotel * Bangkok—The Dusit Thani * Boston—The Colonnade * Cape Co Chatham, MA—Wequassett Inn * Carmel—Quail Lodge * Charlotte—The Park Hotel * Chicago—The Barclay Chicago Chicago/Oak Brook—Oak Brook Hills Hotel * Cincinnati—The Cincinnatian Hotel * Cologne—Excelsior Hotel Ernst * Dallas Hotel Crescent Court * Dallas—The Mansion on Turtle Creek * Denver—The Brown Palace Hotel * Düsseldorf—Ho Breidenbacher Hof * Fort Lauderdale—Pier 66 Hotel and Marina * Frankfurt/Wiesbaden—Hotel Nassauer Hof * Hong Kong The Peninsula * Honolulu—Halekulani * Houston—The Warwick * Indianapolis—The Canterbury Hotel * Kansas City Alameda Plaza Hotel * Keystone, CO—Keystone Lodge * Las Vegas—Desert Inn Hotel & Casino * London—The Dorchester Los Angeles—Westwood Marquis Hotel & Gardens * Lucerne—Grand Hotel National * Lucerne/Vitznau—Park Hotel Vitzn * Madrid—Palace Hotel * Malaga—Hotel Byblos Andaluz * Manila—The Manila Peninsula * Maui—Maui Prince Hotel Memphis—The Peabody * Milwaukee—The Pfister Hotel * Minneapolis—The Whitney Hotel * Montreal—Le Grand Ho * Munich—Hotel Bayerischer Hof * Napa Valley/St. Helena—Meadowood Resort Hotel * New York City—Grand Bay Hotel Equitable Center * New York City—United Nations Plaza Hotel * New York City/Long Island—The Garden City Hotel Orlando—The Peabody * Osaka—Royal Hotel * Palm Beach—The Breakers * Paris—Hotel Le Bristol * Phoenix—The Pointe South Mountain * Portland—The Heathman Hotel * Rome—Ambasciatori Palace Hotel * San Antonio—La Mansión del Rio San Diego—U.S. Grant Hotel * San Diego/La Jolla—La Valencia Hotel—San Francisco—The Stanford Court Hotel * S Francisco/Oakland—The Claremont Resort Hotel & Tennis Club * San Juan—El San Juan Hotel & Casino * Seattle—T Sorrento Hotel * Seoul—Hotel Lotte * Singapore—Goodwood Park Hotel * Sonoma—Sonoma Mission Inn & Spa * Tokyo Imperial Hotel * Toronto—Park Plaza Hotel * Toronto—The Prince Hotel * Vienna—Hotel Im Palais Schwarzenberg Washington, D.C.—The Hay-Adams Hotel * Washington, D.C.—The Watergate Hotel * Washington, D.C./Alexandria Morrison House * Wilmington—Hotel du Pont * Zurich—Hotel Baur Au Lac * Anchorage—Hotel Captain Cook * Atlanta Colony Square Hotel * Atlanta—The Ritz-Carlton Atlanta * Baden-Baden—Brenner's Park-Hotel * Baltimore—Harbor Co Hotel * Bangkok—The Dusit Thani * Boston—The Colonnade * Cape Cod/Chatham, MA—Wequassett Inn * Carmel—Qu Lodge * Charlotte—The Park Hotel * Chicago—The Barclay Chicago * Chicago/Oak Brook—Oak Brook Hills Hotel Cincinnati—The Cincinnatian Hotel * Cologne—Excelsior Hotel Ernst * Dallas—Hotel Crescent Court * Dallas—The Mansi on Turtle Creek * Denver—The Brown Palace Hotel * Düsseldorf—Hotel Breidenbacher Hof * Fort Lauderdale—Pier 66 Ho and Marina * Frankfurt/Wiesbaden—Hotel Nassauer Hof * Hong Kong—The Peninsula * Honolulu—Halekulani * Houston The Warwick * Indianapolis—The Canterbury Hotel * Kansas City—Alameda Plaza Hotel * Keystone, CO—Keystone Lodge Las Vegas—Desert Inn Hotel & Casino * London—The Dorchester * Los Angeles—Westwood Marquis Hotel & Garde * Lucerne—Grand Hotel National * Lucerne/Vitznau—Park Hotel Vitznau * Madrid—Palace Hotel * Malaga—Hotel Bybl Andaluz * Manila—The Manila Peninsula * Maui—Maui Prince Hotel * Memphis—The Peabody * Milwaukee—The Pfis Hotel * Minneapolis—The Whitney Hotel * Montreal—Le Grand Hotel * Munich—Hotel Bayerischer Hof * Napa Valley/ Helena—Meadowood Resort Hotel * New York City—Grand Bay Hotel at Equitable Center * New York City—United Natio Plaza Hotel * New York City/Long Island—The Garden City Hotel * Orlando—The Peabody * Osaka—Royal Hotel * Pa Beach—The Breakers * Paris—Hotel Le Bristol * Phoenix—The Pointe at South Mountain * Portland—The Heathman Hotel Rome—Ambasciatori Palace Hotel * San Antonio—La Mansión del Rio * San Diego—U.S. Grant Hotel * San Diego/La Jolla Valencia Hotel—San Francisco—The Stanford Court Hotel * San Francisco/Oakland—The Claremont Resort Hotel & Tennis Cl * San Juan—El San Juan Hotel & Casino * Seattle—The Sorrento Hotel * Seoul—Hotel Lotte * Singapore—Goodwood Pa Hotel * Sonoma—Sonoma Mission Inn & Spa * Tokyo—Imperial Hotel * Toronto—Park Plaza Hotel * Toronto—The Prin Hotel * Vienna—Hotel Im Palais Schwarzenberg * Washington, D.C.—The Hay-Adams Hotel * Washington, D.C.—T Watergate Hotel * Washington, D.C./Alexandria—Morrison House * Wilmington—Hotel du Pont * Zurich—Hotel Baur Au Lac Denver—The Brown Palace Hotel * Düsseldorf—Hotel Breidenbacher Hof * Fort Lauderdale—Pier 66 Hotel and Marl * Frankfurt/Wiesbaden—Hotel Nassauer Hof * Hong Kong—The Peninsula * Honolulu—Halekulani * Houston—The Warwi * Indianapolis—The Canterbury Hotel * Kansas City—Alameda Plaza Hotel * Keystone, CO—Keystone Lod Anchorage—Hotel Captain Cook * Atlanta—Colony Square Hotel * Atlanta—The Ritz-Carlton Atlanta * Baden-Baden Brenner's Park-Hotel * Baltimore—Harbor Court Hotel * Bangkok—The Dusit Thani * Boston—The Colonnade * Cape Co Chatham, MA—Wequassett Inn * Carmel—Quail Lodge * Charlotte—The Park Hotel * Chicago—The Barclay Chicago Chicago/Oak Brook—Oak Brook Hills Hotel * Cincinnati—The Cincinnatian Hotel * Cologne—Excelsior Hotel Ernst * Dallas Hotel Crescent Court * Dallas—The Mansion on Turtle Creek * Denver—The Brown Palace Hotel * Düsseldorf—Ho Breidenbacher Hof * Fort Lauderdale—Pier 66 Hotel and Marina * Frankfurt/Wiesbaden—Hotel Nassauer Hof * Hong Kong The Peninsula * Honolulu—Halekulani * Houston—The Warwick * Indianapolis—The Canterbury Hotel * Kansas City Alameda Plaza Hotel * Keystone, CO—Keystone Lodge * Las Vegas—Desert Inn Hotel & Casino * London—The Dorchester Los Angeles—Westwood Marquis Hotel & Gardens * Lucerne—Grand Hotel National * Lucerne/Vitznau—Park Hotel Vitzn * Madrid—Palace Hotel * Malaga—Hotel Byblos Andaluz * Manila—The Manila Peninsula * Maui—Maui Prince Hotel Memphis—The Peabody * Milwaukee—The Pfister Hotel * Minneapolis—The Whitney Hotel * Montreal—Le Grand Ho * Munich—Hotel Bayerischer Hof * Napa Valley/St. Helena—Meadowood Resort Hotel * New York City—Grand Bay Hotel Equitable Center * New York City—United Nations Plaza Hotel * New York City/Long Island—The Garden City Hotel Orlando—The Peabody * Osaka—Royal Hotel * Palm Beach—The Breakers * Paris—Hotel Le Bristol * Phoenix—The Pointe South Mountain * Portland—The Heathman Hotel * Rome—Ambasciatori Palace Hotel * San Antonio—La Mansión del Rio San Diego—U.S. Grant Hotel * San Diego/La Jolla—La Valencia Hotel—San Francisco—The Stanford Court Hotel * S Francisco/Oakland—The Claremont Resort Hotel & Tennis Club * San Juan—El San Juan Hotel & Casino * Seattle—T Sorrento Hotel * Seoul—Hotel Lotte * Singapore—Goodwood Park Hotel * Sonoma—Sonoma Mission Inn & Spa * Tokyo Imperial Hotel * Toronto—Park Plaza Hotel * Toronto—The Prince Hotel * Vienna—Hotel Im Palais Schwarzenberg Washington, D.C.—The Hay-Adams Hotel * Washington, D.C.—The Watergate Hotel * Washington, D.C./Alexandria—Mo rison House * Wilmington—Hotel du Pont * Zurich—Hotel Baur Au Lac * Anchorage—Hotel Captain Cook * Atlanta—Colo